Borg versus McEnroe

Wimbledon, 5 July 1980. Bjorn Borg is beating
John McEnroe by two sets to one. The players enter
into the most dramatic tie-break in tennis history. With
exquisite play, Borg creates three Championship points,
only to squander each one of them. McEnroe finally
converts his seventh set point to take the match into the
decider. Borg is chasing a record-breaking fifth title,
McEnroe desperately seeking his first.

From these two characters emerged an intense
professional rivalry which developed into a strong
friendship. In *Borg versus McEnroe*, Malcolm Folley
explores the essence of their competitiveness,
encapsulated in the epic encounter of Wimbledon 1980.
He interviews many of the key characters involved
including Connors, Fleming, McEnroe's brother Patrick
and Borg's ex-wife Mariana. In this defining moment
in the careers of both men, new light is cast on one of
the greatest rivalries of sporting history.

To Miranda
I think your champion!
Happy Birthday
Steve "Angelo" Bony x

Malcolm Folley is Chief Sports Reporter for the *Mail on Sunday* with almost 30 years' experience on national newspapers, including a period as *Daily Mail* tennis correspondent. He has been Sports Reporter of the Year and continues to cover major tennis events across the world. He has written *A Time to Jump*, the authorised biography of Olympic gold medallist Jonathan Edwards, collaborated on tennis champion Hana Mandlikova's and racehorse trainer Ginger McCain's autobiographies and co-authored the acclaimed autobiography of Jason Robinson, a member of England's World Cup winning rugby team. He lives in Surrey with his wife Rachel and daughters, Sian and Megan.

BORG VERSUS McENROE

The Greatest Rivalry
The Greatest Match

Malcolm Folley

headline

First published in 2005
by HEADLINE BOOK PUBLISHING

First published in paperback in 2006
by HEADLINE BOOK PUBLISHING

1

ISBN 0 7553 1361 5

Typeset in Cantoria by Avon DataSet Ltd,
Bidford-on-Avon, Warwickshire

Designed by Avon DataSet Ltd
Printed and bound in Great Britain by
Mackays of Chatham plc, Chatham, Kent

Headline's policy is to use papers that are natural, renewable and
recyclable products and made from wood grown in sustainable forests.
The logging and manufacturing processes are expected to conform to the
environmental regulations of the country of origin.

HEADLINE BOOK PUBLISHING
A division of Hodder Headline
338 Euston Road
London NW1 3BH

www.headline.co.uk
www.hodderheadline.com

CONTENTS

ACKNOWLEDGEMENTS

I am indebted to a host of people who so willingly shared their time and experiences without a second thought. Without their generosity of spirit this book could not have been written.

Thanks, in no particular order, to those who opened the vaults of their memories to discuss Bjorn Borg and John McEnroe with such candour and affection: Mariana Simionescu, Peter Fleming, Peter Worth, Lennart Bergelin, Jimmy Connors, Patrick McEnroe, Mats Wilander, Air Chief Marshal Sir Brian Burnett, Chris Gorringe, Colin Hess, Ingrid Bentzer, John Lloyd, Peter Harrfey, Sue Barker, John Barrett, Ion Tiriac, Roger Taylor, Jonathan Edwards, Mike Lugg, Bud Collins, Bjorn Hellberg, Mark Edmondson, Kevin Curren, Rod Frawley, Balazs Taroczy, Gene Mayer, Brian Gottfried, Ian Wight, David Lloyd, Stuart Wilson, Bill Norris, Tom Okker and Andre Agassi.

I would like to further thank Alan Little and Audrey Snell at the All England Club for making their archive available to me. I am grateful to the tennis writing of Laurie Pignon, David Irvine and Rex Bellamy, retired and distinguished scribes who wrote respectively for the *Daily Mail*, the *Guardian* and *The Times*, and whose work shone a light on history. Thanks are also necessary to Scott Price of *Sports Illustrated*, Tom Tebbutt, who writes for *The Globe* and *Mail* in Toronto, and to my close friends Richard Russell and Andy Martin for their assistance in elements of research.

I am thankful to my agent Jonathan Harris for having the faith to suggest I write this book. I am fortunate to have had the pleasure of working with David Wilson, Sports Publisher for Headline, who offered an unnerving amount of encouragement throughout and edited the manuscript with great sensitivity. Malcolm Vallerius, Sports Editor of the *Mail on Sunday*, is also deserving of thanks for his support in enabling me to dovetail this project with my day job.

Lastly, I wish to express my eternal gratitude to Rachel, and our daughters Sian and Megan for reasons too many to list.

Sources

Books:
Bjorn Borg and Gene Scott, *Bjorn Borg: My Life and Game* (Sidgwick and Jackson, London 1980)
Richard Evans, *John McEnroe: Taming the Talent* (Bloomsbury, London 1990)
John McEnroe, *Serious: The Autobiography* (Little, Brown, London 2002)
Ilie Nastase, *Mr Nastase: The Autobiography* (HarperCollins Willow, London 2004)

Tape:
Legends of Wimbledon: Bjorn Borg (TWI)

PREFACE

Bjorn Borg is a ghost of summers past. To some, he is symbolic of more innocent times, a man who played to the calls, shook hands and headed for the shower. Only the scoreboard told you if he had won or lost. To others, he was the first player who created hysteria at a tennis tournament without an entourage or a spin-doctor in sight. His hair is still Axminster-thick, if shorter. Borgmania was born on the lawns of Wimbledon. He was a champion and a gentleman. Borg won 11 Grand Slam tournaments.

John McEnroe brought the brashness of his native New York to Centre Court. Each dubious call was challenged as though an injustice to his human rights. McEnroe was scathing in his condemnation of those he judged to be incompetent. He spared no one's blushes in his demand for instant retribution. McEnroe was a perfectionist seeking perfection from all those who crossed his path. He was also blessed with a breathtaking talent, and regarded by sympathisers as a rebel with a cause. McEnroe won seven Grand Slam tournaments.

Borg was a poster on McEnroe's bedroom wall. Later he was best man at McEnroe's second marriage to singer Patty Smyth.

Twenty-five years ago this summer, Borg and McEnroe came together in the Wimbledon final. It was a match that will never be forgotten, a pivotal duel within an impassioned rivalry that illuminated tennis around the world.

It is that rivalry, culminating with that dramatic final, which is the inspiration behind this book.

I have interviewed Borg and McEnroe many, many times. I have had private audiences with them in places as diverse as Monte Carlo, Houston, Paris, London and New York. I have witnessed high points and low moments in their lives. Above all, I have seen the respect with which each man views the other. Against Borg, McEnroe behaved on a tennis court as though in church. Borg always played the supporting role, leaving McEnroe to make the hard sell even when they resumed their rivalry on the Seniors' Tour. 'John does a million things, but that's what makes him happy,' suggests Borg. 'He will be always special to me.'

While McEnroe is omnipresent, behind a microphone one second, striking tennis balls the next, and managing to be a father to six children, Borg has disappeared into the shadows. He lives quietly in Stockholm and Monte Carlo with his third wife, Patricia Oestfeldt, who gave birth to their son Leo two years ago. His old, trusted coach Lennart Bergelin, who has survived heart surgery, is godfather of the child.

For this book, I set out to establish how Borg and McEnroe were seen through the eyes of others. I spoke with Mariana Simionescu in Monte Carlo, and she told of her life as Borg's partner and later his wife. I talked with Peter Fleming, who shared a doubles court and confidences with McEnroe from adolescence spent together in a suburb of New York; I met with Patrick McEnroe, who shared the same house as John, then followed him on tour. I placed my tape recorder in front of a range of old foes, managers and officials from the tennis circuit and I am grateful for the fact that no one declined to speak. Borg and McEnroe, so different, yet with striking similarities most emphatically defined by an eagerness to win, are revered for their achievements. Even McEnroe's dark side was excused as Mats Wilander observed: 'McEnroe was softer off the court than people thought; than I thought. I don't think there has been any player in the history of the game that has been forgiven so many times by his fellow players as McEnroe.'

Through many voices, I came to learn and understand more about Borg and McEnroe. This is the story of their rivalry, not their lives. This is how Borg strode centre stage until McEnroe's ambition, youth and brilliance eclipsed him. Taking my lead from McEnroe himself, there are moments when I do not spare *his* blushes. He would expect no less. Several years ago, I asked him to write his own professional epitaph. He obliged. 'If you loved or hated me, I hope when you look back you feel you got your money's worth,' said McEnroe.

Neither Bjorn Borg nor John McEnroe knew how to short change anyone on a tennis court. That is why their legacy will never die.

Malcolm Folley, West Horsley, 2005

END OF THE ROAD

On 13 September 1981, Bjorn Borg shook hands with John McEnroe in front of 20,000 people in the Louis Armstrong Stadium, Flushing Meadow, New York, collected his bag and walked from the court. While ground staff, oblivious to the Swede's unscheduled departure, made preparations for the on-court presentation ceremony in honour of McEnroe's third straight US Open title, Borg vanished down the tunnel leading from the court into the bowels of the stadium built under the flight path of LaGuardia Airport. He bypassed the locker room and was deaf to those inquiring where he was headed.

'Bjorn, won't you say something?' asked Bud Collins, a distinguished American broadcast and print journalist, who, along with Mike Lupica, a respected columnist with one of the New York tabloids, had trailed the Swede through the labyrinth of corridors. Borg did not utter so much as a goodbye. The reporters in the press box located high above the court were unaware of the drama unfolding below them. Borg went out through the tradesmen's entrance to where a car had been assigned to meet him. In an instant, he had ostensibly left mainstream tennis forever. The Swede was driven to his luxurious home at Sand Point, Long Island. He never looked back. 'We ran away pretty quick, I remember,' recalled Lennart Bergelin, who was Borg's life-long coach and remains his good friend today. 'It was not a good feeling for Bjorn in New York again,' admitted Bergelin, when we spoke in the summer of 2004.

In the stadium, meanwhile, McEnroe accepted his trophy, a tangible symbol of his position as the world's No. 1 tennis player, after his four-set triumph 4–6, 6–2, 6–4, 6–3. Throughout the match, McEnroe had, time after time, demonstrated his superiority through his control of both the baseline and the net. If the voluble American was mystified by Borg's vanishing act on that afternoon, little down the years has truly clarified the picture for him. 'It was one of the great regrets of my career that Borg decided to retire,' admitted McEnroe. 'To come into the game when Bjorn and Jimmy Connors were No. 1 and No. 2 and to be part of it was, in a sense, living a dream. I can't speak for the rest of the world, but it seemed like tennis was at its peak.'

He had first laid eyes on the Swede at the US Open. McEnroe was at Flushing Meadow as a ball boy. Borg was there as a man-child with a reputation already under construction. At sixteen, Borg was just three years older than the spindly kid from Douglas Manor District, an upmarket neighbourhood in the New York borough of Queens, but he had already won Junior Wimbledon. Soon, Borg would become a poster in McEnroe's bedroom, although ultimately McEnroe would become a thorn in Borg's side.

Some will tell you the wounds McEnroe inflicted in the previous twelve months, before that final coup de grace at the 1981 US Open, ran so deep that they caused Borg's career to haemorrhage. Others, like his wife of the time, Mariana Simionescu, and Bergelin, will offer eyewitness testimonies that it was not McEnroe that drove Borg into early retirement. According to them, it was the relentless diet of tennis and not one man's emerging brilliance that pulped the appetite of the Swede. Either way, Borg was passing into history as he was driven away from Louis Armstrong Stadium on that late summer's day. He was twenty-five years old.

The end is where this story begins, because, as in all stories, there is always a climax. And this tale is no different. Rightly, Borg and McEnroe are credited with providing us with the greatest final in Wimbledon's history; an iconic moment in sport that has its twenty-fifth anniversary in summer 2005. That is the destination of our journey, not the point of embarkation.

McEnroe had arrived in our lives like an unannounced summer storm. Dazzling and spectacular as lightning, he also brought with him the threat of thunderous menace from the moment he appeared at Wimbledon as a wild-haired, unknown teenager in 1977. He induced a rivalry with Borg on the tennis court like none seen before or since. Muhammad Ali needed Smokin' Joe Frazier in the ring; Arnold Palmer needed Jack Nicklaus on the golf course; Sebastian Coe needed Steve Ovett on the running track as they drove one another to run middle-distance world records; and four times world motor racing champion Alain Prost needed to feel the searing heat of Ayrton Senna's ambition to analyse his own strengths and weaknesses in a true light. Michael Schumacher may be an imperious Formula One champion, but historians will one day bemoan the fact that the German drove in an age when Ferrari's racing car was in a class of its own and his greatness was never properly examined under stress.

Borg had McEnroe to contend with. From first sight of Borg's magnificent, athletic talent, McEnroe felt compelled to provide the Swede with a sustainable challenge. McEnroe was alike in temperament, but different in most other aspects, to Jimmy Connors, an American raised to play hardball by his mother, Gloria. Connors brought the belligerence of the prize ring to the tennis court, but never against Borg. He had some mighty battles with the Swede, but by the time McEnroe came on the scene Borg could claim to have taken the upper hand.

McEnroe was soon to make Connors look like little Lord Fauntleroy. Connors, who returned to Wimbledon in the summer of 2004 for the first time in a dozen years, said dryly, 'I'm not sure that I changed that much as a player, but Mac just made me look better as he took things to a whole new level!' No conspirators could have manufactured such diametrically opposed adversaries as Borg and McEnroe. Borg had ice-cold blood in his veins, and a slow beating heart. McEnroe played and lived in the eye of his own hurricane. Borg was unemotional in public, cocooned in a bubble where the outside world was a mirage. He wore his hair to his shoulders long after the fashion had passed; he grew a beard for two weeks in an English summer and said little. 'We considered Bjorn the most famous person in the world,' said Mats Wilander, who was in the vanguard of Swedish champions inspired by Borg. 'And I think he probably was at one time. Only Muhammad Ali could claim to be as famous – and that includes presidents of the United States and all prime ministers.'

It is an opinion reinforced by his first wife, Mariana Simionescu. Throughout the peak of Borg's career, she was always there, devoting herself to making sure he had a stable environment in which to work untroubled. 'On one occasion we went from Hong Kong to Canton in a chartered DC10 aeroplane for an exhibition match,' said Simionescu, still living in Monte Carlo, but no longer in the eighteenth floor apartment she shared with Borg on Avenue Princess Grace. China was a closed society; not much that happened inside this vast nation filtered out and very little that was happening outside was allowed to filter in. Yet, Simionescu said revealingly, 'When we arrived in China it was just unbelievable. At a time when there were no cars, just bicycles as far as you could see, it seemed everyone knew who Bjorn was. How incredible is that?'

Wilander, a man talented enough to be ranked world No. 1, is unequivocal about Borg's impact on the game far beyond Sweden's boundaries. 'I guess the fact Bjorn had long hair and a headband in a game like tennis made you want to like him,' he said. 'Tennis is a very likeable sport on television, but the players before Bjorn reminded everybody a little more of their dad, or their uncle, or looked like a rich guy,' he said. 'Bjorn was obviously not rich and he was obviously nobody's uncle.'

Nor was McEnroe. He could be compared to any neighbourhood in his native New York; loud and frayed, but unyielding. He had attitude to sell, an opinion on everything, but his impact on the game was different from Borg's. While McEnroe screamed at umpires, Borg had to contend with a new phenomenon in the tennis world – screaming girls chasing him like he was a rock star. 'Being with Bjorn was like reliving Beatlemania,' recalled Peter Worth, the English accountant who managed Borg on behalf of Mark McCormack's ubiquitous agency, International Management Group (IMG).

Likewise, as Borg introduced the double-handed backhand to tennis, McEnroe became a connoisseur of the double-barrelled insult. The New Yorker burned with a magnificent talent and an uncontrollable rage. At times, he was Superman on court; at times, he was the 'Superbrat' of British tabloid newspaper invention. Unlike Borg, his celebrity – and notoriety – burned hard in the backdraught of the conflagration of his game. McEnroe, yelling and cussing, had demonstrated such a destructive instinct for moving the game from the sports section on to the front pages of newspapers around the globe that critics speculated he had come into the world bawling at the midwife, 'You cannot be serious.'

McEnroe claims the truth is at odds with such cynicism and has said, 'No one will believe you when you write this, but I had never questioned a line call before I first played at Wimbledon.' Even so, according to his doubles partner, Peter Fleming, the chain reaction of McEnroe's behaviour as he journeyed to the summit of the game was to create an image that would stalk him through life. Only Borg seemed totally exempt from McEnroe's ire. 'Due to Wimbledon, McEnroe became as recognisable in England as anybody alive,' said Fleming, a boyhood friend from the Port Washington Tennis Academy, New York. 'But from the first time John saw Bjorn at the US Open as a kid, I think he saw something he could relate to. There was something he didn't want to mess with. He had a very strong respect for Bjorn.'

Borg played tennis with such due diligence from the baseline, he might have been surveying it as a piece of real estate under investigation of purchase. McEnroe played with one purpose: to end the point as fast as humanly possible. Usually, this involved a sleight of hand and a perfect volley dispatched from the net. Their rivalry carbon dates a New Age for tennis. This duel of contrasting styles and complex personalities was born when they first played one another in Stockholm in 1978. People imagined it would last for the duration of their careers – and it did. It was just that no one could have forecast that just three years later Borg would, in effect, bring the curtain down on his side of the deal. Yet the legacy of the matches they played will last forever. Obligingly, there is a perfect symmetry to the rivalry: in fourteen matches, Borg and McEnroe claimed seven victories apiece.

When they met in the 1980 final of the US Open it was only their second meeting in a major final, but it was the beginning of Borg's downward spiral, as we later realised. Not that anyone at Flushing Meadow that fortnight could have known how swift Borg's descent into the abyss would prove, for once more the Swede had shown himself to be the ultimate competitor. In the quarterfinals, Borg had trailed Roscoe Tanner two sets to one, 2–4; and in the semifinal, he gave Johan Kriek a two-sets' lead before suffocating the life from the South African's game. Kriek won just three more games in the remainder of the match.

After twice losing in the US Open final to Connors, once at Forest Hills in 1976, then in the inaugural championships at Flushing Meadow in 1978, Borg was being granted another opportunity to spread his influence beyond the gates of Wimbledon and the French Open Championships at Roland Garros, Paris. McEnroe, however, was defending champion in New York and he possessed a cast-iron will forged on the same anvil of ambition as Borg. In his semifinal with Connors, McEnroe at one point lost eleven games in succession, yet his resolve never wilted and Connors was shown to the airport departure lounge. McEnroe, you see, was dedicated to winning the Open at the expense of the player he regarded as the greatest in the game: Borg. Yet when he appeared across the net from the Swede, McEnroe sensed that Borg was more vulnerable than ever before.

McEnroe's perception was not wrong. 'Bjorn gave me the first set,' commented the American afterwards. His argument cannot be disputed as Borg twice failed to serve out the set – at 5–4 and 6–5. Borg's service, normally a potent, if understated weapon, was in poor condition for the entirety of the match, yet from the hopeless position of being two sets down to McEnroe, Borg contrived to be level with the American at 3–3 in the fifth. But a pitiful next service game, punctuated with two double faults, opened the door to victory for a delirious McEnroe. In his own neighbourhood, he had melted the Ice Borg. He had also shattered Borg's aura of invincibility. The game would never be the same again, although it is doubtful McEnroe was thinking that far ahead as he celebrated with friends and his family.

The New York headlines in 1980 belonged to McEnroe, yet when Borg returned to the city, four months later, for the January Volvo Masters 1981, it was he who would capture the front pages – for reasons no one could ever have predicted. At stake in the eight-man tournament for the world's elite ranked players was a first prize of $100,000, more than twice the amount McEnroe banked for winning the US Open. Even given the size of the reward, no one would have guessed that Borg would have been capable of upstaging Americans McEnroe and Connors by picking a fight in Madison Square Garden, of all places.

But that is precisely what happened. The Swede, who, since his early boyhood, had barely raised an eyebrow in defiance of a close call, became embroiled in a dispute with English umpire, Mike Lugg. He refused to play when asked. He was silently enraged and stubbornly defiant. He was Bjorn Borg trying to impersonate John McEnroe. Under the game's code of conduct, Lugg docked him two penalty points, moving Borg to the precipice of disqualification. In newspaper lore we say, 'Dog bites man, no story; man bites dog, hold the front page.' Borg had just taken a chomp out of Lugg's trouser leg, metaphorically speaking, and the news flashed around the newsrooms of world. During the dramatic impasse, McEnroe looked on bemused and shocked. He had no script for the role of innocent bystander.

No umpire before – or after – had acted against Borg as Lugg did on that evening at the Garden. Lugg still wears the moustache that bristled with sweat that night, though it is greyer than it was. Throughout the match he had sat in the wooden chair with the military-like presence befitting a man who had once been a navigator in the Royal Air Force. He wore a shirt and tie and he would have been picked out of a New York Police Department line-up as an Englishman by any bum lifted from the streets of the Bowery.

'I remember the stadium announcer had said during a change-over, not long before the disputed call arose, "Ladies and gentlemen, I just want you to know you can congratulate yourselves as you are part of the largest indoor audience ever to watch a tennis match! Yes, there are 19,103 of you in Madison Square Garden today!"' recalled Lugg, but he was soon to find out how lonely you can become in a crowd. 'It was the second set tie-break [with Borg up a set] when things came to a head,' he recounted. 'Borg hit a screaming drive with McEnroe at the net. McEnroe let it go and I clearly saw the ball long on the baseline. I looked to the linesman, who was a Belgian-American, who made some sort of gesturing with his hands, that I interpreted as, "Oh, is it me? OK, it's safe." But by then, I had called the ball out. Borg came to the chair, holding out his hand towards me as he queried the call. I said to him: "Mr Borg, the linesman has been over-ruled. I clearly saw the ball out. The score is 4–3. You must play on."

'He continued to look at me, unblinking and with sweat pouring off him. He was in a sort of controlled frenzy. He wasn't with us, though. He wasn't hearing anything I said. I was speaking as slowly and as clearly as possible and all I could hear him saying was, "Ask the linesman. Ask the linesman." At that time, the code of conduct was administered in this sequence: warning, point deduction, point deduction, game deduction, default. I realised I wasn't getting anywhere with Mr Borg and started to invoke the code.'

Lugg was one of the first 'professional' umpires in an era when in all corners of the world officiating at a tennis tournament was still a hobby, a labour of love. 'We weren't salaried as umpires are today, but I was one of the first professionals at a time when we had to find our own work through tournament directors. I would say I have been verbally abused and sworn at by more multi-millionaires than anybody else on this planet.' Now it was the turn of the Swede to question his authority. For all his experience, nothing had prepared Lugg for this ongoing crisis with the tennis player renowned as a sportsman and a gentleman who kept his own counsel, no matter what. Borg listened, but heard nothing as Lugg declared, 'Code violation, delay of game, warning Mr Borg.' Still, the Swede didn't move. 'I'd like to think it was only thirty seconds later [the time a player had to resume playing between points as specified under the code], but it was probably some while later when I gave the first penalty point against Borg.'

That made the score 5–3 in McEnroe's favour. Borg was possibly ignorant to the exact letter of the code. He had no reason to have read it and he had never heard it applied, as even the most volatile of men, like McEnroe and Connors, never misbehaved on a scale serious enough to be reprimanded in his presence. 'Anything you did on court with Bjorn made you look worse,' Connors once told me. 'I always tempered my craziness when I played him. There was no chance of getting inside Bjorn's head.'

Up in the chair, Lugg felt isolated. 'I started to wriggle a bit, because I was alone in front of a crowd that was starting to get hostile.' New Yorkers like to tell you that New York is a 'sports mad town'. Whether screaming for the Yankees in Yankee Stadium, rooting for the Mets at Shea Stadium or watching the New York Knicks playing an NBA home game at Madison Square Garden, these are fans not renowned for their sentimentality.

Sympathy is in short supply for an inept play or poor pass, second place is first of the losers and McEnroe always suspected an antipathy towards him in his own city – perhaps he reminded New Yorkers too much of themselves. During one Masters tournament, McEnroe so incensed someone in the crowd that the man in question had to be physically restrained, then removed from the premises by a security guard. Memorably, a headline in a New York tabloid the next morning read: 'The night the fan almost hit the shit.'

That is the stuff of newspaper legend and so was Borg's temperamental meltdown. With Borg still immobile under Lugg's chair, Grand Prix supervisor, Dick Roberson, the referee for the Masters, came on court. He was judge and jury. As the clock continued to tick, Lugg awarded a second penalty point against Borg, as he was obliged to do. 'Six-three, McEnroe,' he announced. At last, Borg came out of his trance. Had he not, he would have experienced the humiliation of being defaulted. Nevertheless, the Swede forfeited the set with a wild shot on the next point. Lugg recollects there was a further explosive moment in the deciding third set. 'Borg had just hit a winner on a big point, but I had called a let as he hit it,' said Lugg. 'Borg went crazy again. Immediately, Mr Roberson was out on the court. He told Borg he had to play on or I would have to give him a game penalty. Thank goodness, Borg went out and played.'

McEnroe lost the match in the third set tiebreak, but Borg was the man most distressed, it seemed. 'I was very upset . . . very upset,' said Borg, when questioned afterwards in the media room. McEnroe was more forthright: 'I was totally shocked. I didn't even want to win that second set.' At least Borg finished the week as Masters champion, overwhelming Ivan Lendl in the final.

Subsequently, Lugg returned to England to receive a torrent of mail. 'For the next three or four weeks I had letters in the post from friends all over the world enclosing the same picture of Borg standing beneath my chair arguing with me,' he said. Had it been more intimidating to be challenged by Borg as it was so unexpected? 'At the time, it didn't occur to me, but I found out it was greater news that it had been Borg not McEnroe who disputed that call with me. Later, when I trained umpires and line judges, I used the experience as part of my teaching. I told trainees to go on court thinking each player is equal and to forget any previous reputations.'

In retrospect, Borg's outburst did more than simply claim worldwide headlines. His behaviour illustrated that his mind – previously an impenetrable fortress – was no longer closed to the possibility of losing. His focus was now capable of being disturbed. He was on the slide. It was not long afterwards that his historic five-year reign at Wimbledon was to end.

In 1976, when Borg had begun to monopolise the greatest tennis tournament in the world, England was governed by Jim Callaghan's Labour Party and Jimmy Carter, a Democrat, was president of the United States. By 1981, the political landscape had been ploughed upside down. Margaret Thatcher, the Iron Lady of the Conservative Party, was now in No. 10 Downing Street and Republican Ronald Reagan, once a second-rank leading man in Hollywood, was presiding over the most powerful nation on earth. The Cold War raged throughout Borg's Wimbledon reign and in the middle of it momentous events, which were to have a significant impact on the world as it is today, unfolded. The Shah of Iran was driven into exile, the Soviet Union invaded Afghanistan and, as his incredible string of victories marched on, Borg's final twelve months as champion were characterised by senseless murder, attempted assassinations and global celebrations.

In December 1980, shortly before Reagan took residence in the Oval Office as the fortieth president of the United States, John Lennon was murdered outside his apartment on the Upper West Side of New York. The death of the former Beatle, shot by Mark Chapman, caused outrage and created an outpouring of grief all over the world. Within four months an assassination attempt was made on the life of Reagan himself. While leaving the Hilton Hotel in Washington, DC, the president was shot by John Hinckley Jr. Before being anaesthetised for surgery to remove the bullet from his chest, Reagan remarked to his doctors, 'I hope you're all Republicans.' Reagan had already jokingly told his wife, Nancy, 'Honey, I forgot to duck.' Apparently, he was quoting boxer Jack Dempsey, who gave his wife, Estelle Taylor, the same explanation when she asked him how he had lost the heavyweight championship to Gene Tunney in 1926. No office was deemed sacred, it seemed. Only six weeks after Reagan was targeted, Pope John Paul II was shot. Mehmet Ali Agca, a Turk, shot the pontiff as he entered St Peter's Square to address a general audience. A month later a teenager fired six shots at Queen Elizabeth II at the Trooping of the Colour, an historic pageant to celebrate her birthday. That the shots fired were blanks hardly eased the peace of mind of those responsible for maintaining Her Majesty's safety.

Alongside such turmoil, there was also cause for worldwide celebration. In February 1981, Buckingham Palace announced the engagement of Prince Charles, the heir to the throne, to Lady Diana Spencer. Theirs was a fairytale romance that, at the time, captured the heart of much of the world and was seemingly set to move the House of Windsor into a new, modern era. The US, too, was moving into a new age, when in mid-April another frontier of space was breached as the Space Shuttle Colombia successfully completed its maiden voyage. It is unclear how far these defining moments of the twentieth century impacted on Borg as he pursued the boundaries of his own talent, but by the time of Charles and Diana's wedding at St Paul's Cathedral on 29 July 1981, he was no longer king of SW19.

It is unlikely, however, that he did pay much attention to such news events, as he was generally oblivious to the world outside his own orbit. Balazs Taroczy, a Hungarian professional two years older than Borg, was granted an insight into the Swede's tunnel vision. Taroczy often sparred with Borg in practice on the clay courts at Roland Garros, when the ball would be returned over the net shot after shot after shot, like a metronome. 'Already, in the thirty minutes knock-up, I was getting tired before we played for points,' recounted Taroczy, who returned to Wimbledon in summer 2004 for the over forty-five doubles event with his old partner, Heinz Gunthardt. 'Bjorn had a totally different way of playing. He was just a machine, really. One time I asked him a question – and when I think back it could not have been more stupid. I said to him, "What are you thinking when we are doing this warm up?" I had millions of things going through my own mind, but Borg looked amazed. "Nothing," was his reply.' Borg lived, breathed and slept tennis. He could not contemplate otherwise. His regime was sacrosanct: practice morning and afternoon; then play a match; then practice again the next day. He was a tennis machine, as Taroczy said.

Borg's sixth – and last – victim in the final of the French Open was an emerging force in the game, Ivan Lendl, the Czech he had beaten to win the Masters in New York nearly five months earlier. At that time, Lendl was a brooding, unsmiling character. The press christened him the 'Man in the Iron Mask'. His groundstrokes pounded opponents into submission, his racket doing the work of a baseball bat in the hands of a back street mugger. Lendl beat McEnroe in straight sets in the quarterfinals of that French Open – and three years later on the same Roland Garros courts he would inflict a defeat that cut the American to the bone. In the 1984 French Open final, McEnroe led Lendl by two sets and a break with the most devastating brand of attacking tennis ever seen on the slow clay of Court Central. McEnroe was an artist, his game asking to be hung in the Louvre, but unlike those of us watching, Lendl never interpreted his position as hopeless on that suffocatingly hot afternoon. As the match turned, McEnroe's tennis fell apart. His mind unravelled. When he overheard voices on a cameraman's headset left unattended on the side of the court, McEnroe picked it up and screamed, 'Shut up!' He complained to a man smoking a cigar in the open-air stands. He all but barked at the moon. Lendl just kept hitting winner after winner until McEnroe's agony was finally complete. 'I have this unique ability to turn the whole crowd around,' he lamented in a magazine interview afterwards. The disappointment McEnroe carried with him into retirement was that he never came as close to winning the French Open again.

Paris was Borg's garrison. In the fourth round of those 1981 championships – the eleventh and last Grand Slam title he won – the Swede took the first seventeen games from Terry Moor, before the American drew a standing ovation by winning the next game to prevent a total whitewash on the red dirt. 'To win that one game was the biggest thing in my life,' said Moor later. 'The man is on another level. Maybe, it has something to do with who he is, but every ball was so deep, so high. Other guys, once in a while they miss. I felt lost. The thing was he looked bored. I have no idea how people beat him. I don't see how they win games.'

In the final, Lendl pushed Borg hard, but as always the Swede never flinched. And in the decisive fifth set Lendl won just one game. Just as we have become accustomed to Lance Armstrong riding in triumph down the Champs Elysees on the last day of the Tour de France, the sight of Borg raising the French Open trophy was a ritual of Paris in springtime. David Irvine, the tennis correspondent of the *Guardian*, and an entertaining companion for many years on the road, wrote in the *World of Tennis* annual: 'One day, perhaps, they will erect a plaque to commemorate Borg's achievement in Paris. If they do, it should read: "Here was a Caesar. Whence comes such another?" For it is impossible to conceive that we will see his like again.' His point has a validity not eroded by time.

Twenty-four hours after his victory in Paris, Borg, as usual, caught a flight to London. McEnroe would be lying in ambush, but for the American there would be as much pain as pleasure at Wimbledon 1981. Even by his own standards, McEnroe was to offer a production that summer from the Theatre of the Absurd. Perhaps no one should have been overwhelmingly surprised. His image had been cast. Dunlop – the company that paid him to play with their racket – had an advertising poster that framed a drawing of McEnroe's head inside a racket head. The caption underneath read: 'Maxply and McEnroe. The most frightening sight in tennis.'

McEnroe confessed in his hugely successful autobiography, *Serious*: 'I'd been famous for a few years, but Wimbledon 1981 is where I became infamous.' To this day, there are those who argue that McEnroe should have been defaulted in his first round match with Tom Gullikson. 'I was tight as a piano wire,' confessed McEnroe. 'The devils were crawling all over my brain that afternoon.' He involved himself in bitter rows with, first, umpire Edward James, then referee Fred Hoyles, a farmer from Lincolnshire, who died in the spring of 2004. This was the day McEnroe delivered the words synonymous with him: 'Man, you cannot be serious!' He also uttered another indignant phrase: 'You are the pits of the world.' He was ready to implode.

Years afterwards, in the quiet courtyard at the Ritz in Paris, McEnroe offered a reflection of his mindset: 'I wasn't there to bad mouth people, but there was a stuffy attitude at Wimbledon then. If I'd been the referee, no, I wouldn't have thrown out

McEnroe that day, but I would have told him: "We've gone far enough and if you go any further, that's it." We never got to that point. Fred [Hoyles] was like, huffin' and puffin'.' McEnroe was fined $1,500 for an audible obscenity and unsportsmanlike conduct. He faced a $10,000 fine and possible suspension from the tournament if he was adjudged to be guilty of further 'aggravated behaviour'. But by the time McEnroe went to play Rod Frawley in the semifinal, that warning had apparently escaped his memory. 'Seventeen times there was a break in play during that semifinal,' recalled Frawley, reliving the closest he came to the Wimbledon final.

In his book, McEnroe describes the Australian as having 'a big mane of wavy hair, like a rock star, and [with] an edgy attitude'. Frawley had smiled when he read it. 'Rock star? Really?' He had come to Wimbledon to play in the over forty-fives doubles tournament in 2004. His right leg needed to be heavily strapped before he could play and, with the greatest respect, he did not look much like a rock star, but there was an easy, Australian, straight-to-the-point charm about him. He retains an involvement in the game as a coach at tennis camps for tourists in Mediterranean resorts and Africa. At home in Brisbane, he has a child care complex.

On that day he met McEnroe, Frawley was unseeded and dangerous, an Australian ranked No. 110 in the world due to an absence from the game through injury. He might have been a little rusty, but he hadn't forgotten his way around a grass tennis court. 'I broke Mac in the first game of the match,' he said. 'In those days, there was a standing section on the Centre Court. It reminded me of the Hill at Sydney Cricket Ground.' For those who have not been to the Sydney Cricket Ground, the Hill, regrettably no longer there, was a section notorious for larrikin behaviour. By mid-afternoon, empty tinnies were scattered everywhere and the crowd was fond of baying abuse at those not playing for Australia. Of course, when Frawley battled with McEnroe there were no tinnies on Centre Court, but the Australian recalled: 'Those in the standing area definitely came to see fire and blood. And after I broke Mac in that first game, he started to go nuts. Mac was standing in the doubles alley to return my first serve as I could swing it so well. He gave the middle of the court away, because he knew if he didn't he was not going to make the away swinger. Compared to today, I was a colourful player. I went toe to toe with Connors, with Mac. The only guy I couldn't hang with was Lendl, his rallying speed was just too heavy for me. I was handy – I just couldn't beat the top guys. I've watched that semifinal with Mac a couple of times. I had a break in every set. In the third set, I had 3–1 serving with new balls and double-faulted twice. Lack of experience. I was better than that. Anyway, Mac went nuts a lot.

'Referee Fred Hoyles did a bad job. I mean there were seventeen stoppages caused by Mac complaining. At one stage Fred came on the court and I said to him, "You know, Fred, you've got to do your job. Otherwise, I may have to walk off here. This is an important match for me – and it's becoming a bit of a comedy. I am having to wait all the time. You guys have got to do your job, you've got to penalise him." I honestly thought about walking out, but then I knew I would be the one penalised. Everyone would have sympathised, but you just can't walk off.

'You have to be a little upset with the ones who allowed all this shit. Hoyles used to hide behind the backstops on court if he knew there was likely to be trouble. I don't know if it was gamesmanship from Mac – or whether he was just losing it. Wasn't it the time he was breaking up with his girlfriend, Stacy Margolin? I think she had been knocked out of the tournament and gone back to the States. I think he was feeling the pressure. He felt he had to win this one. And a guy like me was a dream draw. But he was losing it under all the stress . . . and he was behaving like a little boy who needed a bit of a spank. In my opinion, what went on was unfair to me.

'Mac's dad was a bit upset, too. He came into the locker room after the match and they had a couple of words. I don't think John was that happy. Let me remember the score . . . 7–6, 6–4, 7–5. I should have won a set at least. Mac will tell you it was a close match.'

McEnroe tells you more than that: 'I was tense and, basically, I acted like a jerk,' he said. But McEnroe also felt that the line of communication between him and the club was virtually non-existent at that point, as he once explained to me: 'Maybe, they felt this young kid didn't respect them. I just wish that I had been able to show them that I did, so they felt able to respect me. Their answer was to fine me, then fine me again.'

Significantly, twenty-three years later the chairman of the All England Club at that time confessed to a blunder that haunts him still. Air Chief Marshal Sir Brian Burnett, GCB, DFC, AFC, admitted over coffee in a private room at the club last May: 'We should have defaulted McEnroe that year. He got away with it twice, against Gullikson and Frawley. He behaved very badly. While McEnroe was playing Frawley I was in the Members' Enclosure entertaining to lunch the Duchess of Gloucester, I think. When I heard about it, I sent my vice-chairman, Bimbi Holt, to try and sort it out. McEnroe should have been disqualified. I am sure he must have put his opponents off.'

Even McEnroe had been burned in the maelstrom of his excessive behaviour. Some years later, as he was fighting against the dying light of a remarkable career, McEnroe acknowledged this fact. 'Winning Wimbledon was a secondary consideration,' he admitted. 'My main goal was not to get into any more confrontations. It had all gotten so ridiculous all I wanted was to get out of the place.'

McEnroe's good fortune was that he would share the Centre Court with Borg in the Wimbledon final on American Independence Day 1981. You could have bet your house on McEnroe not playing up against Borg. Nevertheless, Bud Collins had felt compelled to speak on McEnroe's behalf at the outset of NBC's coverage of the final, which was being broadcast to the United States in a show called *Breakfast at Wimbledon*. 'I defended John at the start of the telecast,' said Collins. 'In my precis when we went on the air, I said, "You've read a lot of criticism about McEnroe, but despite his ill-mannered behaviour, he hasn't killed anybody, he hasn't robbed a bank." Well, I got the worst mail I've ever had as a television commentator for "defending that punk".

'The truth is the Wimbledon people didn't have the guts to throw him out during the Gullikson match. They should have done – it wouldn't have cost Wimbledon a ticket. When we asked Fred [Hoyles] what McEnroe had called him, he said, "Oh, you could never print that." I will never forget my friend Gianni Clerici showing me his column that appeared in Italy the next day. The English words stood out: c***, p****, fag. That would have been the perfect time to have thrown out Mac. Borg would have won again – and everyone would have been happy.'

Instead, Borg was vanquished. His forty-one-match winning streak on the grass courts of London SW19, dating back to the summer of 1976, was ended by McEnroe's ability to put behind him the controversies he had created. His strength of mind could be deemed as important to him as his serve, volley and athleticism. No matter how enraged he became, no matter how many bad headlines had traced his progress through the tournament, McEnroe had the capacity to walk out on the Centre Court without a hint of self-consciousness. Or apparent remorse. After all, what had he done other than be John McEnroe?

In the moment of defeat, Borg said with good grace: 'There is no way I could win all the time, but forty-one wins is something to be proud of.' However, Borg is still of the impression it was a match he could, and should, have won. 'I thought I was ahead all the time, I was the better player in that final,' he said, when interviewed for the film the All England Club commissioned in 2003 to celebrate his life and times at Wimbledon. 'I thought I could win for a sixth time.' In Sweden, Mats Wilander had no doubts about the outcome as he watched from his home in Vaxjo. 'We were brainwashed by Borg winning Wimbledon,' he said. 'It was impossible for us to foresee him losing.'

Yet on court McEnroe sensed he was playing a different Borg to the one he had met on the same premises the previous summer. 'Borg no longer had the same fire,' he told me. 'It was like he needed to be relieved of the pressure. I think it had all got too much for him after five years. It seemed as if it was OK in his mind to lose to me.'

When the Wimbledon championship was his, McEnroe's face became that of a child at Christmas. On the Centre Court, the scoreboard declared his victory: 4–6, 7–6, 7–6, 6–4. Not far away, Borg now stood where in five previous summers he had placed Ilie Nastase, Jimmy Connors, twice, Roscoe Tanner and McEnroe. He stood in the most uncomfortable spot at Wimbledon – the spot where you get the closest view of the man collecting the championship trophy. When he spoke of what it was like to be beaten at Wimbledon or anywhere, Connors said, 'The cameras are right in your face as you walk off, win or lose.

The microphones are thrust in your face, too. It's OK to do that with the winner, but give the guy who has just had a tough day a break to compose himself.' Television contracts tend to be devoid of such a clause.

Of course, Borg watched impassively as McEnroe took his prized possession. Only years later did Borg confirm what McEnroe had suspected. 'I was not really that disappointed.' Borg's passion for the game of tennis was taking flight, even if we didn't know it. 'Of all the Wimbledon finals I played that's the one I should have won. John didn't play well and if I had been a little more focused I could have won in straight sets. But afterwards I wasn't upset. I didn't care. That felt strange . . . I set my goals very high all the time. All the other players wanted to beat me and people expected so much of me. I had to be motivated every day of the week. I was the guy who never wanted to lose.' Or he used to be.

McEnroe had fulfilled his own destiny, for if ever a man was born with a game to win Wimbledon it was this irascible New Yorker whose tennis might have been designed in a laboratory to specifically excel on the Centre Court. Yet even in the hour of his triumph, McEnroe walked headlong into another controversy. He failed to attend the champions' dinner at the Savoy. In turn, the All England Club broke with tradition and withheld membership from McEnroe.

In summer 2004 I asked Patrick McEnroe if his family felt Wimbledon was against them. 'Initially,' said Patrick, who made his own mark as a player and is now a respected television commentator. 'That's why my dad would tell John, "You are just making life tougher for yourself." But John was John and that was part of what made him a great player.'

Sir Brian told what happened from the Club's perspective. 'After he won the final, McEnroe blames me for not going to congratulate him. I went on the court for the presentation and congratulated him there, but I didn't go in the locker room. He thought I ought to have done, and talked to him then about the dinner, but the chairman is a bit tied, because he's looking after the royals, and very often there were half a dozen of them, with all the Kent family present. I sent Bimbi Holt to see him, but McEnroe said he didn't know anything about the dinner. That's what Bambi tells me. We turned up at the Savoy and there was a message that he would only come if he could bring his friends. He had arranged to have a beer with them. The committee deemed that it was inappropriate for McEnroe's friends to be at the dinner. Anyway, McEnroe decided to go and drink beer.'

On US cable network ESPN Classic's SportsCentury series, McEnroe said later: 'I wanted to spend [the night] with my family and friends and the people who had supported me, not a bunch of stiffs who were seventy to eighty years old, telling you that you're acting like a jerk.' McEnroe's version of events was more subtly described in his autobiography, but his conclusion was nonetheless one of antipathy towards the way events unfolded after he had offered to make an appearance for coffee and dessert. He wrote: 'When Mills [assistant tournament referee Alan Mills] relayed the word to Sir Brian Burnett, the head of the tournament, the answer came back like a rocket: "If John does not attend the entire banquet, his invitation is withdrawn." Withdrawn! We simply found that unreasonable. It felt like Wimbledon high-handedness at its worst, so I gave the banquet a miss. I wanted to be with my friends.'

However McEnroe dressed up his absence, Wimbledon still treated it as a gross snub of protocol. 'The standard job was that the new champion was presented with a club tie at the dinner,' said Sir Brian. 'I had the tie with me, but there wasn't anyone to give it to.' The champion's gold trophy was on the table in front of McEnroe's empty chair. 'When the committee next met to discuss and sum up the tournament we all agreed not to make McEnroe a member,' explained Sir Brian. 'It wasn't a hard decision.'

According to Burnett, McEnroe Senior felt aggrieved and hurt by this sanction. 'He called me from New York and said, "If I come over and apologise for John will you then make him an honorary member?" I told him: "If he comes himself, then we would certainly consider it."' It is unclear whether McEnroe Junior was ever made aware of this offer, but he never did make the journey.

As Borg and McEnroe walked off Centre Court that day, it was unthinkable to all who watched them that the rivalry would not be re-ignited the following year, but in fact it would be nineteen years before McEnroe was to see Borg again at Wimbledon. Borg steadfastly refused all invitations to return until, finally, he came back to participate in the champions' parade to celebrate the Millennium at Wimbledon 2000. Chris Gorringe, the delightfully urbane chief executive of the All England Club, who took responsibility for the administration of the tournament in 1980, said, 'Successive chairmen invited Borg back every year and as a member he has the right to a ticket entitlement. He was invited to the royal box, of course. We couldn't understand why he didn't come back, but we're just delighted he was persuaded back in 2000. It would appear he enjoyed that moment. What a reception he received.' Borg was afforded an ovation fit for the return of the prodigal son. As he waved in response to the heartfelt roar of the crowd, Borg was aglow with pride. McEnroe smiled wryly as he greeted his rival and friend on what had once been their battleground.

'For me, it was very hard emotionally to come back to Wimbledon before then,' explained Borg. 'Many people said I had something against Wimbledon. It was untrue. I love the tournament. I love the people. For me, it's so special, it's like holy ground.' As if to emphasise his point, Borg knelt on the Centre Court in that summer of 2000 and kissed the grass. 'I thought that was very touching,' said Gorringe. 'Sadly, we have not been able to find any photographic record of him kissing the turf.' Gorringe played his part in commissioning a film of Borg's remarkable place in Wimbledon history. 'We hadn't done much on him prior to the millennium because we couldn't get hold of him, as it were,' he said. 'We felt the film was filling a void for future generations.' Needless to say, McEnroe gladly contributed.

For McEnroe, even if Wimbledon 1981 had been soured by a succession of controversies, that summer was nonetheless especially sweet. After defeating Borg at Wimbledon, he repeated the accomplishment at the US Open in New York, following which the Swede disappeared into the night a broken, disillusioned man. At the time, there were reports of threatening calls made against Borg in phone conversations to the switchboard at the National Tennis Centre, the site for the US Open. Security guards were assigned to Borg, although he had not been informed of the calls and neither had Bergelin.

Daily Mail tennis correspondent, Laurie Pignon, was mystified by Borg's abrupt departure as McEnroe awaited his prize. 'I've known Borg since he was fifteen and never, even after his most disappointing defeats, have I seen him behave so irrationally. In normal circumstances this gracious man would not dream of offending officials or deserting the crowds, who had given him so much noisy support, even though he was up against the local boy.' Was it the disappointment? Or was it fear that sent him scurrying from the scene of his defeat? I think it was disappointment plus anger at having to play a match that started in brilliant sunshine and ended under floodlights. A year ago Borg had said, "No big championship should do that."'

When McEnroe was asked, in the afterglow of his triumph, 'Have you mastered the master?' he replied with consideration and with respect, a preface to all his comments on Borg. 'I don't think so, because I don't think I can beat him on clay,' said McEnroe. 'Hopefully, some day that will happen. If you want to be one of the greats you have to win the French.' Borg won it six times; McEnroe never did.

Not long after he had fled Flushing Meadow, Borg declared himself burned out and announced he would take a sabbatical before returning for the Monte Carlo Open in April 1982. He had wanted to reduce his playing schedule, but in January 1982 the Pro Council, which ran the game, insisted Borg must play the statutory minimum of ten grand prix tournaments as well as three Grand Slam events. Borg, a stubborn man, refused. Instead, this legendary champion entered the qualifying tournament to gain a place in the main draw at the Monte Carlo Open, played in the beautiful grounds of the Monte Carlo Country Club perched high above the Mediterranean. He won three qualifying rounds and two matches in the main draw, but Yannick Noah ended his tournament in the quarterfinals. Borg put himself through the same routine in Las Vegas, losing in the second round of the main draw to Dick Stockton. After that, Borg restricted himself to playing lucrative exhibition matches. He seemed to be readying himself to launch a comeback in 1983. He was not.

Peter Worth was on a family skiing holiday at Val D'Isere in January 1983, enjoying a short vacation from the office, if not entirely escaping from work. 'It was in the days before mobile phones, so during the half hour over breakfast someone from the hotel would frequently appear and say, "Monsieur Worth, telephone s'il vous plait." We'd get back in from the piste around 5p.m. and the same would happen again. It became a standing joke among the friends that we were on holiday with. Clients don't respect their managers having holidays. That's not part of the deal, nor should it be.' But Worth had no conception that his holiday was about to be interrupted by a phone call that struck with the suddenness of an avalanche. 'Peter, I thought you should know that from the end of the Monte Carlo event in 1983, I am retiring from professional tennis,' said an instantly recognisable voice.

Bjorn Borg had just quit the game that had brought him fame and wealth on an unimaginable scale. Worth, scrambling his mind to respond to this devastating news, offered to abandon his holiday to meet with Borg. 'No, no, I have decided to finish,' said the Swede. Worth understood his position was futile. 'It was true to form of Bjorn,' he said. 'He was a stubborn man and one of the great things about working with him was that when he made a decision, with very rare exceptions, it was final.'

But for Worth – and IMG – Borg had dropped a bombshell. Contracts with tournaments and sponsors and television companies were cloaked around Borg's presence on a tennis court. 'I had absolutely no idea Bjorn was thinking like this,' said Worth. 'What else was he going to do with his life?' Worth and IMG's senior partners went into damage-limitation mode, adopting a policy of appeasement with major stakeholders in Borg's name. 'Bjorn was like David Beckham is today,' said Worth in summer 2004. 'He was at the height of his career. He had around forty endorsement contracts and companies had marketing and advertising campaigns all geared to this phenomenon called Bjorn Borg. He was going to be on television many weeks of the year, possibly winning more Grand Slam titles. He also had commitments to tournaments where he was not only playing for prize money, but also due to receive appearance money, which admittedly was slightly against the rules in those days. I had to go back to these people, as did others handling his affairs in the United States, and try to massage the contracts. It was where IMG's skilful management came to the fore. We never took less money, but we could negotiate extra time on the contracts.'

Worth, nowadays managing director of the Quintus Group, whose offices are on the King's Road, Chelsea, recalled the fallout from Borg's retirement as a 'turgid time'. To exacerbate matters, Mats Wilander was emerging as the next tour de force from Sweden and IMG had to withstand the competition of rival agents to sign him. 'Without going into details, I managed to secure Mats's signature, so here was Wilander as the new kid on the block and here I was renegotiating Bjorn's termination agreements. The point I am making is that Bjorn suddenly realised he was not the No. I guy anymore. I think he felt, probably with some justification, that some of the deals that should have been his, weren't, and one suspects that he felt I wasn't spending as much time on his affairs as I was on the new guy's.

'That was when one suddenly realised there was some fire left in his belly, because he got quite angry with me. Two years after his retirement, he was still making a lot of money, but he fired me anyway. Not IMG – just me. He said that he had lost trust in me and didn't want me to work for him anymore. That was hurtful. I had been with him for seven years, of which five had been fantastic. The last two had been pretty shitty, though. We protected him from all the grief and aggravation – and there was huge aggravation, some of it vicious, quite rightly, too.' Worth heard he had been removed from Borg's file through a colleague at IMG. 'That was pretty pathetic, but, hey, he was the boss. Am I bitter? No. I think I would have done it differently, but, after all, why should he have the aggravation of having to confront me in person?'

At his hour of departure, without an appreciation of the monumental contractual maze that would need to be negotiated by Worth and others, Borg cited boredom and fatigue as the reasons for his exit. To him, a tennis court had become little short of a prison cell. 'My life was tennis, tennis, tennis,' he said, plaintively. 'In the end, I felt I can't do this anymore.' Borg was talking with me in Naples, Florida, some fourteen years after he had taken his leave of the tour. 'I don't know if I was tired of playing or the things surrounding the game,' he said. 'I wanted a life of my own.'

Others felt this was a component of his retirement, but not the complete reason behind his withdrawal from the game. There are those who will tell you Borg knew his reign as monarch of the game had been ended and he would not play at the court of another king; the court of King John. Patrick McEnroe, for one, identified his brother as a symptom of Borg's malaise. 'I think Bjorn realised he was getting passed by someone a little younger and, maybe, more talented,' he suggested. 'Borg was so single-minded, so driven with a twenty-four/seven-type mentality. Maybe, if he had taken some time off, his desire could have come back. He might have tried to practise only three hours a day instead of six. When you are that good, it's not like you need to kill yourself. Pete Sampras proved that.'

McEnroe can actually pinpoint a moment in time when he sensed his brother had broken Borg's iron will forever. 'I think it happened in the 1981 US Open final in one game in the third set,' he explained. The score was set-all with Borg serving at 4–3 when, seated at courtside, Patrick watched his brother smother Borg with his panache and flair. 'In that one game, John hit a couple of genius-like lobs and a dipping passing shot and you could see the look of despair on Bjorn's face. It was a look that said, "This guy's too good – I can't beat him."' John himself admitted afterwards, 'I suddenly felt I could do anything.'

Wilander, who retains immeasurable respect for Borg's contribution not only to Swedish tennis, but also to the game globally, also felt McEnroe had been instrumental in his compatriot's retirement. 'McEnroe came along and suddenly someone was beating him and that wasn't cool for Bjorn,' he commented. 'Bjorn was playing for pleasure, of course, but he was playing to win. I don't think he particularly played to improve. He did what he did and he was just better than everybody else. We saw something similar when Mike Tyson arrived to blast his way to the heavyweight world title. But like Bjorn, Tyson couldn't last.

'Bjorn couldn't leave his hotel room, at least that's what we thought in Sweden. Although he probably doesn't get any more attention than someone like Andre Agassi gets today, Bjorn was the first sports guy who had to deal with it. He didn't know how, other than to lock the door. I could see guys like McEnroe were figuring out how to play him and he was not interested in competing with other Swedes. Once you are done, you are done. So much of Bjorn's strength came from his mentality on court.

You can't switch that off and on. I can relate to Bjorn quitting. That's exactly what happened to me. It's like once you are out of love, you're not going to fall in love with the same person again.'

Swedish journalist Bjorn Hellberg watched Borg's final win on the professional tour, a narrow victory over Jose Luis Clerc in the Monte Carlo Open in April 1983. 'Borg lost to Henri Leconte in the second round,' said Hellberg. 'If he had beaten Leconte, which he was close to doing, he would have played Mats Wilander and it would have been embarrassing. When Wilander played Leconte, he completely thrashed him. Borg's time was over – and he recognised it.'

Ingrid Bentzer had been the number one female Swedish player at the time Borg rose to stardom as a teenager and she had seen the game consume him. 'I think he stunned all of Sweden when he just checked out at the ripe old age of twenty-five,' she commented. 'There was a great sadness. He was our guy, a Swedish icon. He was calm, he was a Viking. Of all things traditionally Swedish, he fulfilled every criteria, but I could tell he was so fed up. It was like he was moulded in a cast. In the end, he just wanted to destroy that cast, smash it to pieces like the glass in a car windscreen. Everybody owned him and I have the feeling he couldn't even breathe. He just wanted to get out.'

John McEnroe's over-riding emotion was one of despondency. The player he most respected in tennis had walked out of his life – and he wanted him back. Mariana Borg recalled with clarity how McEnroe approached her shortly after Borg retired, at a party New York socialite Richard Weisman had thrown at his apartment. Mariana said, 'Bjorn had already decided he wasn't going to play tennis anymore when we went to a party at Richard's place. Everyone was there. John came across to me and said, "Come on, what are you doing? You have to convince Bjorn not to stop playing tennis." I told him, "John, there is nothing I can do. He's made his decision." John didn't understand. Nobody understood, nobody got it.

'Of course, when you stop after you lost a couple of matches, at Wimbledon and the US Open, people will think it has to do with that, but it had been in Bjorn's mind to retire at least one year before he lost those matches with McEnroe. He didn't fight because he didn't want to fight, not because it was John McEnroe.

You could see in Bjorn's attitude it was over. I knew he gave up. Bjorn had given up on tennis. I lived with Bjorn so I know. Life was too much for him. Fame was too much for him. When he told me he was quitting, I was very surprised. I respected his decision, but I thought maybe that he should just take a year out. But that was not Bjorn's way. I was in the room when he called Peter Worth in Val D'Isere. Of course, Peter was shocked. At the time, a lot of people say Bjorn quit because of me. It's the worst thing I ever heard. Also, it is untrue. It was his decision. He was tired. He had never lived his life. He wanted probably to experience what he had never experienced before.'

Lennart Bergelin, like Mariana, had watched the mental disintegration of Borg from close quarters. Their three lives were intertwined. Only Mariana and Bergelin witnessed Borg's sullen moments. Only they felt his anger. Only they knew the gentleman of Centre Court had a breaking point. And so, like Mariana, Bergelin, a man who will celebrate his eightieth birthday in the summer of 2005, had not been the least surprised when Borg told him the game was up. 'When you are together night and day for so many years you feel exactly in the air what is going on,' said Bergelin. 'You don't have to talk about it. Bjorn had no motivation. He was not the same in practice. He had not the same enthusiasm, not the same feelings. He'd had enough of the fighting. I thought he could stop for half a year and come back, but it soon looked like he'd had enough of it all and started other things. That was another life, another story, not this one.' No, this story is one where we travel back in time from the end of the most famous rivalry in tennis to where it all began.

1

TANTRUMS, LENNART AND GARBO

Bjorn Hellberg is bearded, sixty years old and has been responsible for over forty murders. In summer 2004 he visited Wimbledon for the thirty-eighth year in succession. 'I have not missed a day at Wimbledon in that time – not bad considering all the pubs they have in London,' he said, laughing devilishly. He is a greatly respected journalist, broadcaster and writer of Swedish detective stories. In 1971, he was also editing a tennis annual in Sweden. At the Stockholm Open that year, he interviewed a schoolboy called Bjorn Borg: 'My last question was: "Are you going to win Wimbledon?" Borg answered me with one word: "Yes." He was fifteen years old, but already he had such confidence in himself.'

Hellberg is a man immersed in Swedish tennis. The country had a status on the international stage prior to Borg's explosive entry: Sven Davidson was French Open champion in 1957 and won the Wimbledon doubles championship with compatriot Ulf Schmidt a year later; and Jan-Eric Lundqvist won the Italian Open on clay in 1964 and twice reached the semis at the French Open, also making it to the last sixteen at Wimbledon twice. 'Tennis was already big in Sweden before Borg, but when he came along it was crazy,' said Hellberg. With an eye for coincidence, he told me, 'Borg was born in the same area in the south of Stockholm as the famous Swedish actress, Greta Garbo.' Two legends from the same place, two people cut from much the same cloth; a coincidence indeed.

Garbo died in 1990, aged 84. She spent almost the last fifty years living as a recluse, having left Hollywood for New York in 1941 after the failure of her film, *Two Faced Woman*. Famously, she is often quoted, inaccurately, as saying she just wanted to be left alone. 'I was always inclined to be melancholy, even when I was a schoolgirl I preferred being alone,' said Garbo in 1928, as her star was rising. Like Borg, she both ended her career abruptly and without explanation and left an enviable body of work: films such as *Flesh of the Devil*, *A Woman of Affairs*, *Camille*, *Queen Christina* and *Ninotchka* are considered classics. She was classically beautiful on screen and intensely private when work was concluded. One critic observed: 'She had a face capable of registering everything . . . and yet nothing.' Borg had just such a face on a tennis court. In 1991, the year after she died, film scholar David Thomson wrote of Garbo: 'In going [on] the journey away from fame into privacy she established herself forever as a magical figure, a true goddess, remote and austere, but intimate and touching.' Garbo and Borg share more than the same place of birth and an unwillingness to live in the public eye. They are to be forever celebrated as part of Sweden's folklore.

Borg, who was born on 6 June 1956, had his destiny shaped when his father, Rune, one of Sweden's leading table tennis players, won the city championships and had first choice of the selection of prizes laid before him. Lennart Bergelin tells the story: 'On the table were fishing rods and other sports goods. Rune was sure about taking some fishing things, but he asked Bjorn what he wanted. Finally, Bjorn took the tennis racket, but as he was just nine years old, the racket was too heavy for him. He couldn't play a backhand shot.' Young Borg was an accomplished ice hockey player for his age, so the solution to the heaviness of the racket was easily resolved. He simply adopted the same grip on his racket as he did on his hockey stick. 'That was how Bjorn's two-handed backhand grip was born,' said Bergelin, laughing at the simplicity of a decision that was to change the game of tennis. No one before had played a two-handed backhand, but since Borg introduced the stroke, those using two hands on their backhand are now two-a-penny.

Borg's father, Rune, and mother, Margaretha, owned a small grocery shop in Sodertalje, near Stockholm. Borg, their only son, took himself and his first racket to the Sondertalje Tennis Club, but was denied entrance to the beginners' class as it was over-subscribed. Instead, he started to hit tennis balls against the garage wall of their home. In his mind, Borg was playing for Sweden in the Davis Cup; the wall was most often the United States. If Borg hit the ball ten times in succession, Sweden won the point; Sweden won the Davis Cup many times that summer. When you think that Steffi Graf was just four years old when she was playing with a customised racket made by her father, Peter, and that Andre Agassi hit balls with Jimmy Connors in Las Vegas at the age of five, Borg could be considered to have come late to tennis. Yet McEnroe was much the same age when he was introduced to the game.

'By the time he was eleven, Borg played in the tournaments on the west coast of Sweden on the summer tour,' said Hellberg. 'He played in almost every event, doubles and mixed doubles as well as singles. His mother arrived with sandwiches between his matches.' Borg's work ethic had been established. He also had that remarkable self-confidence that Hellberg had sensed from his first meeting with him. In an early interview, Borg said, 'I never had a coach for the first three years. That's probably why I have such unconventional strokes – a two-handed backhand and so on. They say you mustn't play like I do, but I just felt right when I played like that. What is important is not the way you hit the ball, but whether or not it goes over the net. And when it does, it is marvellous to watch. If you have a stroke of your own, one that really works, and you feel like playing it, keep it, even if it isn't "classical". Don't try to change it.' Borg won his first tournament at a small competition a three-hour drive south of the family home: 'I can still remember the joy I felt when they gave me the little winner's cup. I was very proud.'

Bergelin first saw Borg when he was thirteen, at which time the young protege was working with coach Percy Rosberg. 'Bergelin was a good player himself and reached the quarterfinals at Wimbledon three times,' said Hellberg. 'He also played some good Davis Cup matches for Sweden. Lennart had a majestic forehand, a good serve and volley, but a poorer backhand.' Bergelin's impact on tennis, however, was to come not from his own exploits on court. At Borg's side, he became part of the game's history. Bergelin recounted how they met: 'We have a handicap tournament in the King's Club in Stockholm and Bjorn lost in the final. I don't remember the name of the boy who beat him. I was the one there to give the prizes and I liked what I saw in Bjorn. He was thirteen years old, but I could see here was a player for the future. He played a double-handed backhand and I had never seen that before. He was very fast. He came with the right feet and I thought that was important. One of the things you watch when you first look at youngsters is how they move. Bjorn was moving really great. He obviously had a good eye for tennis. He always hit the ball at exactly the right speed and in exactly the worst place for his opponent.'

Bergelin began to work with him almost immediately and witnessed a side of Borg's personality that few saw. In his adolescence, Borg would occasionally demonstrate a short fuse. 'I could see he had a temper,' said Bergelin. 'I remember he threw a racket at the back of the court and it smashed into pieces. I told him if he carried on like that, he would run out of rackets.' Borg, in fact, had already been in trouble for his outbursts. 'When I was eleven to twelve I was swearing and throwing rackets,' he has admitted. 'I was the worst a kid could behave on the tennis court.' His local club told his parents they were suspending him for six months as a disciplinary measure. After three months, Borg appealed to be allowed back. He was told he had to complete his suspension: 'Since that point, I hardly opened my mouth again.'

Borg's early travels included a bus journey with other juniors to Monte Carlo and the Riviera and to a tournament in Milan. The oldest kids were sixteen, two years older than Borg. 'Of course, Bjorn beat them all easily,' said Bergelin. 'He won the singles and doubles.' With them in Milan was Swedish junior Helena Anliot, who became Borg's first girlfriend. Clearly, Borg was on a fast track into senior tennis. 'Anyone who had seen Bjorn play when he was thirteen, seen his groundstrokes and how he loved practising, would have realised he would be good,' said Bergelin.

As Sweden's Davis Cup captain, Bergelin took the decision to select Borg for the tie against New Zealand in 1972, to be played in Bastad, a picturesque club on the coast. Borg was one month shy of his sixteenth birthday. 'The youngster was a surprise choice and Bergelin was criticised,' said Hellberg. Even Borg was wrong-footed by Bergelin's selection policy. 'Bjorn had been losing to Ove Bengtson in practice, so he probably did not expect me to choose him to play,' said Bergelin. But play he did – and in his opening match fell behind by two sets to Onny Parun, an experienced and capable professional who had reached the quarterfinals at Wimbledon a year earlier. Yet even at such tender years, Borg never knew when he was beaten. He defeated Parun over five thrilling sets – and suddenly all of Sweden had heard of the boy prince.

Within two months, so had the global village of tennis. Borg's enduring affair with the All England Club began when he won Junior Wimbledon, defeating England's Buster Mottram in the final, from 2–5 down in the decisive third set. He could never have dared dream that this was to be the prologue to a most extraordinary journey on the most famous lawns in the world.

Around this period John Lloyd met Borg on a trip to Australia and New Zealand. Lloyd, who was Britain's own teenage prodigy, albeit a couple of years older than the Swede, remembered the expedition for reasons other than simply tennis. 'At the time, I was going out with Isabelle Larsson, who was No. 2 in Sweden,' said Lloyd. 'Bjorn was going out with Helena [Anliot], who was No. 3. Lennart Bergelin was with them. Bjorn had a glint in his eye around Helena. They were crazy for each other. On the trip I fell madly in love with Isabelle. She had long brown hair, olive skin and long legs. She was a sweetheart and we had a wonderfully romantic time. We got engaged, but as we were both so young it was a mistake.'

Apart from falling in love, Lloyd also benefited from practising with Borg. 'I remember coming back and saying Bjorn was a great guy who will win the French Open one day. But I also added that he would never win Wimbledon. I mean, with those big back swings, there was no chance he could ever win on grass. No way.' Lloyd, now an accomplished tennis analyst for the BBC, as well as a coach, began to laugh as he told the story. 'Win some, lose some,' he smiled.

Borg had ended his formal education by leaving school at fifteen – unlike McEnroe who was academically gifted enough to win a place at Stanford, a highly regarded college in California – and has been defensive about his school record. His argument runs: 'Firstly, I didn't drop school, I left school. In Sweden you stay nine years in your first school, from six to fifteen. After that you can go to another sort of school to continue your studies, and lots of people do, but there are plenty of people who leave school then and go to work. That's what I did. I decided to give tennis a chance for two or three years, to see if I could become a success at it. And if I hadn't had the sort of results I was looking for, I would simply have gone back to school. I think that in life if you see there's a good chance to take, then you have to take it. I liked school very much and I was quite good. I think a good education is very important and I have been very lucky. I have managed to make my way in tennis and have learned a lot by travelling abroad and meeting interesting people. But I repeat: if I hadn't done well at tennis I would have gone back to school.' It was never more than a hypothetical argument, of course. Borg would never need to return to the classroom.

2

A NEW YORK
STATE OF MIND

On a sunlit afternoon at Wimbledon in the summer of 2004, Hana Mandlikova stopped to exchange kisses with a man in a dark suit as they passed on the lawn outside the players' restaurant. Mandlikova, a past US, French and two-times Australian Open champion, as well as twice a finalist at Wimbledon, tells him he looks good. His smile is warm, his manner friendly and polite.

Patrick McEnroe, thirty-eight, has marched confidently and successfully from the shadow of his oldest brother, John. He has made his own mark in the game, climbing to No. 28 in the world in 1995, although he had greater success as a doubles player. Once he was ranked No. 3 doubles player in the world and his sixteen doubles titles include winning the French Open championship with compatriot Jim Grabb. Patrick is imbued with an easy charm and, like his brother, he has a sharp mind. When he reached the semifinals of the Australian Open in 1991, he was asked if it was a surprise. Patrick smiled and said dryly: 'It's just like you all expected – Edberg, Lendl, Becker and McEnroe.'

He was made US Davis Cup captain in succession to his brother and, like John, he is also a broadcaster. He works most frequently for cable network ESPN and CBS. John McEnroe senior and his wife, Kay, clearly, supplied a rich gene pool. Patrick is younger than John by seven years. In childhood, that disqualified him from offering John much of a challenge on the tennis court, but table tennis? That was another matter altogether. 'We had some heated ping pong matches in our garage,' said Patrick, once Mandlikova had melted into the milling throng of players, past and present. 'We needed an inordinate amount of masking tape to re-tape the handles on the paddles because we would wing them against the walls! On the ping pong table I had at least a chance to beat John every now and then – I never did on the tennis court, as I was much younger – so my dad would come running into the garage and shout, "What the hell's going on down here?" We'd say, "What do you think's going on? We're playing ping pong." '

Patrick said that it was only sports that brought John to fever pitch. Together they won the Paris Indoors doubles title in 1992. 'He wasn't like that away from the court, but he has always been extremely competitive and a perfectionist in that way,' said Patrick. 'And still is.' Patrick thinks John's attitude can be traced to his immediate bloodline. 'Where do you think John got his attitude from?' asked Patrick, rhetorically. 'My dad grew up in New York and he was poor. He was lower middle class and worked his butt off. He worked all day in the office of a law firm, then went to law school at night. My dad had that little bit of a street fighter in him. He had New York attitude. My mum is very tough. She has that Irish in her where you never forget anything. Obviously that came over to us in the way we were competitors. We had a combination of mum and dad, but John brought it to another level.'

John McEnroe Junior was born in Wiesbaden, in what was then West Germany, on 16 February 1959. His father was in the US Airforce at the time. His grandfather had emigrated to the United States from Ireland in the early 1900s. His mother was the daughter of a Long Island, New York, deputy sheriff. Between them, his parents were determined to create a happy and prosperous home and future for their family. On returning to Queens, New York, McEnroe Senior studied at Fordham Law School and he finished up a partner in one of the biggest law practices in New York.

When John McEnroe Junior was eight years old, the family moved one mile north to Douglaston Manor, just down the road from the Douglaston Club, which had five tennis courts, a pool and clubhouse. McEnroe – known as Johnny – was small enough to be called 'runt' by his peers. He began to play tennis at the club with his father, with Mark, who was born three years after John, and Patrick joining them when they were old enough to brandish a racket. The McEnroes were loudly enthusiastic over sport. 'We were definitely a family of yellers, my father leading the way blowing off steam or just making a friendly noise,' John Junior has recalled.

Like Borg, McEnroe spent hours perfecting his strokes, honing a featherlight touch that would be integral to his arsenal in later life. At nine, he was enrolled in the Eastern Lawn Tennis Association. Soon, his results entitled him to compete in national tournaments. At twelve, he was No. 7 in the United States in his age group. When he lost, he admitted he had a tendency to cry.

At this time, his parents felt their son needed to be further extended and John switched to the Port Washington Tennis Academy, a twenty-five-minute drive east from Douglaston. The head professional was a man called Tony Palafox, who had played Davis Cup for Mexico and won the Wimbledon doubles championship in 1963. Palafox later became a permanent point of reference in McEnroe's career. McEnroe confesses to another stroke of good fortune when Port Washington acquired the services of Harry Hopman as director of the academy, just a couple of months after he joined. Hopman was a legend in the game; the coach who moulded giants like Rod Laver, Roy Emerson, Ken Rosewall and Lew Hoad to create an era of Australian supremacy.

The star of the day at Port Washington at that time was a blond sixteen-year-old called Vitas Gerulaitis, who would one day forge a close friendship with Borg, but it was another kid at the academy who first befriended McEnroe, a gangly teenager named Peter Fleming. Their relationship, which blossomed and developed to the point where they ruled the world as a doubles team, began in the unlikeliest of circumstances. Fleming was in the coffee shop adjacent to the club when one of the coaches was talking up the potential of a younger boy. Fleming listened to the coach singing his praises until he'd heard enough. 'C'mon, how good can he be?' asked Fleming. The coach insisted he was an exceptional talent. Fleming was unconvinced. 'Tell you what. I'll give him 4–0, 30–0 a set, and we'll play for five bucks,' he challenged. The coach accepted and organised the match to be played the next week. 'Junior came up the next week and we played five sets,' recounted Fleming. 'I didn't win a game.'

Even as they pass through middle age together Fleming has never ceased to call McEnroe anything other than Junior, but the genesis of the nickname has nothing to do with McEnroe being named after his father. As Fleming explained, 'We were playing Fred Stolle and Roy Emerson in doubles when one of them – and I cannot remember which – called out to John, "Hey, Junior." Well, he went mad. He yelled back, "I AM NOT a junior, I am nineteen." To me, that was like a red rag to a bull! From that day on, he was Junior to me.'

McEnroe was junior rather than Junior to Peter Fleming when they played that handicap match at Port Washington. 'At sixteen, I was just a younger version of how I was as a pro,' said Fleming. 'I was wild man. I could hit some great shots, but I didn't keep the ball in very often. He was like a terrier. It was like he had his teeth into you and he wouldn't let go. He just wouldn't miss. He thumped me, but we actually became quite good friends. I used to spend all Saturday and Sunday at the club and so did he. We used to have these marathon chess games and play some touch football.'

Fleming remembered how tenacious McEnroe was back then. 'We didn't actually play that much on the court. Mr Hopman would usually take us on the court once a week for two hours. John and I, and sometimes Vitas and another guy called Horace Reid, would do some drills. There might be another couple of guys around, too. In one of the drills you only got a point if you hit your opponent with the ball. John would be right there and he would get thumped. And he would be hitting us. I mean, he was this skinny little kid. It was pretty impressive. I thought, OK, this kid's got some balls.'

McEnroe's time at Port Washington came to a controversial end when he was suspended for six months, along with his friend Peter Rennert, over what he claims was an innocent misunderstanding. Even before Port Washington went to Princeton for a match, McEnroe had already earned himself something of a reputation for horseplay – much to the non-amusement of those running the academy. This trip was to prove a bridge too far. McEnroe had finished his match and, with tennis still underway on other courts, he and Rennert got involved in a pick-up game of basketball in the gym. When another player was sent to tell them the bus was waiting, instead of ushering them on their way, he also got involved in the game. Another ten minutes passed before the head of the academy, Hy Zausner, arrived. McEnroe took the brunt of his anger and shortly afterwards his parents received a letter telling them that he had been suspended. Rennert met the same fate, but his parents apologised and his ban was lifted. McEnroe's parents were livid with the treatment of their son and he never returned. By good fortune, Palafox had become head professional at another club, Glen Cove. As he had identified and believed in McEnroe's talent, Palafox invited him to his new club on a full scholarship.

As he entered his senior year at high school, at Trinity, McEnroe was No. 2 junior in the country behind Larry Gottfried. He started to travel: to Argentina, to Venezuela, to Brazil. McEnroe in those days was at his best on clay courts, like those habitually used in South America. He was now playing against young men who would follow him along the professional trail, men like Argentine Jose Luis-Clerc, Yannick Noah, Andres Gomez and Ivan Lendl. In March 1977, McEnroe won the Banana Bowl in Brazil and felt entitled to be ranked No. 1 junior in the world. And as his talent began to emerge to a wider world, the cockiness and self-assurance that seemed to go with it was likewise not going unnoticed by some of the key figures in tennis at that time.

In April 1977 McEnroe found his way into a $100,000 event at Virginia Beach. The tournament was being promoted by Ion Tiriac, the Romanian tennis institution who masterminded Boris Becker's ascent to the summit of world tennis and who, during the 1980s, was unrivalled as a tennis entrepreneur (at Wimbledon in 1986 he managed three of the semifinalists: Becker, Henri Leconte and Slobodan 'Bobo' Zivojinovic). That may have been Tiriac's heyday, but he has continued to remain a key figure in the sport and in 2000 was an influential force behind one of the most emotional of all Wimbledon victories – that of the wild card Croatian with the thunderbolt serve, Goran Ivanisevic. Ilie Nastase may be the most famous Romanian tennis player of all time, but Tiriac has had a far more profound influence on the game and his country.

He is a large bear of a man with a bandit moustache, who has never cared much for doing things by half. In the days after the bloody downfall of hated Romanian tyrant, Nicolai Ceaucescu, in December 1989, the nation faced a devastating shortage of electricity. Tiriac persuaded Germany to re-route power to

Romania for two months free of charge. The head of Germany's electricity company just happened to be one of the sponsors of a women's tennis tournament that Tiriac ran. A call to the German foreign minister completed the circuit to switch on the lights.

In May 1990 he returned to Bucharest to promote and organise a Davis Cup tie against Britain. Up to then, he had only been to his homeland for one day in the previous decade of Ceaucescu's monstrous regime, even though he had kept a house in the city, as well as another in the mountains. As we walked through streets with buildings perforated with bullet holes, he was loath to estimate how much he had donated from his personal fortune, although most educated guesswork suggested it ran into hundreds of thousands of pounds. 'Whatever, it's a drop in the ocean to what is needed,' he said. To help combat the chronic shortage of drugs, he created a supply train using staff from his Munich office as couriers. He arranged for the profits from the sales of Coca-Cola and yoghurt during the Davis Cup tie to be given to the city's growing population of orphans. Tiriac explained at the time: 'There are 28,000 orphans in this country. Some are the victims of the revolution, others have just been abandoned because abortion was unheard of as it was a crime. We want to build orphanages for them and this was a gesture.'

Such events were far ahead of Tiriac when he first came across McEnroe at that tournament in Virginia Beach. As well as being there in an official capacity, Tiriac was also in attendance with the Argentine player Guillermo Vilas, with whom he had struck up an alliance. Vilas was a muscular athlete with long hair, who played guitar and wrote poetry in his leisure hours. He wore the air of a man of the night, but with Tiriac in his corner he never shirked his day job, winning the US Open, French Open and Australian Open, twice. He also escorted Princess Caroline of Monaco for some months. Vilas, like Borg, transcended tennis and leapt effortlessly from the sports pages into the social diaries.

As Tiriac recalled, 'I promoted the tournament for the late Bill Riordan and Gene Scott, and it was big deal. Credit to Bill, he asked me to give a wild card to a very young American. I remember I told him that I had too many Americans. Why couldn't he give me a Chinese or something else?' Riordan insisted this young player had a future. Tiriac asked for his name. 'It was

cEnroe celebrates the end of an era as he defeats Borg in the 1981 Wimbledon final

Enroe clan: John, right, with his father John Snr and brother Patrick

Borg receives a trophy from Lennart Bergelin, the man who was to become the most major influence on his career

Borgmania! Bjorn incited hysteria among teenage girls

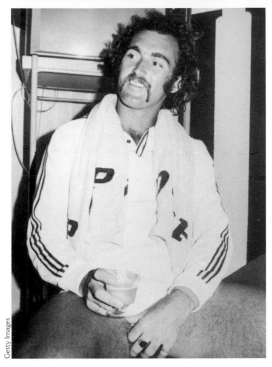

Mark Edmondson, the hirsute, hard-hitting Australian who pushed Borg to the wire at Wimbledon in 1977

Connors at full stretch to cut off a trademark baseline drive from Borg

Michael Cole

Borg's parents Rune and Margaretha sat alongside Mariana and Lennart, who are poker-faced as always

Borg jubilantly acknowledges his defeat of Connors in the 1977 Wimbledon final. Margaretha and Mariana join the crowd in jumping up, top right of photo

Empics

Pain is etched in the eyes of Jimmy Connors after Borg has retained his 1977 Wimbledon title at his expense

British tennis legend Fred Perry congratulates Borg after the Swede emulated his feat of winning Wimbledon for a third consecutive time

'You…

cannot…

be serious…!!'

Michael Cole

vin Curren, who had only ever played McEnroe in college before meeting him at
imbledon in 1980 explained: 'McEnroe had phenomenal skill – but it was
imidating to play him'

Borg trying to impersonate McEnroe... or the night the Swede picked a fight with English umpire Mike Lugg at Madison Square Garden, New York

Michael Cole

Macarow or Macaroni or some such thing. I was still playing four hours a day with Vilas myself, hitting balls here and there. Anyway, a young red-headed guy came up and said, "Hi, guys." I didn't know if he was talking to us or somebody else. Mr Vilas was No. 1 in the world. So, this young guy says, "Can I hit with you guys?" I asked Vilas should I kick his balls off? Vilas said not to do that and he would hit with him for half an hour. Vilas is Vilas.

'I let this kid go out and I saw him hit the tennis ball and I said he is fooling around. It's a joke, he cannot hit a tennis ball the way he hits, with a straight arm. He was moving around and the ball was most of the time coming to him. I said to Vilas, "This is strange, I never saw anything like that."

'Anyhow, he play about five or six minutes and says, "Lobs." No please, no fuck you or anything. "Lobs" to Mr Vilas! They are playing lobs and after five minutes he says, "That's OK for me, see you guys." I remembered watching him in the first round, in the second round and I can't believe what I am seeing. No way, he plays tennis like this and beats one of these guys. Nastase was quick, McEnroe was not quick or fast. He was simply there.' McEnroe, who has said he never needed more than five minutes to warm up before a match, lost that week in a semifinal with Nastase, but at least he stretched him to three sets.

This was not Tiriac's only story. 'In 1978, we played in Basle after Vilas had taken three months off. I show up and he was playing awful. I told the tournament Vilas was going to play qualifying. They said, "Excuse me?" Even if he was a God, I knew Vilas had to play matches. McEnroe arrived in Basle in November in a T-shirt. It was snowing, man. I gave him my jacket as a gift because he was freezing his arse off. He took it and didn't say thank you or fuck you, but anyhow that's McEnroe. He arrives in the final to play Vilas. They have a huge match . . .' Vilas fought off the young pretender's threat, 6–3, 5–7, 7–5, 6–4. 'From now on, I told Guillermo, you have to come prepared when you play him.' It was sound advice from a wise man. The world of tennis at large had to learn to be prepared to meet McEnroe; in every sense the game was placed on guard for the emergence of the New Yorker.

3

BORGMANIA SWEEPS WIMBLEDON

In 1973, Bjorn Borg's career was beginning to take off. That year he reached the final of senior tournaments in Monte Carlo and San Francisco – and the quarterfinals at Wimbledon. At the Monte Carlo Country Club, perched on a rocky ledge with enviable views over the Mediterranean, he was stopped from winning by Ilie Nastase. This was no disgrace, as just the previous summer Nastase had been denied the Wimbledon title after losing in a five-set classic with American Stan Smith. Yet in these formative days of his career, Borg confesses to having been troubled by Nastase's capacity for causing controversy on a tennis court. 'When I was eighteen or nineteen it was tough to play Nastase,' Borg wrote in his book, *My Life and Game*. 'I had no experience and got nervous waiting for him to talk nonsense to the crowd, umpires and even me. In the beginning he was difficult to play because I never knew what he was going to do. Maybe he didn't either. Every stroke was possible. His shots went anywhere with all kinds of spin.' Later, the two men would become friends and Borg could never find it within his soul to be angry with Nastase. 'I've no hard feelings against Nastase when he behaves like a maniac,' he explained. 'When we walk off court everything is fine and we're friends again.'

Nastase, still playing the clown on the seniors' tour, to the amusement of the paying customers, came out of Romania to wreak havoc with the conventions of the game. He broke rackets and hearts; mostly hearts, it has to be said. He stretched the rules and examined the patience of officialdom. He joked, but he also knew how to joust on the court. Nastase was one of a kind.

Connors followed with his own brand of commitment and cussed behaviour, that had as its source a will to win, and then came McEnroe. For a time, Connors played doubles in partnership with Nastase. They were prime-time box office, 'but I figured it was time to call a stop to the arrangement when our fines were becoming greater than our prize money,' Connors told me. He was only half-joking.

Tiriac identifies a succinct difference between Nastase and McEnroe, when he tells you: 'A tennis player is a character of the human being. Some of them keep their feelings inside, some of them throw those feelings outside. McEnroe and Nastase expressed themselves, and Becker was another one who showed all his emotions without keeping anything inside. McEnroe was a guy that put everything on show, yet when it came to business, he didn't fuck up. McEnroe took every possibility he had to win a tennis match. He used the entire book. Somehow, Nastase fucked it up. After twenty minutes of a match something would happen – it was raining or a dog or a cat appeared or some other distraction occurred. You could see the other guy look down the court and he would be thinking, "I cannot beat you, but I'm sure you're going to beat yourself again." That was my friend, Nastase.' Tiriac remains flabbergasted by Nastase's spartan success, given his gift for the game. 'With his talent I think Nastase was the best tennis player ever with the worst results,' he said. 'Two Grand Slam titles . . . that's very little for all that talent.'

In San Francisco late on in 1973, Borg lost to Roy Emerson, a man who had grown up in the Australian school of hard knocks. Emmo knew how to win – and how to live. Like most of the Aussies of the time, he never got lost on the road to the bar. Swedish journalist, Bjorn Hellberg, attached great symbolism to Borg's performance in San Francisco. 'It was the old master against the young pretender; one career stopping and the other beginning,' said Hellberg. 'Emerson won after losing the first set, but years later the great Australian talked with me about how he had been impressed by the stubbornness of Borg.'

But it was at Wimbledon where Borg made international news in that turbulent tennis summer of 1973, when the most famous tournament in the world was controversially boycotted by the players' union, the Association of Tennis Professionals (ATP).

It was a complex, highly charged and extremely political dispute that left the ATP in conflict with the International Lawn Tennis Federation (ILTF). The fallout was felt over London SW19.

The trouble had been brewing for some weeks when, at the end of the French Open, after Nastase had beaten Nikki Pilic in the final, a hastily printed press release was distributed to the international news corps. The release was to rip the tennis world apart. The ILTF announced that they had rejected Pilic's appeal against a nine-month suspension imposed on him by Yugoslavia for his failure to play for his country in a Davis Cup tie against New Zealand three weeks earlier. Pilic had become ineligible to play at Wimbledon. In the eyes of the ATP, Pilic's position made him a cause celebre. They felt it wrong that a man could be ordered to play for his country. Battle lines were drawn.

Of course, the issues ran much deeper, truth and fiction became blurred. The Yugoslavs had announced Pilic's suspension at the start of the French Open, only for the ATP to threaten to boycott Paris. Behind the scenes, the French and the ILTF allowed Pilic to play, pending an appeal. An emergency committee of the ILTF heard the appeal and reduced Pilic's ban to one month – a period which covered the Italian and German Championships and Wimbledon. Pilic doggedly insisted he would play in Rome and under threat of an ATP boycott the Italian Federation permitted him to compete for fear of the financial collapse of their tournament.

Pilic duly arrived in London ahead of Wimbledon. After protracted discussions, the ATP and ILTF reached stalemate. Sir Brian Burnett, a member of the general committee at the All England Club, recalled how an eleventh hour attempt to prevent a player strike had been agreed by all parties. 'We went to arbitration in a London court,' he said. 'The court ruled against Pilic. Then the ATP reneged on an agreement to abide by the decision of the court.'

Seventy-nine members of the ATP withdrew their entries from Wimbledon, but there were three exceptions: Ilie Nastase, Roger Taylor and Ray Keldie. Taylor has never before spoken about the intricacies of the dispute, suspecting that only a few people understood the fine detail behind the Pilic Affair, but in September 2004 he told me, 'It was a complex moment in the game and one that I have constantly refused to comment on. It possibly requires a book in its own right to explain, but two key factors were behind the reason I chose to ignore the ATP boycott. One, the players never got to vote on whether to boycott or not, and two, the ATP totally disregarded the ruling of a London court of law, contrary to what they had promised. I was under an enormous amount of pressure as British No. 1 and a player regarded as world class. I was getting daily phone calls from people urging me to boycott and others urging me to play. I made my own moral judgement – and in the circumstances I felt I had to play.'

Taylor and Nastase were each fined £2,000 by the ATP, while Keldie was fined only £400, perhaps because he was less well known. 'I believe we repaid Roger under the table,' said Sir Brian last year. Taylor countered proudly: 'I would have preferred to have paid the fine myself, but Wimbledon were insistent.' His loyalty seemed to have come at a small price to those in the Wimbledon committee rooms of the day. The great British public voted with their feet. The total attendance for the championships was 300,172, the second highest on record. 'I think this showed that the public were determined to back us,' said Sir Brian.

Taylor, thirty-one, the third seed behind Nastase and Czech Jan Kodes, was renowned as a hard competitor; a man of steel from Sheffield. Twice before Taylor had reached the semifinals at Wimbledon. Now he was received at these championships with patriotic fervour. 'The Yorkshire left-hander was greeted as a hero,' said Lance Tingay, the lawn tennis correspondent of the *Daily Telegraph*, writing in the *World of Tennis* annual, but not even Taylor could compete with the advent of Borgmania. The Swede – just seventeen – duly fulfilled his ranking as sixth seed by arriving to meet Taylor in the quarterfinals. Borg was the teenybopper's new pin-up, suddenly challenging Donny Osmond and David Cassidy for space on many a bedroom wall. Nastase may have been the popular idol at the time, but he didn't boast such a gallery of young girls at his court. Borg was where tennis met rock'n'roll and he was pursued by hysterical females wherever he went. Taylor had never seen anything like it before or since.

After recovering from two sets to one down, Taylor served for the match at 6–5 in the fifth set. At that critical moment, Borg was about to become the beneficiary of an act of sportsmanship from Taylor, who could not allow the significance of the prize at stake to cloud his sense of decency. He explained what happened: 'I was serving at match point to the left court at 40–30. I went for the lefty's trusted wide outswinging service and came in towards the net. I thought the ball had just missed the sideline, but the umpire called, "Game, set and match, Taylor." I looked at him and indicated that I thought the ball was out. On the strength of that, he changed the score to deuce. Borgy won the next point and I remember I had to fight to serve out the match [6–1, 6–8, 3–6, 6–3, 7–5].

'I'd won, but it was Bjorn who was mobbed. Screaming girls stepped on the Centre Court to mob him. It was the first time I had seen that and the last. With his long hair, you could hardly distinguish Bjorn from the teenyboppers around him! You knew then, here was a new personality on the block.' Taylor was subsequently knocked out in the semifinals by Kodes, who defeated Alex Metrevelli to win a tournament that managed to shine, notwithstanding the loss of so many of its stars. Borg's time was coming, though, and his fan base was young, vociferous and causing quite a stir. The following year, Major David Mills, the secretary of the All England Club, wrote to the head teachers of around sixty girls' schools, asking them to keep their students visiting Wimbledon under control!

While Wimbledon 1973 had been a landmark in Borg's development, his real breakthrough into the winners' circle on the pro tour came in the spring of 1974, when he defeated Nastase in straight sets to win the Italian Open at the Foro Italico, next door to the Olympic Stadium in Rome. 'Borg plays like a pawnbroker,' said Nastase, knowingly. 'He doesn't give any points away. Never. Maybe he's the same about his money.'

Already, Borg had won respect as an athlete, a respect that would trail him through his career. He had speed, strength and stamina. His resting heartbeat was forty-six. John Lloyd illustrated the level of Borg's athleticism with this cameo drawn from spells when they travelled together in later life on the champions' tour. 'When Bjorn was forty, he was asked by an institute of sports science in Sweden if he would undertake a cardiovascular test,' said Lloyd. 'Borg said that he would be happy to help, but that he didn't possess any running shoes. It was December and so Borg wasn't in proper shape, as there wasn't any tennis at this time of year. Bjorn got on the running machine and ran. Two hours forty-five minutes later someone tapped him on the shoulder and asked him if he would like to stop. Borg replied, "Up to you." That shows you how phenomenally fit a man he was.'

Nastase took to calling Borg, the Martian. 'In the locker room you'd never know if he had won or lost,' he said. 'He'd come in from the court, peel off his tight Fila outfits, fold them in a neat pile and shuffle off to the showers with that rolling walk of his. Whenever I'd lost I'd tear my clothes off and go to the showers leaving a mess of rackets and clothes behind, talking and some-times screaming at anyone within earshot.'

Having conquered Rome, Borg arrived shortly afterwards in Paris, for the French Open. He would leave a fortnight later with the first of his six French titles. At eighteen, he had become a player to be feared and avoided on a clay court. In winning his first Grand Slam championship, Borg demonstrated the mental tough-ness, stamina and patience that were to become his hallmark. In the fourth round he traded shots for five sets with Eric van Dillen, while in the quarters he went the distance, this time with Raul Ramirez. He required four sets to dispose of his semifinal opponent, Harold Solomon, but he saved his piece de resistance for the final, when he fell two sets behind to Spaniard Manuel Orantes, a twenty-five-year-old left-hander who was a clay court specialist.

Orantes must have felt like he had one hand on the trophy, yet Borg found a rhythm and a purpose in that third set and a final belonging to the Spaniard was stolen from him in broad daylight by an act of tennis larceny. Orantes was not so much beaten as mugged; in the final three sets he took two games as Borg triumphed, 2–6, 6–7, 6–0, 6–1, 6–1. 'Bjorn was killing him,' said Bergelin. 'On that afternoon, Bjorn proved he was a player who could be a champion. He showed he never gives up and gets better and better the longer the match goes on. His name was now all over the world – people may not have known much about Sweden, but they knew about Bjorn Borg.'

A year later Borg defended his French Open championship when he beat Vilas in straight sets, 6–2, 6–3, 6–4. Matches between Borg and Vilas generally turned into a war of attrition.

Rallies could last forty strokes or more. Borg said, 'When I played Vilas it's strange because I felt stronger, which sounds crazy because Guillermo is such a bull, yet I sense if we rally back and forth seventy-five times I am going to outlast him. I have the confidence to stay with him forever. How can he hurt me? He can't serve and volley and I can outlast him.' Even Tiriac, Vilas's loyal coach and mentor, knew the Swede spoke the truth. 'Almost always, Borg had one more ball than Vilas,' he explained. There was a memorable exception to that rule, though.

Some years after that 1975 French Open, Tiriac, a noble Romanian remember, somehow contrived to have himself appointed captain of Argentina in the Nations Cup in Dusseldorf. This allowed him to be seated courtside when Vilas met Borg in 1980. 'I made a deal with Vilas. He was going to play my way even if it meant him going to lose, 6–1, 6–0. Actually, it was one of the few times Vilas beat Borg. What I told him was very simple mathematics, if he could execute the plan. He was not to play thirty-seven balls. After the fourth, fifth, sixth or seventh ball he was to come in with a forehand and . . . smash the ball away. That's what he did. I remember because my relationship with Vilas was different to any other between coach and player. We were close. Anyway, he did as I asked and he got scared after the first set as he won it so easily. In the second set, he pulled back. I said, "OK, I am leaving now." Vilas said to me, "No, no." I stayed – and Guillermo beat Borg over three sets that day.' It ended a painful sequence of nine straight wins for Borg, stretching back over the previous five years. 'But when they were playing the same game, Borg was always one ball better than Vilas,' emphasised Tiriac. In that regard, Vilas was a member of a very big club.

4

LOVE AND HEARTACHE

In the summer of 1976, Borg made a telephone call that was to change the circumstances of his life. Borg's reign as French Open champion had been ended by Adriano Panatta, a matinee idol at home in Italy, when he called Mariana Simionescu on the house phone from his room in the Paris Sofitel Hotel.

Simionescu was nineteen years old and she had been eliminated from the French Open by Britain's Sue Barker, who went on to secure the title. Simionescu, from Romania, was sharing a room with her mother and she answered the phone to find Borg on the line. They knew one another from afar – they would nod and exchange cheery waves at tournaments – but now Borg was on the phone inviting her to dinner with him and Bergelin. The two traditionally shared a joint celebration dinner in Paris as their birthdays are only a handful of days apart. Simionescu placed Borg on hold while she asked her mother's permission to go out with him and his coach. "My mother said it was OK as long as I didn't stay out until six in the morning!' she recalled.

'We went to Montmartre and had dinner with Lennart. It was a coup de foudre – unbelievable really. We had only said hello and goodbye before, but Bjorn told me afterwards that he had been looking out for me all the time. I had no idea. After all, he was already a superstar and I was not even a beauty. I was round. Probably, he liked my personality. We spoke to one another in English, not that either of us could speak good English, but we could understand each other. It was love at first sight.'

Eighteen years later, Simionescu sat at a pavement cafe at the Place des Moulins in Monte Carlo with a cup of coffee, a packet of Marlboro Lights and her memories. Even as a player, Simionescu smoked, and she always smoked to calm her nerves when she watched Borg play. The sun had already risen over the Mediterranean and we were grateful our table was in the shade of an olive tree. Across the street, a road sweeper was collecting the overnight litter as dirt is outlawed in this principality. In front of the Europa Hotel opposite a gardener watered flowers and plants. Even in the week when the principality is defenceless against the noise pollution of Formula One cars practising for the Monaco Grand Prix, there is no slackening of standards. Appearance is everything.

Simionescu has called Monte Carlo home from not long after she met Borg, but these days her apartment is set back a few blocks from the sea, on Places des Moulins, and she shares it with Anthony, her fourteen-year-old son from the relationship with racing driver Jean-Luis Schlesser that ended in 1994. 'My son is my biggest prize,' she said – and smiled. Anthony, who has her undivided love and affection, is addicted to golf and showing real promise at the Monte Carlo Golf Club. 'Anthony has too much energy and in French we have a saying, "les chiens pas de chats" [dogs aren't cats]. He doesn't stay one second in the same place, much like his father, but Anthony is still a little boy and when his energy is channelled with his talent he can become a very good golfer.'

Simionescu is an expert at channelling energy and talent. Borg relied on her stability from the start, it seems. She gave selflessly: 'In 1975 Borg wrote a book – I have it upstairs in my apartment – and on the first page there is a picture of Bjorn playing Roger Taylor at Wimbledon. In the picture is me watching the match. I wanted to watch Bjorn, because I had heard so much about him. Funny, isn't it? It was our destiny to be together.'

After that first dinner date in Paris, unromantically shared with Bergelin, Simionescu flew to Scotland while Borg came to London to begin his preparations for Wimbledon. 'I went to Edinburgh to play, but we were crazy to be together as soon as possible,' she said. 'It was terrible weather in Scotland, but I won the tournament, though don't ask me who I beat in the final. I was so excited to leave to come to London to see Bjorn that I took the cup when I left the club. Apparently, they were looking for me everywhere, but I had rushed to my hotel to pack. Eventually, someone found me and came to get back their cup, that was engraved with all the names of the previous winners of the tournament. I didn't know that it wasn't mine to keep!'

Her priority had been to get to London as fast as possible to be reunited with Borg. 'In London, Bjorn came to where I was staying, but after two days Lennart said this is too much and told Bjorn to tell me to come to the hotel with them. To tell the truth, Bjorn and I did not sleep that much!' She was alongside Borg from the outset of his historic journey through Wimbledon and she knows she was a force for good in his life. Perhaps Borg does now, though she will never know. 'Listen,' she said, quietly, 'it was a destiny. It was not something that you could calculate. You just follow.'

While Borg's emotional needs were suddenly falling into place, his overall game was still not complete, not if he was to achieve his goal of capturing the Wimbledon crown, but in that same summer, that too was about to change. Colin Hess was in his office in the West End of London when he was summoned to meet his boss Peter West, the chairman of sports marketing company West Nally. A representative of Guillermo Vilas had called looking to find some grass courts for the Argentine to practise on before Wimbledon, explained West. As a committee member of the Cumberland Lawn Tennis Club in Hampstead, Hess was just the man to offer advice. He took the request to the Cumberland, an exclusive club in Alvanley Gardens, NW6. 'Everyone jumped at the idea,' he reported to West, who, besides being an astute businessman, was also a well-known sports commentator and television presenter in Britain. Hess was deputed to look after Vilas when he arrived at the club in June 1976. The Cumberland had four manicured grass courts marked parallel to one another outside the members' pavilion; a tennis oasis in the midst of the large, detached homes of this sought-after residential area.

The courts offered perfect – and private – facilities for a man seeking to adapt his game from the slow clay courts of Roland Garros to the sleek grass of Wimbledon. After Vilas's first practice partner had departed, Hess asked him if he had a new sparring partner lined up. Vilas told him, 'I am bringing a young Swedish guy called Bjorn Borg.' For the next five years, Borg would call the Cumberland his home from home in London and so, of course, would Bergelin and Simionescu.

Bergelin had wanted somewhere that he could work with Borg hour after hour in a bid to alter his service action, adapting it to the peculiar needs of playing on grass at Wimbledon. 'In 1975, Bjorn was a little unlucky at Wimbledon,' said Bergelin. 'We were practising and he slipped on grass that had been wet by some sprinklers and he tweaked an ankle. He lost in the quarterfinals to Arthur Ashe (the eventual champion when he upset the odds to beat Jimmy Connors), but we knew then that we were not too happy with Bjorn's serve. He played the ball in one piece, one movement. We changed that. He needed more power. We worked on that for two hours a day at the Cumberland Club that summer in 1976. Another one not happy with his client's serve was Tiriac. He tried to change the serve of Vilas at the same time as I worked on Bjorn's serve. We were serving a lot!'

One of the crucial aspects that Borg and Bergelin appreciated about the Cumberland was that the groundsman, Pepe Villarette, would always endeavour to get them a court, even if it had been raining, which was not exactly an unknown phenomenon in an English summer. This was not the case at Wimbledon as the courts had to be protected for the championships. Another disadvantage at Wimbledon was that court time was severely rationed for the same reasons. 'We could play at the Cumberland even if it was raining, which was fantastic,' said Bergelin. However, if the conditions on the grass were too perilous, Bergelin would obviously not risk Borg slipping and injuring himself so, as insurance, the coach had another court booked a few miles away at the Vanderbilt Club, an indoor tennis centre. 'I had courts booked for 10 to 12a.m. at Cumberland and the Vanderbilt and from 3 to 5p.m. booked in both places again,' said Bergelin, still proud of his eye for detail. Without appreciating it at the time, Bergelin and Tiriac were establishing the ground for an army of coaches who would follow.

Borg's game was constructed around such detail and such long hours. Unlike McEnroe, he chose not to hone his game in doubles match play at tournaments. For the majority of the years Borg spent using the Cumberland, his most frequent practice partner was Vitas Gerulaitis, the star at the Port Washington Academy in New York when McEnroe was making his first moves as a tennis player.

Hess recalled: 'Invariably, Bjorn and Vitas would be hitting and then Lennart would stop and talk to them. It was a real coach-pupil relationship, with Bjorn content to work hard on his game. They were so nice – that's a funny word but it does describe them – and so unassuming and just delighted to be there. Our groundsman, Pepe, who sadly died in the early part of 2004, would ask them to change court sometimes, but he always tried to have a court for them, even if it meant them starting later if it had been raining. At the end of play, Bjorn and Vitas would happily sign autographs for our members who had come to watch.'

Gerulaitis acquired the nickname Broadway Vitas because he had a great love of life, a willingness to live on the edge and a voracity to go out to play after darkness had fallen. He had long blond hair that never looked like he had troubled to brush it and that never changed with the passing of the seasons or the changing of fashion. No one had more street cred in the 1970s. He hung out with the trendiest crowd in New York – his name was a passport to places like Studio 54 where the rock giants of the day chilled out – but Gerulaitis could also play. He won the 1977 Australian Open and finished as runner-up to Borg at the French Open and runner-up to McEnroe at the US Open. He never beat Borg, but business on the tennis court never interfered with their friendship. He also lost sixteen times in succession against Connors before he finally beat the former world No. 1. 'Nobody,' he said, 'beats Vitas Gerulaitis seventeen straight.'

But there was a dark side to Gerulaitis's lifestyle. As his ranking fell, so his addiction to cocaine increased. This was not a secret, and friends feared for him, yet Gerulaitis manfully fought through his problems and seemed to discover a route to salvation through the game of golf. He also returned to his first love, tennis, and pitched up on the seniors' tour that had become good box office across the United States, thanks to the driving ambition of Jimmy Connors, which injected real competition, as well as entertainment, into the tournaments. Gerulaitis was back among friends, men like Borg, Connors and John Lloyd, when tragedy struck. In 1994, aged forty, Gerulaitis died from accidental carbon monoxide poisoning in a guest cottage on a friend's estate on Long Island, New York.

Lloyd was the man who broke the sad news to Borg. Connors, Borg, Lloyd and Gerulaitis had been together for an exhibition in Seattle, Washington. Three thousand people had packed the venue that autumn evening. 'Vitas was on fire that night; every joke he made came off,' said Lloyd. 'That night, the last real big night he was going to have in public, Vitas had the crowd in hysterics. He was coming out with one-liners and interacting with Jimmy and Bjorn. He was just fantastic. But then I hit a lob and, as Vitas went back for a swing at the ball, he felt a twinge in his back. Afterwards, rather than stay in Seattle with us, he went back to the East Coast two days earlier than planned for some treatment. But he also went to a charity tennis event, a corporate night which the organisers begged him to do. Vitas agreed, then went back for a nap to the place where he was staying, because he wanted a rest before he had to return for a cocktail party later the same evening. He went to sleep and never woke up.

'The first I heard of the terrible news was when I came off the court in Seattle and received a phone call from my wife, Deborah. She told me Vitas was dead. My first thought was, "Oh no, Vitas what have you done?" I was devastated. I went to find Jimmy and Bjorn to break the news to them. I was told Jimmy was in an amusement arcade with his daughter, but I couldn't find him. Bjorn was in the restaurant with his girlfriend. I grabbed him and said, quietly, "Bjorn, Vitas is dead."

'Bjorn asked, incredulously, "What are you talking about?" I told him about the phone call and as he listened to what I was saying Bjorn went grey. He went upstairs and called Vitas's mother. She came on the phone and he was in hysterics. She was still in shock, she didn't know what had happened. Vitas had been Bjorn's closest friend. That week in Seattle they were great together. Vitas had really cleaned himself up and he was as good as he had been in a long while. His career in television was going well and he had become a golf nut. Vitas was a compulsive man. He had to do everything one hundred and ten per cent. That was why, perhaps, he had his problems. I admit we all thought at first he had died because of drugs. All Bjorn kept asking was, "Why has he done it?" When we found out what had actually happened, it didn't make sense. How could it?'

Almost 500 people went to Gerulaitis's funeral. Borg, Connors and Vilas helped carry his coffin. 'McEnroe was in tears the whole time, like most of us,' said Lloyd. Connors and Mary Carillo, who won the mixed doubles championship with McEnroe at the French Open in 1977, before creating a successful career in the commentary booth, both delivered memorable eulogies. 'Forty years was not long enough for Vitas to live, but it was long enough to leave a lasting impression on all of us,' said Connors. 'I loved him and I'll miss him.' Sentiments the world of tennis echoed.

After two weeks of intense work on his serve, Borg headed for Wimbledon as No. 4 seed in that sun-blessed summer of 1976. In the first round he met Britain's David Lloyd. At the time we could not have supposed it was the start of an historic tennis odyssey. However, Lloyd, dismissed in straight sets, 6–3, 6–3, 6–1, on Court No. 2, did have an insight that Borg was an exceptional talent, even before he set foot on court with him. Lloyd explained: 'I had been at the Scandinavian Open a few years earlier and, as usual, I was out watching the tennis when I came across this teenager with long blond hair and a bloody great bandanna. The kid was playing a different way, not a way I'd seen before. I thought, this is a good way of playing, the net doesn't come into play, because the ball travelled so high over it with its spin. I thought here was a kid who was going to change the game.'

John Barrett, promotions director for tennis company, Slazenger, and an institution in British tennis after a lifetime in the game as a player, team captain and broadcaster, shared Lloyd's enthusiasm. 'Our agent in Sweden, Gilles Templeman, had told us about Borg and we placed him on a contract to use our racket.' Borg won Junior Wimbledon playing with a Slazenger racket in 1972. Then he returned a few years afterwards to play at the pre-Wimbledon tournament at Beckenham. A man named Ceslaw Spychala, known as Spike to all and sundry, was the tournament director for Slazenger and was requested to look after the needs of the teenage Swede. When Barrett appeared, he asked Spike if Borg lacked for anything. 'All he ever asks is for more time on the practice courts,' said Spike. Barrett later sought out Borg in the players' tea room. 'Anything you need, Bjorn?' he said. Laughing, Barrett recalled Borg's response. 'He said, "Can you help me get more time on the practice courts?" Even then, Borg was a perfectionist, very driven.'

Borg was still using a Slazenger racket when he won his first French Open in 1974, but not long afterwards Mark McCormack, Mister IMG himself, came to London to meet Barrett and Ian Peacock, managing director of Slazenger. 'The money McCormack wanted for worldwide rights was far too much for a company like ours,' said Barrett. Subsequently, McCormack negotiated a deal for Borg to play with Donnay rackets.

If that disappointed Barrett, he felt even more appalled when Slazenger were forced to let McEnroe slip through their fingers as well. After McEnroe's deal with Wilson ended, Peacock and Barrett made a presentation to John McEnroe Senior at Slazenger's advertising agency in London. 'We had rackets with McEnroe's name on, a clothing line, bags and an advertising campaign in place,' said Barrett. 'McEnroe senior was knocked out and we won an approval of an agreement with them. He was definitely coming to us, but then Dunlop, the parent company, decided McEnroe had to play under their brand, and that's what happened. We were absolutely mortified, it sent shock waves right through the company.' On such whim in the boardroom is history changed. McEnroe and Dunlop Maxply, and later a graphite version designed to the American's preferences, became synonymous with tennis success around the world.

By the time David Lloyd met Borg at Wimbledon, the Swede was starting to swing his Donnay with its double-length grip to devastating effect. 'When I went to play him, I knew what a good player Borg was, but I admit I didn't think he could win Wimbledon,' said Lloyd. 'He must have been a little nervous, first match on grass for a year, and I was a pretty good grass court player. I was experienced and thought I had a shot. All I remember is that whenever I got to a big point on his serve, he got his first serve in every time. Boff! It went straight in a corner. He had an unbelievable first serve. It was heavy and he served a high percentage. If you analysed his game, at the beginning he could hardly volley, but he came to the net behind ground strokes that put you out of the court and he was left only to poke the ball over the net.'

Lloyd was not alone in being bemused by Borg. In the next two rounds, the Swede brushed aside Marty Riessen and Colin Dibley without loss of a set, but then his body threatened to let him down. 'Bjorn was feeling a muscle strain from all the serving he had done,' said Bergelin. 'It was bad. As he prepared for his round sixteen match with Brian Gottfried, Bjorn couldn't serve.'

Swedish journalist, Lennart Eriksson, recommended a London-based doctor called Richard Rushman to manage the crisis. 'Before the match with Gottfried, Bjorn had an injection to deaden the pain,' said Bergelin. Borg's mental strength allowed him to success-fully compete against both his American opponent and his injury, but from that match on, Borg required pain-killing injections to survive the tournament. 'I remember the needle for every match got bigger and bigger,' explained Bergelin. Between end changes Borg could be seen lifting his shirt to spray his sore stomach with an aerosol to deaden the pain. Yet pain or no pain, Borg was a class apart for first Vilas in the quarters, then hard-serving Roscoe Tanner in the semifinals. At twenty, the Swede with the headband and double-handed backhand had arrived in the Wimbledon final.

Just one man stood between Borg and the championship – the wildly unpredictable Ilie Nastase. And this presented Mariana Simionescu with a dilemma. 'Ilie was my idol,' she recalled. 'In Romania, he was a God for us. I was madly in love with Ilie when I was twelve or thirteen. I would take a bus to wherever he was playing in Bucharest and if I couldn't get there I would cry. My heart was divided, as I had only known Bjorn for three weeks.'

Nastase, part court jester, part genius, had a fantastic fan base in Britain, but they tended to be older and slightly more reserved than the fanatical following Borg had acquired without trying. As they waited to walk out on to the Centre Court, Borg wore the blank expression of a man about to take his seat at a poker table. Nastase fussed with his appearance. 'Ilie's last action before going on court was to brush his hair,' said Borg.

Four years earlier, Nastase had played beautifully and lost a thrilling five-set final with Stan Smith, a one-time corporal in the

US Army. He was not to get that close to the championship against Borg. 'Bjorn was like a wall, every ball you hit comes back,' said Nastase. More often than not, Borg returned the ball with interest, too. On that summer afternoon, the world witnessed Borg's speed and athleticism on the grandest stage of all. Nastase's own repertoire was exhausted and extinguished, and the Romanian went down, 6–4, 6–2, 9–7.

At his moment of triumph, the unshaven Borg threw his racket skywards in a cameo of joy that was to become his hallmark. In the competitors' box where family and friends sat, Mariana joined the applause echoing around Centre Court, but she had mixed emotions. 'I was falling in love with Bjorn, but I was still very reserved when he won,' she said. 'I wouldn't have minded if he had lost that first final, because Nastase would have won and I would have been happy for him and for Romania, but it was incredible for Bjorn to become champion without losing a set – and without sleeping that much either!'

Borg, a tall, muscular man, released his first meaningful smile of the fortnight as he held aloft the trophy for the photographers assembled on Centre Court, but he admitted, 'I think it took me at least a week afterwards to realise what I had done. Yeah, at least a week. A lot of people said I couldn't play on grass.' Well, a lot of people had to readjust their thinking.

5

TEAM BORG

Peter Worth had been with IMG in their European headquarters in Geneva for barely three weeks when he was told the company had a client for him to meet. If Bjorn Borg liked him, Worth was told he would be given responsibility for his account. Worth, a twenty-five-year-old Englishman, was a chartered accountant who spoke French. Borg was the rising European star in McCormack's galaxy of sportsmen and women. 'For reasons I won't go into, his previous managers could no longer handle Bjorn,' said Worth. 'To be handed Bjorn as a client within three weeks of joining IMG was a dream come true. In those days, Mark McCormack only employed professional people; you were either a lawyer or an accountant. His philosophy being, you worked for IMG and you were the hotshot businessman managing the hotshot sportsman. The sportsman played the sport and the businessman took care of business. Not only that, but McCormack wanted to do away with agents being portrayed in the image of a fat-cat, ten-per-cent, cigar-smoking, Lew Grade-like character. The idea was like for like, with twenty-five to twenty-seven-year-olds managing the same age group – and it worked. It was a magic formula.'

Worth's initial task was to unravel problems that had developed after Borg had moved out of Sweden. 'There were big shenanigans going on . . .' he said. 'Bjorn had a shop in Monte Carlo and a house in Cap Ferrat [a short distance along the Cote D'Azure, but, critically, in France]. For tax reasons, Bjorn had to have a flat in Monte Carlo. I walked into that situation as the voice of reason.'

For the next seven years, Worth managed Borg's business affairs in Europe, during which time Bob Kain became the overlord at IMG's global HQ in Cleveland, Ohio. After Borg won Wimbledon for the first time, Kain said, without fear of contradiction, 'This made Bjorn a worldwide celebrity making money in America, Europe and Japan. He made the numbers jump from little to pretty damn big.' Worth fitted into the plan on the ground and, in his own way, he was as integral to Borg's growth and increasing success as Bergelin and Simionescu.

While they looked after his professional and emotional needs without complaint, Worth took care of business, just as IMG envisaged, and was overwhelmed with offers. 'I did the Fila, Diadora, SAS, Saab and Donnay deals for Bjorn,' he said. 'This was not IMG's skill in unearthing deals, they just came to us. That was the easy bit. The difficult bit, and where the skill comes in, is structuring the deals to get the best amount of money while committing the athlete to the least amount of time. The secret was to make sure your sportsman only has to concentrate on his sport and then, a few times a year, do his TV commercials, do some shop openings, that sort of thing. On the whole, I think we did a good job for Borg. We sheltered him. He was hugely rewarded, quite rightly, because the companies who paid him a huge amount of money got a huge amount of value out of him. There is not a single company out there who would say, "We overpaid for Bjorn Borg." He delivered in spades.'

The strategy expanded as Borg became a global brand in the manner of American golfers Arnold Palmer (McCormack's original treasure) and Jack Nicklaus. 'Bjorn had separate contracts in the tennis sector for the USA and the rest of the world,' explained Worth. 'In America, Borg was contracted to play with Bankcroft rackets, while he used Donnay in the rest of the world. Actually, he played in the US with a Donnay racket that had Bankcroft markings. It was perhaps a bit naughty, but everybody was happy. Borg liked a very stiff shaft, with a double-length handle. No one else played with a racket like that. It had no give in it at all.'

Worth's relationship with Borg was sound, but he never considered himself part of the Swede's entourage, unlike so many agents in the modern era. Worth focused on business. 'The deals were done for him, he signed them and we got a commission. I wasn't a friend of Borg in the true sense of the word. He wouldn't call me up and say, "Peter, Mariana and I had a flaming row and I was bad and I shouldn't have done that." I wasn't in that loop. I didn't want to be. I don't think many were. For support, Bjorn had Mariana and Lennart and his parents.'

After Borg triumphed at Wimbledon, Mariana rarely left him. She marginalised her own career for the sake of his. She recognised in Borg a man of exceptional talent and a man who required constant support. 'I tried to play my own tournaments, but Bjorn needed me very much,' she said. 'I gave him balance in his life. To live with a champion – someone so good at something – you have to have an unbelievable mentality. You can't be selfish. You have to think of him.'

His life became her life. 'We had a certain way of living, we were very precise,' she said. Mariana means their lives were dictated by Borg's practice regime. He never compromised the time he spent on the court. Mariana never protested. Once she did request support from him, however, asking him to come and watch her play at a Virginia Slims tournament in Seattle. 'Bjorn went crazy,' she said, laughing at the memory of Borg playing cheerleader. 'He said to me, "I don't know how you do it." I think he spent most of the time in the hotel room. Afterwards I said to him, "See how difficult it is to live with somebody like this."'

When Borg returned to Wimbledon as defending champion in 1977, Mariana fought her way into the fourth round, where she was drawn to meet Britain's Virginia Wade, the No. 3 seed. 'I wanted Bjorn to come and watch me,' she said, even though she knew it was an impractical wish. 'If he comes to the court, there would probably be a riot! The girls were crazy for Bjorn, but I still wished he was there. I needed someone myself. I was playing so well and, perhaps, I would have won, but I had no one to look at like he has.' Wade, incidentally, won 9–7, 6–3, and went on to win the championship in front of Queen Elizabeth II, in her Silver Jubilee year and on the only occasion that Her Majesty has visited Wimbledon.

Mariana was comfortable in her relationship with Borg, so she wasn't jealous of the girls who besieged their hotel or pursued him at tournaments. 'He was a good looking boy – and he was fit,' she smiled. 'Sure, it was crazy, but I was not jealous. I had him. I was proud. Besides, it was nice for him to be appreciated that way. I was not jealous of people looking at him, taking advantage of his game or his physique, because it was something beautiful to see. His physique was even better without clothes!'

Borg's charisma came entirely from his look, not from his lifestyle or from his opinions. Worth recalled, 'Where Bjorn was incredibly clever – and I don't think it was by design or intention – was that he didn't say anything. If you think about it, that's so clever. Journalists then created his personna: the Iceman or Mr Cool, the man who never shouted at umpires.'

Borg, in reality, never much cared for the media side of his business. In contrast, McEnroe often took the first question at his post-match press conference as an invitation to address the troubles of the game or the world at large. American journalist, Bud Collins, observed, 'We should have charged John for coming into the press conference as he treated it like a session on a psychiatrist's couch.' Those of us with press passes loved McEnroe for that, naturally.

Borg's relationship with the Swedish press was almost non-existent. His decision to base himself in Monte Carlo made logical sense to Borg, but was treated at home as a near-treasonable offence. He argued he lived in a climate more conducive to playing tennis, he had the convenience of Nice Airport close at hand and, of course, he benefited from the advantage of the tax laws. The Swedish media took an alternate view. 'I was called unpatriotic, selfish and money-hungry, which didn't ease my distrust of tennis writers,' said Borg.

Bjorn Hellberg tells the other side of the coin. 'Borg was a difficult man in some respects. For instance, he would not speak with the Swedish press. His press conferences were in English. We have to accept people are different. Borg is a stubborn man and that stubbornness took him to exceptional, faraway places on a tennis court, but this did not make it easy for us at Wimbledon, for example. Remember, we were dealing with a man who was a very big star in Sweden, a man more important than our prime minister.' Worth admitted, 'Borg had a non-relationship with the Swedish press. There seemed to be a series of issues.'

Monte Carlo was one such issue certainly, as was an unwilling-ness, at the height of his powers, to represent Sweden in the Davis Cup. After making his Davis Cup debut in 1972 at the age of fifteen, Borg won thirty-seven of his forty singles matches for Sweden. In 1976, Borg was on the squad, but never played as he claimed to be injured. Without him, Sweden's defence of the Davis Cup, a victory Borg had inspired, ended in defeat against Italy in Rome. Borg finally returned to the team in 1978 and played again in 1979, but brought his Davis Cup career to an abrupt close after he beat German Klaus Eberhard in 1980. That match took place in Bastad, so he finished playing Davis Cup where he had started, and it ended in controversy, in disputes over contracts and money.

According to Worth, 'IMG and Bjorn had huge problems with the Swedish Tennis Federation, because it was still at the stage when amateurs were running tennis in individual countries. It was expected that the players should participate for their countries for nothing. We were at the forefront of saying to some of the federations, the directors, that this was not acceptable. These guys are professionals. You go to work, you get paid for it. There were contracts to be respected, too. Borg had a contract with Fila, they [the Swedish Federation] didn't want him to wear Fila clothes. That would have left Borg in breach of contract with Fila. Stupidly, in my view, the Swedish Federation had signed with a rival clothing company and I told them he wouldn't play Davis Cup in those clothes, because of his own contractual obligation.'

Unsurprisingly, the Swedish press vented their anger on Borg. He made himself an unwitting target for vitriolic condemnation on at least one other occasion. Worth recalled, 'Bjorn and Vitas [Gerulaitis] went to Israel to play some exhibition matches and, as they drove from one venue to another, some Israeli Army guys stopped them. They got chatting and the soldiers asked them if they'd mind putting on some army fatigues and have their picture taken holding guns.' Borg and Gerulaitis happily posed for some photographs, supposing they would be no more than a souvenir for the guys they had met. Instead the photographs were distributed worldwide, to the disgust of Palestinian freedom fighters.

'The Swedish press were appalled that Borg had posed in Israeli uniform,' said Worth. 'Worse, Borg got a death threat from a Lebanese militia group that had a base in Sweden. I got heavily involved. There were tense negotiations with the militia. The Swedish press were not helpful.' Borg, it was reported later, felt in grave danger, after the threat against his life. He took the precaution of hiring armed guards. Eventually, an apology appeased the terrorist organisation, to the relief of Borg and Worth. For Hellberg, the whole episode was regrettable. 'Borg was perhaps guilty of no more than bad judgement, but in Sweden he received a lot of criticism and there were problems,' said Hellberg. 'I think the overall opinion was that he shouldn't interfere with politics.'

According to Worth, Borg cared little for what was written about him at home, even if he considered himself a victim. His values could be measured twofold: winning tennis matches and massaging the bottom line. Worth commented: 'The money interested him, quite rightly so, as he recognised this was a business, but he didn't have much to say. Sometimes, I sat in a corner when he was interviewed and I could almost give the answers verbatim. They were banal and uninteresting. You must accept that English for Borg was a foreign language and, however much we thought he spoke it well, he was limited in his vocabulary. It seems he had the same problem in Swedish.'

For Borg, tennis was the language he spoke most fluently. And through his game and success, the money rolled in from a diversity of sources. Dolls, key rings, headbands, notebooks, jigsaw puzzles, calendars and posters were all marketed under his name, alongside his contracts with blue chip companies. He was becoming seriously wealthy. 'At the height of his game, it could be argued he was the wealthiest sportsman around,' claimed Worth. 'He was an Arnold Palmer in the making. Arnold never said that much either, besides, "Hi, really nice to see you." Actually, that is what makes a star, that ability to keep their head below the parapet while continuing to smile. Borg was doing that nicely.'

Outside his tournament schedule, Borg was now central to a series of lucrative exhibition matches that IMG began to promote. Worth explained, 'We created an exhibition tour that was lucrative for him and other players in the IMG stable, naturally. They'd be making more in a week of playing one-night stands than they would make in a month of playing tennis on the tour. The players loved it. It was a money-making exercise – and one we did with our mates.' Regulars aboard this gravy train with Borg were Gerulaitis, Panatta and Nastase. Other players, costing far less to hire, were booked as required. For instance, Per Herqvist, an old friend of Borg from Sweden, often played. 'Per did a lot as a fill-in, as you want a guy who is going to do it for almost nothing,' said Worth, acknowledging the cynicism at work. The big percentage of the promotion was always reserved for Borg.

These one-offs were an exhaustive merry-go-round of airports, hotels and arenas. The official tour was sceptical of the arrangement and feared the players were being over stretched. 'It was an argument,' conceded Worth, 'although I don't think that is the case. I defy anyone in the world of sport to say that the manager ever forces his players to do anything. That was not the way IMG worked. You worked for your client and said, "Right, this is the opportunity. Do you want to take advantage? Here are the pros and here are the cons. You make the decision." Yes, we would take the flak. We don't mind journalists accusing IMG of overworking people. We'd rather that than have the criticism aimed at the player. It wasn't going to affect our money-making capacity if we were criticised, but if, for example, Borg was criticised, it was. It was quite a good strategy.

'Borg was never resistant to it. He loved it. I can't, for professional reasons, divulge individual contracts, but I would think Borg would gross something like a quarter of a million dollars a week. Courts sold out wherever we went. It was a licence to print money, it really was. In Geneva, we did a couple of exhibitions that sold out 7,000 seats a night. That was the beginning of the Martini Open, which became an IMG event. Same happened in Milan and Kitzbuhel.'

In time, McEnroe became part of Borg's circle on the exhibition circuit. Together, they were a marketing man's dream. One night they were playing in Milan, before a sell-out crowd in the old Palazio della Sport, and Mike Lugg had been hired to umpire the match. However, the evening did not go entirely to plan, although it wasn't, for Lugg, the international incident that he later experienced with Borg. Lugg has a photographic recollection of the incident. He is an ebullient man, ably qualified for his current part-time role on the highlights programme that is broadcast each night from the French Open Championships at Roland Garros. 'This was my first real experience of big stars in an exhibition,' recalled Lugg. 'At the time, McEnroe had signed big contracts in Italy through Sergio Palmieri, who was then in

IMG's Milan office and was a good friend of John. I had steered clear of exhibitions, not through choice but through circumstance, but Palmieri wanted me to umpire this one. Before the tournament I sat with Sergio and he instructed me to employ the code of conduct in the match. I said, "Are you sure?" He insisted we play the code, end of story.

'In those days, we shared the same lounge as the players. I heard Borg say to McEnroe in the lounge, "You have the first, I have the second and we play the third." At the time, that really didn't make too much sense to me, but about fifteen minutes after we started, McEnroe won the first set, 6–1. Borg hadn't done anything. At this stage, of course, Borg was the super hero. He didn't sit down at the changeover at 6–1, he went straight out and stood on the service line, almost encouraging the crowd to pick him up. And they did. They went crazy for Borg. Eventually, McEnroe gets up and about forty seconds later they are sitting down at the side of me again, because Borg has served three aces and had a service return put in the net. Thirteen minutes later it was one set-all.

'In the third set, it was magnificent tennis. Here were two guys who were really determined to put on a good show and competing with all their might. I forget the exact instance, but McEnroe had a service called a fault. I stuck with the call. He was naughty to me and I said, "Code violation, audible obscenity, warning Mr McEnroe." McEnroe went ballistic. "What? This is an exxo, we don't do the code." I told him it had been cleared beforehand. John called out for Sergio, so Palmieri came to the court with me sitting in the chair, totally bemused at what was happening.

'McEnroe says, "Sergio, this is absolute bullshit. This is an exhibition." Palmieri told him we were playing the code of conduct, to which McEnroe says, "Sergio, if you don't take that code violation away you are going to see the biggest double fault you have ever seen." Palmieri insisted the warning stood. McEnroe went back and his first service is in the first row of the balcony. The linesman, of course, is looking at the service line and he doesn't know what has happened. Eventually, he looks at me. I point to where the ball has gone. He shouts, "Fault!" This brought the house down, but then McEnroe did it again . . . Honestly, I cannot remember who won that night, but it was a tremendous experience.

'After the match, we met outside, waiting for a car to go back to the same hotel. I went up to McEnroe and said, "John, will you ever forgive me for being an arsehole like that?" He looked up and replied, "I forgive you." McEnroe was always a pleasure to work with. What he would say to you on the court never influenced how he behaved with you outside. In fact, I'd like to think I am a friend of his. I have great respect for him as a player and even more respect for him as a television commentator. As a person, I love him to bits. Even so, I decided that night in Milan was the last exhibition I would work!'

Executives at IMG never had a shortage of ideas, broadening exhibition events into a format television networks found irresistible. Sue Barker found herself invited to partner Borg in one such event at Hilton Head Island, South Carolina. Barker, who grew up in Devon, was viewed on the tennis circuit as being as English as strawberries and cream. As a consequence, she was popular in the United States. 'Believe it or not, I still have the tape of that event in Hilton Head,' she volunteered, with a hint of embarrassment in her voice. 'I roared with laughter when I last watched it with my husband, Lance. It helps to have had a couple of drinks beforehand! I have the poshest English accent you have ever heard. I sound so terribly sweet. Whatever happened!

'Anyway, I think Bjorn and I were both eighteen or nineteen and I was there because I had just signed with IMG. The event involved playing singles, doubles and mixed doubles and you got points for each match you won. Basically, if we won the mixed, Bjorn would win the overall title . . . and $50,000. We beat Evonne Goolagong and Arthur Ashe, leaving us to play Martina Navratilova and Ilie Nastase in the final. Well, Nasty began threatening me, because I had passed him a couple of times down the line. I didn't think he was joking as Nasty was really trying to intimidate me. And that was when Bjorn became my absolute hero. He went straight up to Nasty and stood nose to nose with him. Nasty shut up and never said another word. Bjorn had terrified him. I was grateful, but I think Bjorn could see his dollars going out the window unless he acted! Fifty thousand dollars was a huge amount of money in the 1970s.'

Barker, later to share a successful broadcasting partnership with McEnroe during Wimbledon, admitted to being spellbound by Borg. 'Because we were the same age, he was such an inspiration,' she said. 'Bjorn, and later Jimmy Connors, when he was in his mid-thirties, stirring the crowds at the US Open, had the most effect on me. At seventeen I used to go to see Bjorn play because he was a joy to watch. We thought that we couldn't beat the oldies, that the Billie Jean Kings of this world were far better than us, but Bjorn had no such inhibitions. He believed he could beat anyone. I think he just proved a heck of a point for us.'

Yet even to Barker, Borg remained an enigma. 'Bjorn was gorgeous looking, but I never thought of him as sexy. It's funny, but he had this aura that made everyone in awe of him. He was different to the others. He was just like this untouchable, God-like person. Even when you played with him, he would not say a word when you sat together at the changeovers. The only time he might say something was on the court, when he suggested where you should try to hit your return or something. That was fine; that was how Bjorn was. That was why, in a way, it was so bizarre when he got together with Mariana. He always said he was never going to play that long and you almost thought he was going to stay as he was until he finished playing tennis, then get married. But Mariana brought out so much more of Bjorn. She is a lovely person. She had no side to her personality, she wasn't after anything. Although Bjorn was successful, I wondered how happy tennis was making him. We had a lot of fun on the women's tour. I had a great time with people like Chris Evert, Evonne Goolagong and Virginia Ruzici, but I worried at the kind of unnatural life Bjorn was leading. I think Mariana really made him happy. They seemed so well suited.'

Better than anyone – with the exception of Bergelin, perhaps – Mariana knew what made Borg tick. She was also one of the few who knew that Borg the Iceman had a meltdown point. Mariana explained: 'To live with him was nice, pleasant, but sometimes it was like this . . .' She banged her fist hard against the table. 'Bjorn was very stubborn. Oh my God, you don't know how stubborn, but he was never bad tempered or violent. No, never. If he shouted, sometimes I shouted louder. You just had to walk away. Even when you have right on your side, you have to be psychological and realise that some things do not matter.' During a match that was displeasing him, Borg would use a secret signal to vent his anger on Mariana. 'No one could see him do it, but he would tell me to leave the court.' She flicked her right hand across her thigh in a demonstration of Borg's sign language. 'As he didn't get upset on the court, he had to get upset with something. That was me.'

Bergelin, too, could be in the line of fire. He was intelligent enough to appreciate that even a man as level-headed as Borg had to have an occasional outburst. He looked on it as Borg's safety valve. Bergelin's one real bone of contention was Borg's exhibition schedule. 'Four times a year, he takes off on an exhibition binge, where he'll play four matches in five nights all in different cities,' Bergelin told Gene Scott, who, as well as being a lawyer and publisher, also played Davis Cup for the United States. 'The exhibitions are killers. Each night he finishes at midnight and by the time he has had a meal and gone to sleep, it's 2.30a.m. The next day he has to get up at 8a.m. to go on to the next city. It's too much. The body doesn't recover from that sort of strain easily. Bjorn's a baseline player, so the exhibitions are tougher on him physically than the net-rushers. I should go to the exhibitions, too. Bjorn doesn't want to lose to McEnroe even in an exhibition, because there will be a carry-over effect against John in tournaments. If someone beats you a few times even in practice, it's easy for him to lose respect for you.'

But as Worth said, the exhibitions were where a player made serious money. When Connors won Wimbledon in 1974, he received £10,000; thirty years later, Roger Federer received £602,000. 'We made our money after winning Wimbledon or the US Open, not for winning it alone,' explained Connors. 'Our money came from exxos or special events. Typically, I would play seven weeks of exhibitions and eight weeks of special events, but always turn up for the tournaments on the regular tour. I'd only have to play eight to ten weeks a year if I was playing today! I talked to Bjorn years after we had finished playing and I asked him how he thought we would do if we were on the market now. You know what Bjorn said? "Jimmy, they couldn't afford us." Who said Bjorn never said anything?'

So, Bergelin had to accept that the exhibition circuit was going to be part of Borg's life; and if it was part of Borg's existence, it was part of his own. Bergelin never thought of himself before he thought of Borg, even if he acted as a sergeant major when it came to ensuring discipline and dedication on the court. Also, it seems he provided Borg with a secret weapon. 'Bjorn was very lucky to have Bergelin,' said Balazs Taroczy, his Hungarian practice partner in Paris. 'That made a hell of a difference as to how Bjorn was seen in the eyes of the other players. It gave him an extra edge. He was the guy with a coach.'

While his value to Borg was immense, Bergelin was paid a pittance. 'Lennart was appallingly paid,' said Worth. 'I know, as I negotiated the contract. In today's terms, this guy should have been a multimillionaire. Having coached a five times Wimbledon champion, he should never have had to work again, but Borg was my client and I am proud of the negotiations I did on his behalf. I think Lennart was paid $20,000 a year; anyway, it was some ridiculously small amount.' Bergelin laughed at such a public revelation. 'If I coached today I would be a millionaire, it is true,' he said, 'but money was never that important to me. It was the tennis. What mattered was having the chance to be together with a real, real champion. That was great.'

His contribution ran deep. Once Borg had signed with Donnay, Bergelin travelled to their factory in Belgium to custom-build a racket Borg liked. 'Before we got to Bjorn's racket, he tried thirty-seven models,' explained Bergelin. 'I was at the factory a lot. I had never seen anyone with that double-handed backhand. He came up with a much longer grip than anyone else played with.' Borg would arrive in Paris for the French Open armed with forty rackets. How many did he take on court? 'A dozen,' said Bergelin, all of them numbered to correlate with the tension in their strings. 'Very often I had to jump on them to test the tension was right for Bjorn. If one was broken, we had maybe up to four in reserve with the same tension. In Paris, the rackets could be strung to 30 kilos. At Wimbledon, you would want a racket with less tension. When you play on grass, the balls can be a little wet, fluffy. In that case, you had to play a little bit more of a catapult system. Usually at Wimbledon, Bjorn had his rackets strung between 17 and 22 kilos. If it was very dry, you could go up a little.'

Bergelin fulfilled many roles. On the road, he had all Borg's calls diverted to his room for screening. On the court, Borg looked to

Bergelin for reassurance in moments of crisis. 'I had to sit there with a poker face, no matter what,' said Bergelin. Down there on the court, Borg had turned just such a look into an art form.

6

JUNIOR COMES OF AGE

In May 1977, the United States Tennis Association (USTA) handed John McEnroe $500 and gave him a plane ticket to Europe. He was entered for the juniors at the French Open and Wimbledon, but as he had a couple of ATP ranking points, McEnroe thought he would take his chances in that tennis crap-shoot known more formally as qualifying for the main draw. In Paris he succeeded in winning the requisite three matches and drew Australian Alvin Gardiner in the first round proper. Alvin who? McEnroe never stopped to inquire, although at this point Gardiner would have been entitled to ask, 'John who?' McEnroe breezed through for the loss of a mere six games over three, one-sided sets, in a match that attracted only close relatives and friends.

However, a reality check was just around the corner, in the form of his second-round opponent, Phil Dent, an Australian with a Davis Cup pedigree and a hardened professional veneer. McEnroe was about to get a lesson he would not forget. Disturbed by the incompetence of the line judges, McEnroe sportingly refused to accept the worst of the dubious calls and invited Dent to play a let on more than one occasion. Dent, meanwhile, never reacted to any of the suspect calls that occurred on his side of the court. After five sets, Dent's experience allowed him to prevail. At the net afterwards, the Australian told McEnroe, 'Listen, sonny, this is the pros and we don't give away calls.' The message was filed in McEnroe's mind – for life.

Even if his adventure in the men's singles was at an end, McEnroe still had the juniors' championship to contemplate and, through a stroke of good fortune, he was to find another outlet for his burgeoning talent. At Stade Roland Garros, he met Mary Carillo, a childhood friend from Douglaston, who was playing in the women's draw. On a whim, they decided to enter the mixed doubles. Carillo, one year older than McEnroe, had joined in the boys' games back in their neighbourhood days together. 'We played everything – basketball, football, ice-hockey,' said Mary. 'John was by far the best athlete around. His was the team you definitely felt like being on! But we also used to play a lot of tennis against each other when he was eleven and twelve.' She later played at Port Washington, where Harry Hopman occasionally disciplined McEnroe for his sometimes irreverent approach to training by making him play with the girls. 'Hop used to get mad because John would start dinking around and using all that loose-wristed stuff to produce outrageous spins in the middle of some straightforward drill,' said Mary, who, like her doubles partner of 1977, later made a reputation as a distinguished broadcaster on American television. 'So Hop told him that if he wanted to play like a girl he could come over to our court and play with real girls!'

Their partnership in Paris was to prove fruitful. As the tournament unfolded, McEnroe progressed unimpeded in the juniors and mixed doubles. Indeed, the final of the mixed was scheduled for just one hour after McEnroe had defeated Australian Ray Kelly in the junior boys' final. McEnroe's regret was that few people watched him play either match. His final with Kelly was played at the same time as the duel between Guillermo Vilas and Brian Gottfried for the French Open crown. By the time McEnroe and Carillo were beating Romanian Florenta Mihai and Brazilian Ivan Molina in straight sets to win the Mixed Open title, the crowd was already heading for home having seen Vilas crowned champion.

No matter, the two teenagers from New York were not going to allow such a comparatively small disappointment to deflect them from partying. Carillo recalled how they responded. 'Mixed doubles champions at the French Open!' she exclaimed. 'Wow, we could hardly believe it. Four of our friends from Douglaston just happened to be in Europe and we all sat around the table and popped the champagne and made jokes about how half the town had come to Paris to see us win the mixed. It was a great evening.' McEnroe left Paris for London in ebullient mood. At eighteen, he was the winner of a Grand Slam championship. Unbeknown to him, his excursion to London was to prove even more eventful.

The 'qualies' were held at Roehampton, a twenty-minute drive from the All England Club. Some competitors arrive in the downward spiral of their careers, rolling the dice one last time in the hope of being able to walk through the gates of Wimbledon again. Others come to Roehampton harbouring dreams of making a break into the big time. Tempers fray, tears are shed, hearts are broken. It is a hard place to win, but an even tougher place to lose. McEnroe was at home in just such an environment. After Paris, he was ready to make another move and, unlike so many who pitched up at Roehampton, his game was tailored for grass. Also, he felt more comfortable in London than he had in France, because he didn't have a foreign language to contend with. At Roehampton, he beat Christopher Roger-Vasselin, Uli Marten and then, in the rain, overcame Gilles Moreton. He was qualified to play at Wimbledon for the first time.

It was also the first time he was in the same main draw as Borg, the Swede having missed the French Open. Borg, the defending champion, was seeded No. 2, behind Connors. The Swede had no desire to change a winning formula. He asked his management to ensure the courts at the Cumberland Club were at his daily disposal and he booked into the Holiday Inn at Swiss Cottage, a short journey away. He shared a suite with Mariana, with Bergelin along the corridor. All telephone calls for Borg were diverted to his coach's room.

While Borg had a courtesy car supplied by Saab, McEnroe was on a tight budget. He travelled on the tube and, like any student in London, he stretched his dollars by eating pizza and pasta at cheap and cheerful restaurants. In the first round, McEnroe started like a dream, taking a love-set from Ismail El Shafei of Egypt. El Shafei, a burly left-hander, who had won the Wimbledon junior invitation event thirteen years earlier, made McEnroe work a little harder after that, but the American teenager still cruised in straight sets into the second round, where he had to meet Colin Dowdeswell.

Borg's second round opponent was Mark Edmondson, who had stunned the tennis world by claiming the scalps of Ken Rosewall and John Newcombe as he won the 1976 Australian Open championship. (Who would have guessed that twenty-nine years later the Australians would still be waiting for their next home-born champion?) By now Borg's reputation as a player of outstanding ability and remarkable resilience went before him, yet his rivals on tour did not feel an overwhelming sense of hopelessness against him at Wimbledon as, clearly, they did on the slow clay in Paris. Within the locker room there remained a communal belief that Borg was vulnerable on grass, especially in the early rounds. Edmondson, two years older than the Swede, was quietly confident that his attacking game would ask questions of Borg's counter-attacking strategy. As events transpired, his confidence was not misplaced.

'Without sounding as though I am blowing my own horn, I knew how to win on a grass court,' said Edmondson. Not that he had learned to play on the surface, as he had grown up in Gosford, New South Wales, some fifty miles north of Sydney. In his childhood, Gosford had a population of 30,000; today, it is close to one million. 'I only saw a grass court when I went to the city for the state age group championships,' he explained. 'Borg was basically the best player in the world – and on a clay court I think he was almost unbeatable – but I believed that in tennis the ultimate aggressor should always be able to beat the ultimate defensive player. I'd won the Australian Open out of the blue, beating Rosewall and Newcs, and then won another grass court tournament in Brisbane. I figured I had a strong serve, reasonable returns and, if my ground strokes were a little erratic, I believed that if I had only to hit one of them I could usually pick a spot.'

Edmondson had known from the moment that the draw was made that he would meet Borg, provided he could beat a British player called Michael Wayman. In actual fact, Edmondson hurt his shoulder playing Wayman on a miserably damp day. As the drizzle fell, the game became too tight to call. Momentarily, Edmondson considered retiring as the pain bit deep. 'I was really struggling,' he said, 'but, to tell you the truth, the other Aussie boys and me didn't like him. We called him Whinger Wayman. He was disliked because he didn't show much respect, so I wasn't going to give up against him.' Edmondson held out to win, 7–5 in the fifth.

With play severely disrupted by rain, the Australian had an extra day to receive treatment and declared himself fit to play

Borg. They were scheduled to meet on Court 14, in the far corner of the grounds, where some temporary stands had been erected. 'The court wasn't flat,' said Edmondson. 'It was a bit like a paddock, rising and falling, and there were bound to be a few more bad bounces. That was an advantage for me.' Edmondson had never played Borg before, but he had watched him a great deal. His strategy was clearly defined in his mind. 'I was going to play him in a way I thought he was weakest. I was going to serve and volley on both balls. I told myself I would have to grin and bear it when he hit a winner past me. The pressure has to build on the other guy if you keep coming to the net. Borg had an out-standing first serve and he could volley, but he didn't do so all the time. And if he missed his first serve, you knew he wasn't coming in, so when I made a return on his second serve I just ran in. Every time. I was prepared to take my chances.' Edmondson won the first set, 6–3. Then he took the second, 9–7. His game plan was working a treat.

The defending champion was in a hole. 'I saw him shaking his head,' recalled Edmondson. 'He turned to look at Lennart Bergelin, not to be coached, but for some kind of support I suppose. Lennart shrugged his shoulders.' In reality, Bergelin and Mariana were fearing the worst. Bergelin's recollections are vivid: 'It was one of the most nerve-racking matches ever. It was a new court, it was wet and I could see that it was difficult to play on. There was not a regular bounce.' Mariana made it sound like a visit to the Chamber of Horrors. 'Oh, my God, that was horrible,' she exclaimed. 'Horrible! From matches like this, I don't know how I didn't get an ulcer. Edmondson served so well, a serve you couldn't touch. I never thought Bjorn could win. Nothing worked for him that day.' Her cigarette count was high as she tried to soothe her nerves. 'I left the court at least once,' she said.

Edmondson, meanwhile, kept in his groove until he served at 1–2 in the third set. 'Borg hit four cold winners. I didn't touch the ball,' he remembered. 'That was a bit of a bummer.' The third set fell to Borg. 'I regrouped and for the fourth set the gloves were off... We were both fighting like hell.' Borg could not get away from Edmondson, who cut a menacing figure at the net through his sheer size and evident exuberance for the battle. At 4–4, Edmondson had a break point on the Swede's serve; a break point which, if converted, would allow him to serve for the match. 'I hit the ball deep to the backhand corner and followed it to the net,' said Edmondson. 'In that corner of the court, Borg always looked like he was going to hit cross-court, but, at the last moment, he drove the ball down the line. As he hit the ball, he was outside the lines, but I picked his shot. The trouble was he hit it so well that I had to dive to my right to play the volley. Yes, I was diving around before Boris Becker came along! Usually, Borg is so fast to cover the court, but at this moment he isn't moving. I'd hit the ball over to the forehand corner of the court and he was still in the backhand corner. I had him . . . Didn't I?'

Edmondson was still on the grass, following the flight of the ball. 'As I looked up from the ground, the ball was landing a few inches out,' he said. 'I could have been serving for the match, I could have been serving to put out the Wimbledon champion. Instead it was deuce. I admit for a moment or two I was psychologically flattened.'

Borg held, then broke, Edmondson's serve to level the match at two sets all. Now the Australian was on the back foot. His reserves of energy were being rapidly depleted. 'I was used to serving and volleying every second game,' he explained. 'But against Borg I was going to the net a huge amount on his serve, too. In essence, I was volleying every game. It's a lot further from the back of the court to the net than it is to cover the court from side to side as Borg did. I felt like I'd already played eight sets, not four. When do you play eight sets? I started to feel fatigue. I was becoming a fraction slower to the ball and there was Borg still fresh. He's used to playing for ten hours on clay! Eventually, I was just worn down. By the end I felt I'd played ten sets.' Borg took the day, 3–6, 7–9, 6–2, 6–4, 6–1. 'I had in my mind I could beat him,' lamented Edmondson, more in admiration for Borg's strength than his own demise. Borg's father, Rune, had watched alongside Bergelin and Mariana. 'We were so nervous,' admitted Bergelin. 'Bjorn was really happy to get over that match. Sometimes, one man ends up just a little luckier on the day.' Sometimes, history hangs by such a thin thread.

McEnroe may have arrived at Wimbledon as an unknown teenager, but he was not to preserve his anonymity for long, on court or off. 'The first time I met McEnroe was in the secretary's office here with Major David Mills. I happened to come down to speak to David about something and there was McEnroe arguing with him.' So said Sir Brian Burnett, the Wimbledon chairman of the day. 'McEnroe had been fined after he'd got stroppy and slashed his racket into something or other on Court No. 1, I think. Anyway, if memory serves he was told he was fined five hundred pounds. McEnroe was arguing against it. I talked to him for a long time and tried to convince him he'd play much better if he could control his temper. As I recall, he promised not to do it again, so I let him off, which was a great mistake. He never said thank you either.'

When we met for coffee, Sir Brian had just played his weekly game of tennis. At ninety-one, he was the oldest of the four men on court by almost a decade. When pressed, he modestly admitted to being on the winning side. Unwittingly, the McEnroes, father and son, had chosen a formidable opponent when they crossed the path of Burnett, a man medium of height, but giant of stature.

After graduating from Oxford, Burnett joined the Royal Air Force in 1934 to begin a thirty-eight-year career, as distinguished as it was long. As a young navigator, he was selected to join the crews being assembled in the Long Range Development Unit. 'To impress the Germans,' said Sir Brian, 'Air Minister Kingsley Wood issued a creed that the RAF had to achieve a world record for flying at altitude, at speed and long distance by the end of 1938. In those days, one had to specialise and I specialised in navigation.'

Burnett became involved in a project that was to extend the boundaries of flight. In November 1938, three RAF aircraft with three crewmen aboard each, all of them pilots, with two of them, respectively, specialists in navigation and wireless operation, left Egypt bound for Darwin, Australia, almost 7,200 miles away. It was a pioneering journey into the unknown; a journey that would take over two days in a single engine aircraft made by Vickers. 'We weren't flying very high – never more than 18,000 feet – as we didn't have any oxygen,' explained Burnett. 'We were saving weight, you see; no oxygen, no parachutes, no dinghies, no safety aids at all. We were saving all the weight for fuel in the wings.'

His voice is unmistakably Oxbridge, but he talked about an extraordinary time in his life with great humility. 'First night over

India, it was completely overcast. Never saw the country at all until just as we were leaving the Indian coast at dawn. Took our navigation from the stars – luckily there had been plenty of stars visible. We spent the second day over the Arabian Sea and the second night over Malaysia and Borneo. That's where we encountered the really bad weather. We were caught in a big storm, electrical sparks – St Elmo's Fire – running up the wings, very frightening. I must admit I did fear we might not make it, pretty dicey. There was torrential rain and the engine wasn't covered in. We learned from the great aviators that you should never attempt these sort of flights with one engine. They recommended three, but the Vickers was the only aircraft that could do the job at the time.

'It was a quite a narrow cockpit, three seats one behind the other. To change positions, the pilot at the controls had to climb out backwards, still holding the stick. The planes were fitted with autopilot, but, unfortunately, ours wasn't working. As we had been forced to push back the flight from September to November, we didn't quite get the weather we had hoped for. Anyway, over Timor we had to decide whether we had the fuel to make the last 400 miles across to Darwin. Number one aircraft was OK because he could fly at the right speed and so on to get the most economic consumption. Number two and ourselves had to fly in formation on him and that meant throttling back and forth with a loss of fuel. Number two aircraft decided that with the fuel they had left it was not worth the risk and landed at Timor.

'By my calculations, I reckoned we could make it to Darwin with half an hour to spare. Over the Timor Sea, we were able to communicate with the other aircraft and he slowed a touch and we opened our throttle a bit when we were sure we would make it. We landed together at Darwin. Can't quite remember what amount of fuel we had left – it was seven or seventeen gallons. Pretty close, anyway. The flight was news all over the world.' Little wonder. Burnett and his fellow pilots had flown 7,158 miles and had been airborne for forty-eight hours and five minutes to establish a world record for the longest non-stop flight.

Sir Brian was invited to apply for membership of the All England Club in 1946, after he had been to Wimbledon to play for the RAF against the club. The match was rained off, so instead of tennis the two teams reconvened for a game of bridge. 'I was asked why I wasn't a member of the club and I explained that no one had asked me to join,' he said. 'I was made a member the same year; very lucky as usually one has to wait a bit.' Some, like Ilie Nastase, twice a beaten Wimbledon finalist, are still waiting after almost thirty years.

After club chairman Herman David died in 1974, Burnett was elected to assume the chairmanship. 'I suppose I was a fairly natural choice as the age group of the committee was much too old, with a lot of them in their seventies,' said Sir Brian. His elevation coincided with the game moving into a new era, as men like Nastase and Connors arrived with swaggering confidence and a disregard for convention. They wished to play by rules of their invention. And then on their heels came McEnroe. 'I sensed the McEnroes had a problem with the club in the beginning, very much so,' said Sir Brian. 'Mr McEnroe could be quite rude. He was a difficult chap, a brash New York lawyer.'

As a family, the McEnroes felt almost from the beginning of their association with Wimbledon that the All England Club epitomised a class structure they abhorred. Over many years, there was much evidence to support this argument, although through the modernisation policies of a succession of chairmen, from Buzzer Haddingham to John Currie to Tim Phillips, this is an accusation that holds no water today. Nowadays, the All England Club organises a vibrant, progressive tournament celebrated across the world, in a facility that is modern and designed with the players' needs in mind.

In 1977, this was not necessarily the case. After beating Dowdeswell, McEnroe set up a third round match with German, Karl Meiler. By now, McEnroe had become reacquainted with his old friend from New York, Peter Fleming. 'It was like I hadn't seen Junior for a week rather than three years,' said Fleming, who had graduated from UCLA and entered the ranks of professional tennis. 'He was eighteen, I was twenty-two, but to me it was a case of, "Wow, this kid's pretty mature." The real shock was how confident he was. Yeah, just how secure he was in his own game. It was a revelation to me.'

Fleming, having been already knocked out of the singles by seventh seed Raul Ramirez, found himself one day hanging out with McEnroe, Mary Carillo and Elliot Teltscher in one of the booths in the players' restaurant. 'Junior and Elliot had both made it into the third round and Junior had to play Meiler, a solid player probably ranked between forty and sixty in the world, which is what my ranking was at the time. Junior was talking disparagingly about Meiler, suggesting he wasn't very good. He didn't think he was in for such a tough match. I was unsure about that, telling him, "This guy's not bad, I've seen him play a decent match or two." To this day, I remember Junior's response: "If I lose to Karl Meiler, I'm quitting the game." He's like eighteen years old and still in the juniors. I just said, "Yeah, well OK, we'll see. I hope you don't get a shock."'

McEnroe beat Meiler, 6–2, 6–2, 5–7, 6–3. 'For most of the match, Junior thumped him, he really did,' said Fleming, smiling at the memory. 'Clearly, he watched Meiler play a little and thought, "I can do this and this against him and it should be all right." I think John saw the game a whole lot differently than most of us. He just understood the game – and just had a strong belief that he could pull off most of what he tried.' In the fourth round, McEnroe overcame Sandy Mayer in four sets to confirm a quarterfinal assignation: against Phil Dent. 'I went in with Dent this time with a changed attitude,' admitted McEnroe.

Borg had to meet Poland's multi-lingual Wojtek Fibak, who was once summoned to the Vatican to give tennis lessons to the Pope, but undoubtedly the biggest match of the last eight pitched two former Wimbledon champions – Connors and Stan Smith – against one another.

For the first time McEnroe was scheduled to play on a show court – No. 1. It has vanished now, to be replaced by a state of the art stadium, but then it was a tight, rectangular arena. The front row of the crowd was only a step or two away from the players. In the press seats opposite the umpire's chair you sat almost at ground level. You could hear the players' feet landing on the grass. You could hear them breathing deeply after a sprint to the net. Sometimes, you could catch a word or two exchanged between them on the court. In later years, McEnroe's presence on Court No. 1 caused a media stampede to get the seats closest to the action. You never missed a single word of his protest speeches or his stage whispers. On either side of the umpire's chair, cameramen filled the narrow trench separating the players from the crowd. They pointed their hardware over the low wall in front of the playing surface. This was tennis in its most intimate environment.

McEnroe's first foray on to this court was, surprise, surprise, dramatic. After he won the first set from Dent, he dropped the second. McEnroe's disappointment with himself was evident to all and sundry. At the end of the set, he tried to snap his racket under his foot. The crowd booed this public display of petulance, yet McEnroe was genuinely confounded by this reaction. 'What the hell are these people booing for,' he thought. 'I'm the one who lost a set.' He was not done. 'To rile them further, I kicked the racket across the court. I thought the whole thing was hysterically funny, a joke.'

No one else was laughing. For the first time – but definitely not the last – McEnroe's temperament had overshadowed his talent at Wimbledon. While McEnroe's tantrum may not have won him an instant fan club, his tenacity in fighting back against Dent had to be admired. Having been down two sets to one, McEnroe conceded his service at the beginning of the fourth, but recovered to level the match. Court No. 1 was now a cauldron. Not once did he offer Dent a let and the Australian left the court a disgruntled and disgusted loser as McEnroe won the day. 'Suddenly, I was a different human being than the one he had seen just three weeks before at the French. What monster had he created? Suddenly, the punk kid was questioning calls, kicking his racket.' That was how McEnroe summed it up in his autobiography.

The legend of the man to be christened 'Superbrat' in the British tabloid newspapers was taking shape. At eighteen he was a Wimbledon semifinalist; and he would never again travel to a tennis tournament incognito. McEnroe's semifinal opponent was Connors, who, having beaten Smith, needed four sets to repel the challenge of unseeded South African Byron Betram in the quarters. Meanwhile, Borg cruised past Fibak and then overcame Nastase in a re-match of the previous year's final to clinch a semifinal against his close friend, Gerulaitis.

It was a landmark moment: for the first-time Borg, Connors and McEnroe were together in the semifinals of a Grand Slam championship. Borg and Gerulaitis delivered a five-set classic that the Swede eventually survived, 6–4, 3–6, 6–3, 3–6, 8–6, to reach his second successive final. Gerulaitis pushed him hard until the very end. 'I had a break in the fifth set and had a chance for another and also had a chance to hold my serve to keep the break alive, but he played good percentage shots each time,' recalled Gerulaitis.

'Everyone is puzzled how a clay-courter like Bjorn plays so well at Wimbledon. It's simple. First, he returns solidly, plus the grass makes his volley better than it really is. Balls that he hits short or mis-hits – flub volleys – are great volleys on grass. He also plays the bounces beautifully on grass. Everyone else is worried about bad hops, but they don't affect Bjorn. You need a lot of patience on grass, because sometimes you get so frustrated with the way the court is playing, yet nothing fazes him. I think Bjorn does have emotions, but he has a special talent for masking them. He doesn't let his opponent know what he is feeling. I've never seen him change his expression in all the matches I've played him. I've been there on an outside court when he lets off steam, but his emotions run at a low level and usually the most sign of excitement you get from him is a faint smile. But that's his way, even though I might go into hysterical laughter over the same thing.'

Borg has fond memories of the game for reasons other than the exciting tennis played. He said, 'Vitas rang me the next day to say that if I needed someone to practise with he was available.' Their friendship was cemented for eternity.

In the other semifinal, Connors perceived McEnroe as a kid trespassing on his turf. Aged twenty-four, Connors had already won Wimbledon (1974) and been runner-up to Arthur Ashe (1975). Connors felt McEnroe needed to be put firmly in his place. He was not about to lose his hard-earned street cred to a player who came to Wimbledon as an anonymous member of the chorus line, not a star like him. When it came to tennis, Connors was a man without sentiment.

And McEnroe felt a cold rush of fear from the moment he came into contact with Connors in the main locker room at Wimbledon. 'Jimmy said nothing, but he had this look and I was petrified,' said McEnroe. He would never feel like that again, of course, but this was an overwhelming experience for a young man, who had come to London to play in the juniors. Instead, because of his extraordinary run of success, McEnroe had never hit a ball in the juniors and his world ranking had risen from 233 to seventy-one in recognition of his journey to the semifinals. In tennis terms, he had been launched into outer space. Connors was to assure him a bumpy landing, but once McEnroe overcame his understandably nervy start, he created enough of an impression to take a set from the No. 1 seed before he was shown the exit. John Patrick McEnroe had arrived – and he would never be forgotten.

Connors and Borg were left to meet in their second Grand Slam final, the American having been the victor when they contested the 1976 US Open. The top two seeds provided a memorable contest to commemorate Wimbledon's centenary. As in most great dramas, the plot thickened without warning in the last scene. When Borg jumped out to a 4–0 lead in the fifth set, he seemed in total control. His second coronation was all but a formality and the presentation party readied themselves to leave the royal box, but Connors was stirred, not fried. A pugnacious man, he started to bombard Borg with unanswerable shots.

Like a fighter behind on the judges scorecards, the American made point after point count. Borg was the man starting to reel as Connors won one game, then two, then three. Connors was throwing punches in the air as the crowd crowed for more. And, then, he levelled the match at four games all. 'Every single point in all his matches was like a match point to Jimmy,' argued Borg. Connors agreed: 'If two guys are the two best in the world, every time they go out they are at each other's nuts all the time. I'm in there fighting my butt off and he's doing the same. There's no riding out hot streaks and no waiting for cold streaks to end. You just stay in there and hope, and if that's not good enough you're finished. I was down four games, but I got back to 4–4 and the match could have been very easily mine.'

No one, however, could have predicted the final twist. In the ninth game, Connors led 15–0 when he double-faulted. A lone voice heckled him – and Connors's concentration was shattered. 'It seemed everyone was cheering for me except this one guy,' he recalled. As if the on-court battle was not enough, Connors could not resist getting involved with the heckler. 'I had to hear him, didn't I? I got involved in a needless row and, suddenly, the final was over thirty seconds later. I won one more point.'

Borg stepped forward to receive the Wimbledon trophy for a second time, a relieved man after his triumph, 3–6, 6–2, 6–1, 5–7, 6–4. 'After three and a half hours on the Centre Court, I couldn't have played another game,' said Borg. 'Following the mental strain of beating Gerulaitis, 8–6, in the fifth set on Thursday, I have never been so tired on a tennis court as I was today. If Jimmy doesn't double-fault in that ninth game, I think he would have won the championship.' As champion, Borg received a cheque for £15,000.

On 23 August, Borg became world No. 1 at the age of twenty-one, when he ended Connors's 160–week long reign at the top of the rankings. But the Swede's first visit to the summit of the game lasted a mere week, as Connors surged back to reclaim the No. 1 ranking for another eighty-four weeks. Yet that summer Borg had been shown a glimpse of the future in the guise of another, younger American. 'The events at that Wimbledon entirely changed my life,' said John McEnroe.

Twenty years later and it's 1997. Picture the scene in the dining room at the Kensington Golf & Country Club in Naples, Florida. Bjorn Borg, John McEnroe and Jimmy Connors are sitting together, laughing and reminiscing about when they were young, feisty and at war on a tennis court. For a memorable decade from 1974, Wimbledon belonged to them.

Borg, forty, twice divorced, has a teenage son, Robin; McEnroe, thirty-eight, also divorced, has three children, Kevin, Sean and Emily; while Connors, forty-four, remains married to Patty, the mother of their two children, Brett and Aubree-Leigh. I was witness to this unique reunion having persuaded them to share a round table discussion during the Masters of the Champions' Tour that Connors had masterminded. All three men are still lean and fit and still driven on a tennis court. They still command a crowd, too. The conversation – never published in full before now – unfolded like this:

McEnroe: For me, the most exciting part of tennis was when the three of us were at the top in the late 1970s and early 1980s. Maybe I am biased, but to come into the game when these two guys were No. 1 and No. 2 and to be part of it, I felt like tennis was at its peak. It's always been the most exciting time in my career. You live a dream, in a sense. As the youngest, I tried to emulate things about these guys. In practice, I tried to emulate the way Bjorn was, but I wasn't able to be successful. Jimmy's intensity was something I had a better shot at! Whatever you try in your life, he was the ultimate guy to look up to. And then there was the aura Bjorn brought on the court; the dignity he had. It was something I was always chasing, but never quite got close to imitating. [Cue laughter from Borg and Connors.]

Connors: We had three guys who stepped up at once . . . Can you imagine what any one of us might have won if there had just been one of us out there by ourselves? It would have been clean-up time. We created an interest in tennis, not only on the court, but off the court as well. We all had our own personalities, our own mysteries. Borg was sneaking out the back windows of Wimbledon. Where the hell did he go? Who did he go with?

Borg: For me to play against these two guys was something special. Winning or losing, it kept you going. To have played John and Jimmy is something that will be in the back of my mind for the rest of my life. Maybe Jimmy and me have a similar style; John was the more aggressive one. John is the player who had the best hands ever. Even today, Jimmy is the best fighter on the court. He never, ever gives up, no matter what. He never gives less than one hundred per cent. We respected each other.

McEnroe: Bjorn questioned a call once. [Cue more giggling.]

Connors: We needed each other. Bjorn and I had our style, but we needed Mac to come in because of his different style. People enjoyed watching Bjorn and me play. They loved the rallies. I might have been a little more aggressive, tried to force the action a little, but we needed a different style to come along to uplift our battles. When Mac arrived, he gave us a new dimension. It was not just me playing Borg and people knowing what to expect. With Mac around, you never knew what to expect, which in turn made me a more complete player. I had not only to keep my groundstrokes humming for Borg, but I had to fight Mac's style of game.

Mac and me had the same attitude towards the game, plus we had the same inner rage. He was an American, he was younger than I was and he was coming after my territory. I had to do whatever it took to stay on top. I didn't invite him for a beer, but I didn't ask any other player for a beer either. Back then, mostly you sealed yourself off with close friends.

Borg: We all kept ourselves very distant.

Connors: It wasn't like when we walked into the locker rooms we avoided each other. We were cordial, but business was business. We understood more than anybody the importance of being the best. Forget the money. If keeping them at arm's length, trying to stay one step ahead, was the right way . . . who the hell knows? The one thing we did was have respect for each other. Whether you got along or not was really irrelevant.

McEnroe: I come from a different perspective. Bjorn was the first guy who, in a sense, was a matinee idol. He made you want to play tennis. Jimmy, too. They were the two guys who made you want to play the game. They were not from an upper class background, not from the country clubs. And girls were jumping all over Bjorn. So, tennis became more acceptable as something you'd want to do for a living. As a kid, tennis was considered as a cissy sport. These two guys brought down the barriers. They took the game to a lot more people. Then I was able to bring in my flavour.

I noticed that the one person Jimmy befriended early on was Nastase. In some ways, he struggled with that when they played. Nastase would get under his skin, because he knew him better. To me, it seemed that thereafter Jimmy made a point of keeping business as business. At the same time, if you're the three best players in the world, you're not hanging out. That's a bunch of crap to see guys say, 'We're friends. We get along.' To have the intensity we had, looking back now, I wouldn't have had it any other way. The good times or the bad.

I had to go out there knowing I could feel I wanted to kill the other guy. Everything becomes personal. To me, when I look back, that's the beauty of it. That's the fun. Even now, I want to play these guys. I know if I lose, I'll be pissed off, but it's not as if the world comes to an end. Who would I rather play – Bjorn Borg, Jimmy Connors or Mel Purcell? If I'm going to lose, I'd rather lose to these guys.

Connors: Hell, Bjorn, we know why you're back, but why did you go away?

Borg: I don't know. Perhaps I was just tired of the whole thing. It was a chance to be yourself, to have a life of your own. There was no life. I just wanted to be more myself; even if I was myself playing tennis. I wanted to get away from everything. My life was, like, tennis, tennis, tennis. In the end, I felt I can't do this anymore. That's why I admire these two guys. They stuck around for a long time. Especially Jimmy. It's unbelievable how many years he has been playing. John played doubles because he hated practice. I was laughing about this with Gerulaitis. Here we were playing for five hours – we needed to spend a lot of time on the court – and this guy [looking at McEnroe] would practise for ten minutes and come out and play unbelievable tennis. No, it didn't get inside my head, but it is more of an advantage if some guys have more talent! I think I needed to work more. So did Jimmy.

McEnroe: It's true that I used doubles as a practice tool. In 1979, for example, I played 240 matches. Admittedly, like, 125 were doubles matches. These guys were playing seventy-five to a hundred matches. I had a lot of time on a court in competitive conditions. To me, that was better than practice. These guys chose not to play doubles, yet I think Bjorn was probably the most fit tennis player of all time. He was fitter than I was – and I don't think I was unfit. Bjorn had an amazingly athletic body. In Jimmy, you are talking about the gutsiest player who ever played. When you compare yourself to these two, I think I'd be a small notch down on them, but if you compare me with everyone else, I think I was fitter than most, physically and mentally.

Connors: It was interesting to hear Bjorn say he didn't want to put up with it any more, that he wanted to go and live a normal life. I was lucky enough to find that. I had a happy medium between tennis and returning to home life. It's not an easy transition. It took me a couple of years worrying if I was playing too much tennis and screwing up my family life. I don't think the three of us tried to pump up our fame. We did our job and we were very good at it. It gets you in a lot of restaurants, but there are a lot of disadvantages. Yet it's all been a part of what we do. You look at the people who came to watch us play and, you know, they made us what we are financially and they contributed to any fame we may have. It's not unusual for kids to yell out to me,

'Hey, Connors.' It's not Mr Connors or Jimmy. It's a familiarity that comes from their parents saying, 'I watched Connors. I watched Borg and McEnroe.' If my kids went up and said, 'Hey, McEnroe,' I'd be disappointed, but that's the way they think of us. The crowds are real close at tennis; people think they know us.

Borg: I wanted more of a quiet life when I stepped away from tennis. I was hoping so, but it never really happened. Maybe I am part of the reason. I've been through divorces and business failures. Still, I see it as a learning process. At forty, I know what I want to do. If I look back, I don't regret anything, but it has taken me forty years to understand myself. That's weird.

McEnroe: In a sense, I think I am still finding the way. I was very fortunate to meet a great lady [singer Patty Smyth] who has become part of my life. That's really picked me up from a difficult period, but I have been separated from my ex-wife [Tatum O'Neal] for almost five years. I don't think people realise how long it has been. Only the last two and a half years I have been with Patty have been real positive for me, but as to what makes me happy today, I still feel it's a learning process. How much tennis do I play? Do you want to do commentary? More or less, if at all? I love music, but how seriously should I take it? There is my art gallery . . . and trying to do the best I can with the children, do the right thing. It's a complicated mix.

Then you feel like people are looking over your shoulder. Like Bjorn said, it would be good to find your way without that, but the reality is that's not going to happen for the time being, if at all. You have to deal with the fact that every decision you make is analysed by people who don't know you. That's not easy, but, as Jimmy says, we have gotten a lot, we still get a lot. You can't have your cake and eat it, I guess. Like he says, you may get into a restaurant, but then they want you to sign autographs and go and meet the chef and say hello to everyone in the restaurant.

Connors: And still pay for your dinner. [Cue laughter all round.]

McEnroe: Am I embarrassed by some of the things I did in the past? Some of it embarrasses me, yet some of the things I did yesterday embarrasses me! The job is to look in the mirror each day and say, 'I'll attempt to make myself point nought nought one per cent a better person.' I think I've done that. I'm really different to Bjorn. He says he doesn't regret anything. I certainly do regret things, but I can't change them and, for the most part, I feel more positive than negative about what I've done.

[The conversation switches to how McEnroe and Connors always treated Borg with total respect on court, never losing their cool when he was on the other side of the net.]

Connors: I gave Bjorn some of my best material and he never even smiled, but I admit I always tempered my crazy spells when I played him. It was interesting playing John, because everything about us clashed: his game against my game, his serve and volley against my return; his psychological make-up against mine. There was just no chance of getting in Bjorn's head. It calmed me down. Whereas playing Mac, the smallest thing in the world would bring me to the boil, but every time I went out there I knew they were going to have to play their absolute best tennis against me. They never gave me one per cent less than they had. It was a strong compliment.

McEnroe: Anything you did against Bjorn would be magnified. There was nothing coming back. Like Jimmy said, it naturally forced you to bring it down. You looked that much worse. Especially at Wimbledon, where Bjorn was placed on a really high pedestal, so, they were all over me. Ultimately, you just had to play your best. Against Jimmy, the intensity was just oozing out of us. You wanted to shoulder the guy at the changeover. We were ready for battle in the warm-up. It didn't take long to get going . . .

Borg: I think maybe that I missed tennis without realising it. Tennis is always going to be part of my life.

McEnroe: It's always going to be part of my life, too. You have to face up to that, just embrace it. I've always been tortured. No, tortured is not the right word. I've always had trouble finding the middle ground. Even when I was playing my best. It's an ongoing search for that elusive middle ground. I am determined to find it.

Connors: You don't put the kind of effort we have put into this and just throw it away. Even if we just do it with our kids for fun, we are going to play some tennis. I'm almost forty-five, Borg is forty, Mac, you're thirty-eight, right? We have our priorities rearranged and tennis is no longer number one, not for me anyway, but there's no story like ours in tennis. I don't think there ever will be.

Borg: I have tapes from all the matches, from all the majors with these guys, and I have had to watch every single tape, every match, every set for the last three years with my son, Robin. He knows these guys so well! He enjoys it so much. It's a nice thing.

McEnroe: My kids are totally the opposite. They don't give a damn. They have never sat and watched a match. I couldn't pay them to do it! I call home and – I don't want to admit this –I tell them I just lost to Mel Purcell and a voice says, 'You lost! You used to be good . . . a long time ago.' [Borg and Connors share his laughter.] In some ways I wish my kids were more aware. I'm not sure I want them quite as aware as Robin is, but definitely it wouldn't be bad if they were aware of the past. One good thing about me is that I respected my elders. Maybe these guys will disagree, but I worked my way in.

Connors: It's interesting your kids don't give you the credit outsiders do. Brett's watched me play many matches. He didn't make anything of it. My daughter didn't know what I did until a couple of years ago. She went to school and one her little friends came up to her and said, 'Gee, your daddy's famous.' So she came and saw my wife and said, 'Mom, did you know daddy's famous?' The kids look at their parents as mom and dad who take them to the store and buy them this and that. We play a game and that's the way they look at it. What a nice thing to do, they probably think. You're going to get some exercise and a tan. It's interesting to hear Robin watches the games. If I say to my kids, 'Want to play some tennis?' they go, 'Phew, must we?'

McEnroe: They do you a favour, I know.

[Finally, the conversation drifts to the intensity of competition and the need to be selfish if you wished to be a champion.]

McEnroe: You don't go off court after the final of Wimbledon and say, 'Let's have dinner.' Nastase was the only guy who ever did something remotely like that to me. At the 1979 US Open, he got defaulted as he was going crazy. Afterwards, he said, 'Macaroni, what are you doing for dinner?' He used to drive me crazy on purpose. He knew it'd take about two seconds to get under my skin. Then, the guy wants to go out to eat.

Borg: Did I ever get mad? Yeah, many times. Lennart took most of my shit. On the court, I only got really mad once – in New York against John – but I had to release my feelings somewhere. I took them out on Lennart and Mariana. They understood. They knew. Sometimes, I was boiling for no reason at all. I could do some stupid things. We had so many fights, me and Lennart, but he knew me so well. He took all the rubbish from me and the next day it was OK.

Connors: If you want to be the best, I don't think a lot of people realise how selfish a game this is. Everything is done to prepare you to play the next day. Day after day, tournament after tournament – it all revolves around you . . .

McEnroe: That's why the divorce rate is so high.

A few months after the three men shared the round table at the Kensington Golf & Country Club, John McEnroe married Patty Smyth on the lawn of a friend's home in Maui, Hawaii. His best man was Bjorn Borg.

7

'I'LL FOLLOW BORG TO THE ENDS OF THE EARTH . . .'

After his unforgettable Wimbledon baptism, John McEnroe spent the rest of that summer playing a succession of professional tournaments across the United States as an amateur. He also began to spend more time with Peter Fleming, as they travelled from city to city. Their friendship developed and from this came the notion that they should team up to play doubles. McEnroe had played some doubles with South African, Bertie Mitton, while Fleming was partnering fellow American, Gene Mayer, but neither pairing was set in stone.

So, in September 1977, McEnroe and Fleming established a double act that was to win world renown. They would become to tennis what Laurel and Hardy were to comedy and Astaire and Rogers were to dance – an incomparable team. 'Junior used doubles as preparation for his singles and never gave less than one hundred per cent,' said Fleming. 'That's why it was great preparation. That's where players today miss the point. The reason Junior was so great was he just had a habit of hitting the right shot at the right time. That's not something you can train by doing drills. It was just a question of him saying, "Put me in a certain situation and I will make the right decision in an instant." It trains your mind in a really well balanced way to make decisions. Junior was better than anyone else at making the right ones very quickly most of the time.

'For Junior, doubles was one of the things that allowed him to relax. We did have a few times when he lost it, but far less than in singles. Because we were a team, I could help him. I could probably help carry some of the stress that in singles he felt one hundred per cent on his own. This gave him a chance to compete at quite an intense level without going over the top. Sometimes in his singles, like when he played that match with Tom Gullikson at Wimbledon in 1981, his stress levels went way over the top. You can't play your best tennis when that's the case. Practice can only take you so far, but winning matches – no matter what the match is – builds your confidence.'

Once, when asked who were the best doubles team in the world, Fleming replied: 'John McEnroe and anyone.' To his credit, McEnroe reacted swiftly to correct the record. As soon as Fleming had uttered those words, McEnroe insisted: 'That's not true.' Fleming was a perfect foil for McEnroe. He was someone who understood him, well, almost understood him, and he was not intimidated by his presence on the court. Fleming, six foot five inches tall and right-handed, locked the deuce side of the court and had a natural instinct to get forward. McEnroe dealt his magic from the ad court with a style not easy to disarm. Together, they would win the Wimbledon championship four times and the US Open on three occasions; together, they would accumulate a grand total of fifty-seven titles plundered from all around the world; together, they played as one.

Another of Fleming's strengths was the sense of loyalty he showed his friend, no matter what deteriorating circumstances he found himself in on court with McEnroe. On one occasion, McEnroe managed to irritate Hank Pfister and Victor Amaya beyond the limit of their patience. Pfister is six foot four inches and Amaya six foot seven inches and they were generating a lot of bad attitude in the confined space of a tennis court. Fleming recalled: 'I thought, "I'm going to get my lights clocked because Junior has gotten us into something . . ." but I knew I couldn't run away. I knew I had to stick by my man. He defended me, too. It was a team effort. We were always loyal to one another, no matter what.'

Another time the temperature rose to boiling point was when McEnroe and Fleming played Mark Edmondson and Steve Denton in the Canadian Open. 'Denton wanted to smash McEnroe in the teeth,' said Edmondson. 'Something had happened between them in a singles somewhere. Mac had been mimicking Steve, who was a bit of an ungainly bloke. Steve asked me to look out to see if he was doing it again. Mac in all honesty was being a bit disrespectful. Denton was going to round the net posts this day and have a go at Mac. Steam was coming out of his nostrils!' But in the event public order was not disturbed.

Notwithstanding the odd controversial exchange, McEnroe's record as a doubles player is quite outstanding. 'John is the best doubles player there has ever been,' said David Lloyd. 'He could make you look stupid.'

Edmondson offered this neat analysis: 'I like to put forward a golfing analogy to describe the differences between the most talented players around,' he said. 'Someone like Newcombe had fourteen clubs in his bag and he could use six or seven of them very well. Henri Leconte had fourteen to eighteen clubs in his bag, but rarely knows which one to get out. Borg carried just seven or eight clubs and used them all unbelievably well. McEnroe, though, is a man with twenty-seven clubs in his bag and he knows which one to pick out at any given moment.'

McEnroe went to college in the autumn of 1977, reporting to Stanford in California. His original coursework proved too burdensome, so in his second semester he studied parapsychology and psychic phenomena. Studied is too strong a word, in truth. McEnroe attended class when he wasn't playing tennis or on a road trip. He was the number one college player in the USA and was determined to climax his short career at Stanford by winning the college championship, the NCAAs, which that year were being staged in Athens, Georgia. His opponent in the final in May 1978 was John Sadri, from North Carolina State, who walked on court wearing a blue blazer, white tennis shorts, a shirt and a ten-gallon hat. The good ol' Southern boys in Athens just had to love that. McEnroe may not have had many fans that day, but that did not trouble him. However, pains in his lower back did. He needed repeated treatment, but he weathered the discomfort to end his amateur playing career as NCAA champion.

In June, he made his professional debut at the pre-Wimbledon grass court championships at Queen's Club in London – against Fleming. No one likes to play a friend, so the occasion was awkward for both men. McEnroe, however, had the resolve to come from a set behind to defeat Fleming, before eventually going on to lose in the final to Tony Roche, a hard, competitive and wily veteran from Australia. McEnroe's hope that he may have sown the seeds for a successful reappearance at Wimbledon was instantly destroyed, however. He was a first-round victim of Eric van Dillen. After his spectacular entrance at the tournament in the previous summer, his level of expectation was high and he was hugely disappointed, but at least he still had the doubles with Fleming to keep him in town.

Borg had returned to Wimbledon having, a fortnight earlier, won his third French Open championship by routing Guillermo Vilas, 6–1 6–1 6–3. In Paris, Borg was a man cloaked in an aura of invincibility. It was the second time Vilas had been beaten in the final by Borg and over those two matches the strong man from Argentina, who had won fifty straight matches in 1977, including the French and US Open championships, took a total of fourteen games.

At home in Vaxjo, Sweden, Mats Wilander watched and he filed the lessons away in his subconscious. 'I was already playing tennis, but Bjorn fuelled the fire, for sure,' said Wilander. 'We used to have just two channels on television and we didn't have that much sport to watch. Our two international stars were Borg and Ingmar Stenmark [a champion slalom skier]. Even though I play very similar to Bjorn I was never trying to play like he played. I think it just happened, because we watched him so much that you get brainwashed.'

As Borg was placing his marker on the world of tennis, a Swedish pop group called Abba was selling records and playing at sold-out concerts around the world. Bjorn Ulvaeus and Benny Andersson, both wearing their hair long like Borg, and Agnetha Faltskog and Anni-Frid Lyngstad, two alluring women, became to Sweden what the Beatles were to Britain in the 1960s. Abba had won the 1974 Eurovision Song Contest in Brighton with their song, *Waterloo*, which became an immediate number one hit in the UK charts. Abba was a cocktail of saccharine and sassiness. The group's colourful stage costumes, the epitome of 1970s fashion, provided huge visual impact on the videos that accompanied its hits. And there was a romantic thread to the story, too, for Bjorn and Agnetha were married, as were Benny and Anni-Frid, known as Frida. By 1978, the members of Abba were megastars, with a long string of hits behind them. They built a state-of-the-art studio in Stockholm that was in demand from other bands. Led Zeppelin recorded there, for example. By remarkable coincidence, Abba disbanded in 1982, much the same time as Borg slipped from centre stage. Like Borg, Abba's legacy lives on. The band has sold over 370 million albums worldwide. Only the Beatles and Elvis Presley have ever sold more.

At home in Sweden, Wilander confesses this led to a conundrum for kids like him, growing up with an endless stream of stories and pictures of these superstars of the pop world. 'You didn't like Abba because they were from Sweden,' he explained, 'so it's cool to like Slade or Sweet or one of those kind of bands, and Borg was kind of like the same thing. You can't like Bjorn Borg because he was too big and too good and he wins everything, so you have to like Jimmy Connors. That's where I was, but I would never have been a professional tennis player if it wasn't for Borg. I'm not sure any of us that followed him would have been. There was never a programme in place in Swedish tennis as we grew up. Just everybody played and had a good style. We could stand out there on the court for days. We wouldn't miss. I think we were good athletes and had a really good mentality and that was through Bjorn. Brainwashed again.'

Four years years after Borg annihilated Vilas in that 1978 French Open final, the Argentine disputed the title with Wilander, who was still only seventeen. To the media, Wilander was the new Bjorn Borg. To the players on the tennis tour, he was a ghost of nightmares past. To get to the final, Wilander's fourth-round victim was Ivan Lendl, runner-up the previous year to Borg. Wilander's memory of his own emergence from the giant shadow Borg cast over the game has humour and self-deprecation: 'I think by the end of the match with me Lendl thought, "I'm not fucking even trying any more against this Swedish little shit. I won't be humiliated again. Borg did that last year and I just beat myself and I don't want to do it again."'

Understandably, Wilander rejected the media's predictable insistence on presenting him as Borg mark two. He wanted his own identity, not to be coloured as a clone of the great man. 'I am not the new Borg,' he repeated like a stuck vinyl record. Of course, he was whistling down the Champs Elysees. After all, he was Swedish, he had a two-handed backhand, he barely missed a ball and he had the stamina of a man who saw tennis as a marathon not a middle-distance event. Oh, and he hardly said a word in public. He was a shy, introverted teenager. Other than that he had no similarities to Borg whatsoever.

That was all to change. Over the years travelling on the circuit I came to know Wilander well. He has been unfailingly good company over a beer or two, has a fund of stories and is a man whose outstanding success on a tennis court never blurred his own humble perspective of his place in the world. His willingness to give something back – along with men like McEnroe and Pat Cash – is done without fanfare or trumpet. On an occasion when he won a Porsche at a particular tournament, Wilander instantly donated it to GOAL, a Dublin-based charity dedicated to sending medical assistance to poverty-stricken areas of the Third World.

On another, memorable night, Wilander and McEnroe met one another in a boxing ring constructed in a Dublin hotel, at the instigation of John O'Shea, the driving force at the heart of GOAL. The fight took place in the summer of 1988. 'John hit me a lot more than I hit him,' said Wilander, 'but the best punch of the night was mine!'

McEnroe's respect for Wilander on a tennis court ensured that he very rarely misbehaved on any serious scale against him, but Wilander's old coach, John-Anders Sjogren, recalled the Swede's epic Davis Cup match with McEnroe in 1982 was played in an atmosphere of high intensity. 'McEnroe tried everything against Mats in an unbelievable tie lasting more than six hours. We had to give the referee the rule book!'

At forty, Wilander still meets McEnroe on the Delta Tour of Champions, where the American still has the capacity to rage at officials as well as charm the crowd who marvel at his touch and remain captivated by his passion for winning. Wilander smiled benevolently when he suggested, 'I find it amazing that he has that fire still burning, but he has to be careful . . . I respect that he cares so much, and he can behave as badly as he wants, but you can't go after everybody. Well, I don't think you can, but I am not John McEnroe.'

However, Wilander acknowledges that McEnroe is two men. There is the man who plays tennis with an insatiable hunger and there is the other McEnroe, who is humorous and generous with a smart take on life. 'John was softer off the court than people thought; at least softer than I first thought,' said Wilander. 'Once I saw that side of him, it was not so difficult to like him or become friendly with him, no matter what happened. Jimmy Connors was different, because I think some players thought what he did was intentional. Some players thought he was trying to kind of drag the other guy down, but with McEnroe it was so clear there was no intention to disturb the other guy. It was so clear to most of us, "Hey, he can't help it!" John walked the genius/lunatic line, then. Once I met him off the court, I understood that, but I don't think there has been any player in the history of the game that has been forgiven so many times by his fellow players as McEnroe.'

Wilander's own selection as current captain of the Swedish Davis Cup team is not only a reflection of the role he played in the post-Borg era, but is testimony to the values he holds. He is an ambassador for tennis, yet still a man of the people, still a guy without pretensions, and the next generation of Swedish players can relate to him. And, of course, the man could play.

Twenty-two years on, Wilander gave a wry grin when he thought back to the time he announced himself at that French Open in 1982, the year after Borg had quietly disappeared. 'Before the tournament, the others must have been thinking to themselves, "Thank God, Borg's not playing,"' he said. 'The greatest example of this was the final itself. Vilas must have thought without Borg in the tournament that he had the biggest chance of his life. But, suddenly, he sees there is some guy who looks exactly like the man he hates to play and this is a guy who is not missing. He's not as good, but he's just not missing. So, these guys beat themselves. Honestly, I think the reason I won my first French Open was because the others lost it! But the real reason the French Open appeared easy for me was because Borg had made it look easy on television. When I got there I felt a sense of deja vu.'

Without question, Borg left an imprint on the clay that everyone in the game recognised. 'Our biggest nightmare on the tour was to play Bjorn on the clay, in the rain, on a day when he decided he didn't like you,' said Rod Frawley, the Australian who ran McEnroe so close in the Wimbledon semifinals in 1981. 'He could make you hit balls for as long as he liked. He was the fittest guy in the world, the fastest and had the best concentration. He didn't worry about serving too many big first serves on the clay, he just rolled it in.'

And then he dared you to think about duelling with him. Balazs Taroczy, often used as a sparring partner by Borg in Paris, said without embarrassment: 'For me, Bjorn was like a god. I lost to him twice at Roland Garros, once in the quarters and once in the last sixteen. Those were the years I could have done my best. I was just unlucky to play him! He was really too good, plus, like almost everyone else, I had so much respect for him. Even if he played badly, I think I would have no chance. Borg had that feeling that no matter what happened he was going to win somehow.' Gene Mayer, who, in partnership with fellow American Hank Pfister, won the French Open Doubles Championship in 1978, added: 'For someone to beat Bjorn at the French was almost inconceivable. No one would be surprised if he won twelve French Opens.'

Yet when he came across the English Channel, Borg had adjustments to make to ensure he could successfully transfer his game from the clay courts of Roland Garros on to grass. And it didn't seem to come easily. Having just defeated Vilas in the French Open, in 1978 the Swede once more showed early signs of vulnerability at Wimbledon. For Mark Edmondson read Victor Amaya. The twenty-three-year-old from Holland, Michigan, led Borg two sets to one, 3–1, and had a break point to extend his advantage even further. This may have seemed incongruous to those who had paid to come through the gate, but in the locker room there was no real sense of shock. John Lloyd explained: 'Bjorn was funny, because when you saw him get into a tournament he was like a machine, yet for the first three or four days of practice on grass he was so baaaaad. When I suggested that, people thought I was on drugs. He was mis-hitting balls and you'd think, "Jeez, I'd love to play him in the first round."

'He needed time to adjust his technique from clay to grass. A guy like McEnroe or Henman walks on grass and it literally takes them no more than a couple of minutes to adjust. At my level, it only took five to ten minutes. I understand the bounce is lower, I know you have to take the racket back shorter and you have to stay with the ball longer. Piece of cake. Except it wasn't for Borg. He had to put an intense amount of work into his practice, but that was the man. He was precise in the number of hours he worked. He knew practice would make perfect – or as near perfect as damn well mattered.'

Borg had a sense of his own vulnerability in the opening rounds of a tournament and those feelings intensified on the grandest stage of all. His self-analysis read like a visit to the psychiatrist's couch: 'I hate playing first rounds. Everything is strange: the courts, the weather, the grounds, the crowd, the scene. It takes almost a week to get used to.' At the French Open or the US Open, the leading players could always arrange to have some practice time on the centre court to acclimatise to the pace of the ball and the environment. At Wimbledon that has never been an option.

But, like Edmonson before him, Amaya's chance came and went. Borg was never afraid to rake risks when he was behind. Against Amaya, he saved that critical break point against him at 1– 3 in the fourth set with a bullet-like service down the middle of the court. Borg ran in the final two sets without further drama. Wilander suggested, 'At the time, Borg was faster than the evolution of the materials. It was so hard to get the ball past him – and that was one of the reasons he won those matches he could so easily have lost.' The Swede lost one more set – against Jaime Fillol in the third round – as he assured himself a place in the final for a third consecutive summer, against the man he had replaced as No. 1 seed. Connors himself only lost two sets on his journey to the final, dropping one against Kim Warwick in the second round and one against Tom Gorman in the third.

Up to this point, Connors had won seven of the nine matches he had played against Borg. Significantly, however, he had lost the one game they had disputed on grass. For Connors, Borg remained the rival he most respected. 'From the beginning we had some wars,' recalled Connors. 'I was established and he was this little kid from Sweden who could play the hell out of the game. My attitude was totally different to his. I was the fire, he was the ice. I played the all-out aggressive game, a straightforward strategy to come at you all the time. He was content to stay back and run down a lot of balls with patience for point after point. That's why we enjoyed playing against one another. Not only did our attitudes clash, but our games clashed, too. Every time I played him I'd tell myself, "It's going to be a battle. It's going to take a long time and you are going to come out with a lot of scars." You just hoped you weren't bleeding too badly at the end.'

From the beginning, Connors viewed tennis as a battleground. 'Tennis was a cissy sport in my neighbourhood,' he explained. 'It was a fairly rough place, but I wouldn't trade it for anywhere in the world. It's where I came from, where I grew up and the way I am. Most of the kids played football and baseball, although tennis is becoming accepted a little more and seen as becoming big business. But as far as running around in a pair of white shorts . . . you just didn't do that back then!'

His formative years in the game were spent under the tuition of his mother, Gloria, and his grandmother in Belleville, Illinois, on the other side of the Mississippi from St Louis, Missouri. His father managed the Veterans' Bridge. 'I had a normal childhood, I had some horses, some little motorbikes and go-karts as a kid,' said Connors. 'I just happened to have some tennis mixed in.' He told me that he could not beat his mother until he was sixteen. It was around that time that Gloria Connors felt it appropriate to move her son out west to California, to broaden his tennis education on the fast hard courts in Los Angeles. 'I ended up going to school with Pancho Segura's son and I was able to play tennis at the club where Pancho was the professional,' said Connors. He also practised and played on the tennis team at UCLA. 'At that time, I think my mom and grandmother thought they had given me everything two women could. I needed the influence of men, not to fool with my game, but to give me a man's outlook. My two-handed backhand came from me being too small to hold a racket in one hand. I play a very compact, woman's style of game. There is not much excess motion in my game. It's straight back and straight forward.

'The part I put in myself is the grunting and groaning and the way I lead my feet into every ball. That's the man's part of the game they gave me, which, in turn, is the way I want to play. The grunts and groans have been around for as long as I remember, but that's not done with any intention, it's just the way I breathe. I inhale at a certain point and I exhale at the time I hit the ball and it comes out as a grunt and a groan.'

However, even as Connors was making a name in the game,

there was a sinister cloud hanging over American men of his age, whether at college or at work. In the late 1960s and early 1970s, young men in America were being drafted into the armed forces to serve in the Vietnam War. 'I missed the draft by the skin of my teeth,' said Connors. 'The way it worked was this. Your birthday was thrown into a bowl. I had a very, very low number and that could have been difficult. I was number forty or something, but, because of a holiday, I got thrown into a bigger pot where my number became 365 plus forty. At that time, it was enough to keep me out, as they only picked the first one hundred or so. Those were nerve-racking days. I would have accepted the duty, that's for sure, but it was a very dangerous time for a lot of kids. A lot of my friends were in Vietnam – and a lot of them didn't come back. I lost a lot of buddies over there.'

Connors counted his blessings and, soon, he was climbing the peaks of the tennis world from the humblest of base camps. 'For the first tournament I won [in 1972], I got $1,200 and I was ecstatic,' he said. 'I could buy my own clothes. I felt a little more independent.' By 1974, Connors was ranked No. 1 and he won Wimbledon a month after Borg captured his first French Open.

For a time, Connors combined singles with doubles, as McEnroe would when he came on the scene. Connors graduated into a short, but highly entertaining and inevitably controversial doubles partnership with Nastase. Their friendship began in the most curious of circumstances as far as Connors was concerned. 'I was fifteen when Nastase beat me in the second round of the National Indoor Championships in Maryland. I went to the locker room and my head was down. I realised I'd have to go back to school and I was not in good humour about that. Nasty came in – and at this point he could barely speak English. He looks at me and goes, "You . . . me . . . dinner." I looked up and said, "Oh yeah, why not? We'll have a hell of a conversation!" We became very good friends from that moment. One year, I think we played fifteen tournaments and we won five and were defaulted from the rest. That was just when the fines were being introduced, but there wasn't huge prize money about. I was losing money! So we dissolved our doubles partnership, but I can't claim Nasty was responsible for all of the problems.'

When Connors walked on to Wimbledon's Centre Court for

the 1978 championship final, he had four Grand Slam titles to his name to Borg's five. 'For me to play Bjorn, I had to be on the tenth floor with my game,' argued Connors. 'I couldn't play him if I was on the intermediate floors. I had to be playing my absolute best or it was no contest. I had to go out there and get pumped. I'd yell and scream and moan at myself, but there was never any conflict or controversy with Borg. He went about his own business, I went about mine. He would let what I did on my side of the net go by and I let what he did go by.' But on that day, Connors never made it to the top floor of his game, because Borg never allowed him that luxury. Borg played an exceptional final, eclipsing his American rival, 6–2, 6–2, 6–3. For the first time, the Swede dropped to his knees on the Centre Court in celebration of his triumph.

Daily Telegraph correspondent, Lance Tingay, wrote in the *World of Tennis* annual: 'Connors took the first two games of the match and was beaten in the next six, being passed, lobbed, out-served, out-volleyed and out-generalled. Never, probably, has a fine player performed so well and yet been so routed. Borg took lawn tennis to new heights in the final.' This was Borg's twenty-first consecutive win at Wimbledon. His third successive championship had enabled him to equal the achievement of Britain's Fred Perry in 1936. 'When Borg left Wimbledon in 1978 there was no doubt about his candidature for joining the all time greats of the game,' argued Tingay.

Typically, Connors still had the final word. He recognised the brilliance of Borg, but promised: 'I'll follow Borg to the ends of the earth. I'll stay with the son of a bitch until I beat him. Every time he looks round, he will see my shadow.' Less than three months later, Connors was as good as his word. He defeated McEnroe in straight sets in the semifinals of the US Open, then eclipsed Borg, 6–4, 6–2, 6–2, to become US Open champion for a third time.

Connors always relished playing in front of the partisan crowds in New York. He was their type of guy. He revelled in the bedlam; no, he encouraged it. He brought the menace of the prize ring to the Louis Armstrong Stadium. Borg never looked the same man in New York as he did at Wimbledon. Connors later told me: 'I happened to play very well that day. Roy Emerson saw me that evening and said, "It's unbelievable, Jimmy! How is it that Borg pounds you three months earlier and you turn round and beat him just as bad today?" I think the atmosphere has something to do with it. He felt very comfortable on the Centre Court at Wimbledon with the crowd there. The crowd in New York made me comfortable. That kind of crazy, wild atmosphere was like my upbringing. A little thing like that in a game of that magnitude will make it possible to raise your game a little higher.' Borg and Connors would never meet in a Grand Slam final again.

⊟

FIRST BLOOD McENROE

The post-1978 US Open season was to prove extremely profitable for John McEnroe. In a breathless few months, he won four singles titles and six doubles titles. He also went head to head for the first time with Borg. At the epicentre of McEnroe's storming end to the year was his decision to remodel his service action. During the Open, he had changed his serve, primarily as a response to the tightness he was still feeling in his lower back. For reasons he has never properly understood, McEnroe opted to turn completely sideways on the baseline when he served.

Instantly, the action felt natural and the discomfort he had been experiencing disappeared. Instantly, his service became a more vindictive weapon. He left the ground as he made contact with the ball and moved instinctively into the court on the wave of his own momentum. As McEnroe possessed uncanny directional control of the ball, this sideways-on action made it increasingly difficult for rivals to 'read' where he was serving. The final piece of the jigsaw had been put in place.

The results started to flow. Two weeks after the Open, McEnroe won his first professional title, the United Technologies Classic in Hartford, Connecticut, beating Johan Kriek in the final. A week later he defeated Dick Stockton to win the Transamerica Open in San Francisco, but it was his return to Europe that was to provide the game with a landmark moment. In the semifinals at the Stockholm Open in early November, McEnroe came face to face with the man he most admired: Borg. 'I thought he was magical – like some kind of Viking God who'd landed on the tennis court,' said McEnroe. 'Even before he won Wimbledon, there were hundreds of girls round him: tennis groupies, like the Beatles and the Stones had! Who could have imagined such a player coming out of Sweden, a country of only eight million people with a sub-Arctic climate?' Who indeed?

Ingrid Bentzer was an eyewitness to this piece of history when Borg came home to be drawn in the same half of the Stockholm Open as McEnroe. 'Bjorn and I were No. 1s in Sweden at the same time, even though I am ten years older than him,' she said. 'I played for the King's Club in Stockholm and he played for SALK, from the suburbs. The first time I came across him was when he played on centre court at the King's Club. Everyone was talking about this little guy with one eye – well, that's how it seems, because Bjorn's eyes are so close together.'

As she spoke, Bentzer was sipping tea in her large family house on the banks of the Thames at Chiswick, west London. In many respects, Bentzer had been a maternal influence on Borg all those years before. She smiled, 'Bjorn means bear in Swedish. I have always called him Nalle, which means Teddy bear.

'My first real memory of him was when we played the Scandinavian Championships in Copenhagen and Kjell Johansson had to play him. Everyone was buzzing about Bjorn, who was no more than fourteen. I remember Kjell came to see me – all the Swedish players were close, like the Australian tennis set-up. He said he didn't know how to play this little bugger. Everyone was getting so nervous. I told Kjell that as Bjorn only hit the ball half-court, he should come in and smack it. "Really?" said Kjell. He took the advice and absolutely polished off Bjorn!'

No one did that again, of course. 'Bjorn was soon like a wall,' she said. It was traditional for the Scandinavian Championships to move around between countries and Bentzer recalled travelling with Borg to Helsinki, when it was Finland's turn to host the tournament. 'Bjorn was great fun. He has a gift for one-liners. Not droll humour, but on the ball. Anyway, that week I won the singles, the doubles and the mixed doubles. Bjorn won the men's singles. When we flew home, we were picked up at Stockholm Airport by Bjorn's parents. His mother, Margaretha, asked me in her heavy Stockholm accent, "Poor you, Ingrid. What happened? How did you do?"' Bentzer soon realised that there was only one story the Swedish newspapers were interested in reporting: the rise and rise of Borg.

Bentzer had another story from Borg's formative years. In 1973, she had won in Monte Carlo, so when she arrived at the French Open she was 'hot-shit Madame Bentzer'. She went to see Madame de Bombardier, the woman who distributed the practice balls. Bentzer asked for the balls to go out to practice on court 13. 'Ah, Madame Bentzer, pas de probleme,' said Madame de Bombardier, respectfully. Politely, she wondered who Bentzer was going to hit with. Bentzer replied that it was one of the Swedish players. 'Comment s'appelle-t-il?' said de Bombardier. 'Bjorn Borg.' Bentzer recalled Madame de Bombardier tossing her head dismissively and suddenly remembering she had more pressing business to attend to. In the event, Bentzer lost early in the championships. 'I became the practice bag for Bjorn and Virginia Wade,' she explained. 'My god, I was so fit by the end. I'd take Bjorn for lunch and he won round after round.' Eventually, Borg's run came to an end when Italian Adriano Panatta beat him in the fourth round, but the Swede had made an impression. When Bentzer returned to Roland Garros a year later, Madame de Bombardier spoke with respect as she asked if another Swedish player was with Bentzer. 'It was funny because she had been so dismissive of Bjorn!' said Bentzer. Of course, on that second visit to Roland Garros, Borg was crowned champion.

Four years later, in 1978, Borg's participation in the Stockholm Open assured a great deal of excitement in Sweden. He had just won the Seiko World Super Tennis Tournament, a $200,000 event in Tokyo, and was favourite to win in his home town – but it didn't quite work out that way. The Swedes played the Stockholm Open on a super-fast indoor tile surface; a surface more receptive to McEnroe's serve and volley game than Borg's baseline strategy. Mats Wilander, a teenager in Vaxjo at the time, commented years afterwards, 'I remember that court was almost unfairly fast. You could see Borg *could* lose to McEnroe. He was caught so far behind the baseline.'

McEnroe could hardly believe his luck that he would be playing Borg for the first time in the Swede's homeland, yet have the advantage of playing on a surface that favoured his game. No matter how much respect the young American might privately reserve for Borg, by this stage of his career McEnroe had enough self-assurance to consider himself capable of meeting him on level terms. The American took first blood in some style.

Swedish journalist Bjorn Hellberg remembered the tennis carnage McEnroe's game visited on Borg that day in Stockholm. 'Despite the fact that Borg had such a wonderful return, he got just seven points on McEnroe's serve in two sets,' he said – and had no need to look to reference books to confirm such statistics. The memory and shape of Borg's defeat was burned in his mind. 'Borg lost, 3–6, 4–6, and was completely outclassed. It was the first time Borg lost in a professional match against a younger opponent. McEnroe was so fast.'

That day in Stockholm, McEnroe understood he had crossed the Rubicon. He recognised the significance of his achievement. He had proved to himself that he was equipped for the big time, mentally as well as physically. 'I think he felt the pressure playing me in his hometown, in front of a Swedish crowd who'd gotten excited about the game because of him,' said McEnroe. 'I actually won the match pretty easily. The win was a huge victory for me, but it didn't make me think one bit less of Bjorn. I just felt I was with the big boys now and this was the official coronation.' Borg admitted afterwards, 'There was little I could do. John simply played too well for me.' McEnroe clinched the title when, after a night on the tiles, and not those on the court, he returned to the office to overwhelm Tim Gullikson.

Almost from the start, Bentzer found an easy alliance with McEnroe. 'I always liked John, though I hated his petulance,' she said. 'I really think from that first match, Bjorn brought out the best in him. His intensity was different to Bjorn's, but measured just as big. I am only half-Swedish – my mother was from Czechoslovakia – and John was much more my cup of tea. Bjorn was always in character on and off the court. The difference was that you could get through to John after he left the court. You couldn't get through to Bjorn, not really through to him. The wall is always up.

'Bjorn never had a proper childhood and ran into serious personal problems in later life because he was trying to find himself and went completely on the wrong track. I don't think he had any points of reference and that was a pity for Bjorn. His parents were taken out of their environment and, in the nicest terms, they are very simple people. I also think he might have hugely profited from a calmer relationship with the press.

'I went on to work on the Volvo Grand Prix [the men's tour] and ran the press room at the Stockholm Open. After Borg's matches, I'd go to the changing room where he would be sitting there and tell him, "Bjorn, press!" He would reply, "Bentzer, no!" and laugh with his one eye. This went on until Bjorn at last won the final in 1980. He did it by beating McEnroe [6–3, 6–4]. This time the court was so slow, you wondered if the ball would ever arrive! It was diabolical and everyone was laughing – apart from McEnroe. Bjorn was on the treatment table that day when I came to the changing room. I implored him to come to speak to the press. At last he agreed. There is a famous photograph in Sweden of pressmen hanging from the rafters as the conference was so crowded.'

The next morning, as winter began to bite in those early days of November, Mariana opened the door to suite 550 in Stockholm's Grand Hotel to allow access to a handful of reporters to hear Borg talk in an upbeat and positive manner after his triumph over McEnroe. Laurie Pignon, from the *Daily Mail*, reported, 'Mariana, in jeans and T-shirt, was smiling sweetly through slightly tired eyes. She pointed to an empty bottle and a thawed out ice bucket and said, "You won't often see that in a Borg room. We don't normally drink champagne." But this was the morning after a special night before, when in front of friends, family and his king, Bjorn Borg had climbed a tennis hillock that was fast becoming a mountain in his mind: he had won the Stockholm Open at the seventh attempt.'

Borg, unshaven, and surrounded by discarded breakfast crockery, spoke of the future with enthusiasm and innocence. 'I intend to be around for a while yet,' he said. 'If anything I am more hungry for success than when I was fifteen, for I realise I have the chance to achieve those things I want most. That is to win as many big titles as possible. I think I can still improve and that is a challenge that is more important these days than the money. I feel I am getting better because I am not playing more than seven months a year. Three or four years ago, I would be eager for a couple of tournaments, then I got tired and lost matches because of that.'

His distrust and dislike of the press in Sweden made him a constant moving target. Under the rules of the tour, Borg was fined four times that week for failing to attend a post-match press conference. He had been strongly attacked in Scandinavia's largest circulation newspaper for contemplating meeting McEnroe in South Africa, still governed under apartheid. Swedish television had to apologise for their anti-Borg reportage. 'The trouble wasn't really about playing in South Africa, but it happens all the time with so many things,' argued Borg. 'All the journalists everywhere I am playing are very positive and very nice except in my own country.'

Bentzer had seen Borg grow ever-distant with the Swedish media. She places a portion of the blame on Bergelin. 'It was a pity that Bjorn developed paranoia with the press,' she said. 'I think much of that had to do with Lennart Bergelin. Lennart was a massive influence – both positive and negative. In later years, Lennart would tell Bjorn, "Don't talk to those bastards from the press." They annihilated some Swedish pressmen. They would go through the papers with a fine toothcomb and find any word that was not complimentary.

'Money was never the issue for Lennart. Coaching was his oxygen – and Bjorn his champion. Bjorn and I used to take the piss out of Lennart something fierce. Bjorn could wind him up. But Lennart is larger than life. He has two sons of his own, Erik and Nicolas, and a lovely wife, Rosemary, yet his relationship with Bjorn was very much a father-son relationship. They were very close, but for other people he was Bjorn Iceborg – he was ice through and through.'

Bentzer had played doubles with Mariana Simionescu, but their arrangement was to run aground as the Romanian woman's infatuation with Borg coloured her decision-making. 'Mariana dumped me because she wanted to be with her "scumpule" as she called Bjorn,' recalled Bentzer. In Romanian, scumpule means darling. 'Mariana was head over heels in love with him. For Bjorn, she provided stability, a comforting shoulder, a good friend and a ball plank. She was a spunky girl, incredibly forthcoming, yet she was totally and utterly unselfish. Whatever Bjorn wanted to do, she fitted in with him.

'But I believe Borg was crazy about Helena Anliot. He always was, yet it has to be said that Bjorn is not the most amusing man in the world and he liked to be in bed most nights by 9. He was up early to get ready to practise. Helena wanted to go out and have fun. Mariana shacked up with Helena on the road to be close to Bjorn. She was a good tennis player herself, with a thumping forehand and a good mind, but the truth was she would drop anything for Bjorn.'

After that first triumph over Borg at Stockholm in 1978, McEnroe's year had a final flourish. He went to London and claimed victory in the Benson & Hedges Championships at Wembley, where Tim Gullikson was his victim in the final, as he had been in Stockholm, and this rich vein of form won McEnroe a berth as a singles player on the US Davis Cup team for the final against Great Britain. McEnroe exuded a passion for the Davis Cup unlike some others from the United States. Connors, for instance, could blow hot and cold, but McEnroe liked the team aspect of the competition – possibly a throw back to his school days when he played soccer in Queens – and he took an immense pride in playing for his country. That USTA only paid their players $2,000 a week for being selected to play singles was never an issue for him.

He had been given his debut earlier in the year in Santiago, where the United States had travelled to meet Chile in the final of the American zone group stage of the Davis Cup. It would be safe to say that nerves didn't get the better of him on this trip and he slept blithely through the earthquake that shook Santiago when the US players were in the city. He went on to make a winning debut, taking the doubles rubber in partnership with Brian Gottfried. The United States defeated Chile, 4–1, and McEnroe revelled in the hysterical atmosphere. In Latin America, it was not uncommon for coins or seat cushions to be hurled on court if the crowd felt their man had been dealt a bad call. 'Nobody in South America seemed to think tennis was a sissy sport,' said McEnroe.

Gottfried's younger brother, Larry, was a contemporary of McEnroe, so Brian had seen him mature as a player over the years. 'In the last year they were in the juniors, John and my brother were given a wild card into the doubles at the US Open,' said Gottfried. 'I watched them against John Alexander and Phil Dent, one of the best doubles partnerships at the time. What

McEnroe could do on a doubles court was just phenomenal.' Yet Gottfried had reservations about McEnroe's temperament. 'We were different types on the court,' he commented. 'I'm old school. I wasn't always crazy about what John did out there. He thought anything to win the match was OK, but I think he did things, verbally, at critical times in matches that didn't need to be done. He was too good, but John always said that it was just part of the game. Shall we say, if I was the owner of a sports team and he was the manager we would have had philosophical differences of opinion.' Gottfried chuckled gently as he spoke.

McEnroe was not on the US Davis Cup team that defeated Sweden in the semifinals of the competition in the autumn of 1978. Borg beat Arthur Ashe and Vitas Gerulaitis in his two singles rubbers, but with Ashe and Gerulaitis each scoring a point off Kjell Johannson, the tie was decided by the doubles. And over five, tense sets, Stan Smith and Bob Lutz edged out Borg and Ove Bengtson, whose father was the first chairman of the Swedish Parliament. Bengtson was a qualified PE teacher, who, intriguingly, wrote his thesis on the behaviour pattern of the world's top players, although McEnroe was born too late to be one of the subjects of his academic scrutiny.

For the Davis Cup Final, McEnroe was chosen to make his singles debut for the United States against the surprise nation of the tournament, Great Britain. After beating the Czech team of Ivan Lendl, Jiri Hrebec, Jan Kodes and Tomas Smid in the European A zone final, Britain then ambushed Australia on a fast indoor court at Crystal Palace. Remarkably, Britain had the tie sewn up by the end of the second day. In the singles, Buster Mottram overcame Tony Roche and John Lloyd eclipsed John Alexander, before David Lloyd and Mark Cox defeated Ross Case and Geoff Masters in the doubles. Such acts of bravado put the British boys on the plane to Palm Springs, California, for the final, due to be played between 8 and 10 December. Palm Springs is a resort community in the middle of the Californian desert where Frank Sinatra and Bob Hope kept homes. It was an altogether strange location to play the Davis Cup final – as golf was the predominant game of choice in this area – but the fact that the USTA chose Palm Springs was a compliment to the British. American captain, Tony Trabert, wanted to play on an outdoor hard court rather than stage the tie indoors, as they had seen how the Australians had been undone with a roof, rather than sky, over their heads.

McEnroe, still only nineteen years old, had become pivotal to the US cause. 'The court was made lightning fast, especially for Mac,' remembered David Lloyd. 'It was like lino. His left-handed serve was around 120 miles per hour and it moved in the air a couple of yards and it moved off the court. The ball was in the wall before he'd finished his swing.' Lloyd's younger brother, John, became McEnroe's first ever victim in the singles of the Davis Cup. The score line told its own story: 6–1, 6–2, 6–2. John Lloyd felt he had been professionally mugged. 'I've never been made to look like an idiot on the court before,' he admitted afterwards. 'Not by Borg, not by Connors, not by anyone, until I played McEnroe today.'

Yet Mottram responded to the challenge staring the British team in the face. As the sun dropped behind the San Jacinto Mountains and the temperature fell, Mottram recovered from two sets down to beat Brian Gottfried, saving a match point in the third. At the end of day one, the British team went to bed still harbouring dreams of winning the Davis Cup for the first time since 1936 and the halcyon era of Fred Perry. Those dreams of fantasy were soon to fade in the hard light of daybreak. The next afternoon Stan Smith and Bob Lutz crushed David Lloyd and Mark Cox in straight sets.

The stage was established for McEnroe to earn the roaring approval of his nation. He ground Mottram into the desert, 6–2, 6–2, 6–1. In his first two Davis Cup rubbers, McEnroe had lost just ten games. Gottfried was mesmerised. 'I think he lost six points on serve against Mottram in three sets and maybe ten points against Lloyd. The way John handled pressure was so impressive.' McEnroe had just made himself the youngest player in history to clinch the Davis Cup. He had lost two fewer games than American Bill Tilden in the challenge round of 1924 and two fewer games than Borg had lost in the 1975 final.

9

BLOSSOMING
IN THE GARDEN

Bjorn Borg opted to miss the 1978 Masters – the year-end tournament reserved for the most successful eight men in the world – for reasons that were never made public. Perhaps he was simply disinclined to travel to New York in early January. Clearly, money was no longer a motivating factor. What other professional would take a rain check on a tournament offering $100,000 to the winner? Well, Guillermo Vilas, actually, but Vilas would have had no realistic expectation of success in Madison Square Garden.

John McEnroe, however, accepted his place in the Masters for the first time in those wintry days of 1979. The tournament was played in a round-robin format with McEnroe in the blue group alongside Arthur Ashe, Jimmy Connors and Harold Solomon. The red group comprised Brian Gottfried, Eddie Dibbs, Raul Ramirez and Corrado Barazzutti. Under new rules, written after Borg and Vilas threw the Masters into confusion twelve months earlier when they failed to play their final round-robin matches, having already won a place in the semifinals, each player had to fulfil their three group matches. Failure to do so was to invite instant elimination.

McEnroe crunched Ashe in his first match and when Connors disposed of Solomon, the scene was set for a showdown between the two volatile lefties. McEnroe had been on a roll since the US Open, whereas Connors had not played for five weeks. And in London the week before the Masters, McEnroe and Fleming had won a sixth title together, claiming a record $80,000 first prize in the World Championship of Tennis (WCT) Braniff World Doubles Championship. Connors, though, could draw strength from the fact that he had won his four previous matches with McEnroe. He was not a man given to conceding an inch to a rival, a position Connors reinforced with his comment before their meeting. 'Yes, he's a good kid,' he said, 'but he's not ready to beat me yet.'

Sixteen thousand people filled Madison Square Garden on the evening of the match. Loyalties were boisterously divided. McEnroe may have been the home town kid, but Connors always connected with a New York crowd. He had attitude. There was a raw intensity to the tennis that was played, a real edge between the two men. 'The opening set of the match was a minor classic,' said broadcaster John Barrett.

McEnroe claimed that all-important first set by breaking Connors in the twelfth game after fifty-six minutes. Connors, it transpired, was in trouble from another source, too. He removed his left shoe and sock to have treatment on something troubling him on the sole of his foot. He was heard to ask umpire Frank Hammond what would happen if he retired. 'You'll be out, Jimmy,' replied Hammond. Connors returned to the court, but he lost the first three games of the second set. At the next changeover, Connors announced, 'I can't play anymore.' Instinctively, a jubilant McEnroe raised his arms aloft on court. He left the court as fighters had left the Garden down the ages – with a victory salute to the crowd. In return, people rose to their feet to acclaim McEnroe. He had Connors's scalp for the first time and, frankly, he couldn't give a damn that the game had ended prematurely.

Afterwards Connors explained that a deep blister had formed under the hard pad of skin on the ball of his left foot five days earlier. He had asked the tournament doctor, Norman Rudy, to try to draw the blister the day before he played McEnroe. He conceded that he had taken too much downtime, a factor that had made his foot susceptible to this type of injury. Rudy confirmed that Connors needed rest. 'I don't believe Jimmy could play tomorrow,' said the doctor. 'It could take up to two weeks to heal completely.' Later McEnroe told his media conference, 'Sure, I would have liked to have finished the match, but I didn't notice anything [wrong with Connors]. I was happy. He had chances to break me, but I hung in there. Beating him – I'll take it anyway I can get it.' McEnroe progressed to the final by overcoming Dibbs, while Ashe beat Gottfried in the other semifinal.

At thirty-five, Ashe, an African-American, was acknowledged as a gentleman of the game. He was also an overwhelming underdog going out to play McEnroe, but he had been similarly written off when he appeared in the 1975 Wimbledon final against Connors. Ashe's response to those telling him he was destined for an afternoon of humiliation at the hands of Connors was to play a game of such subtlety and such cunning that he turned the form book inside out. His variation of pace and the angles he created disorientated Connors, the defending champion, and Ashe stole his crown in broad daylight in front of millions of witnesses watching on television around the globe. Could he rise once more to the occasion against McEnroe? 'Sure, I feel my age,' said Ashe. 'I have to train much harder – lift weights – and I have to stretch for ten minutes and get a massage. Since the US Open, McEnroe has been the best player in the world, but he can be as bad as anyone else.'

On the night before the final, McEnroe warmed up by winning the doubles title in partnership with Fleming. They defeated Wojtek Fibak and Tom Okker in three straight sets to endorse the argument that there was no better doubles team in the world. McEnroe's next assigment was to make himself Masters champion for the first time.

In front of a sell-out crowd at the Garden, McEnroe eased into a 5–4, 40–0 lead, although his game lacked a little lustre, perhaps a reflection of his late-night finish the previous evening. Barrett takes up the story: 'Unaccountably, McEnroe served three consecutive double faults, something none of us could remember seeing in similar circumstances before and, in spite of having a fourth set point, he lost the game. Suddenly, Ashe knew his moment had come.' After each man held serve to love, the set was to be decided on a tie-break. Ultimately, Ashe thumped an overhead out of McEnroe's reach to win the set in a fraction under an hour.

McEnroe levelled the match, however, courtesy of the only break of serve in the second set. The assumption of those inside the Garden was that the young pretender would now sprint to the title. Ashe had other plans. Just as he had against Connors on the Centre Court at Wimbledon, Ashe planted seeds of doubt in McEnroe's mind. He hit some heavy winners, but laced his game plan with some returns that floated over the net. He was the man who raced out to a 4–1 lead, but the pendulum was to swing once more, hard and in the direction of McEnroe. After some uncharacteristic errors from Ashe, McEnroe was back in the final at 4–4. Ashe regrouped to hold serve – and then the drama of the night unfolded. At 15–40 on McEnroe's service, Ashe held double match point. He negligently squandered the first with a sloppy backhand into the net. McEnroe returned to the baseline to serve again. 'The point will be talked of for years,' said Barrett. 'McEnroe threw in a fast first serve to the backhand that Ashe whipped to McEnroe's feet as he lunged hopelessly to his right, but it had been called a fault.' Ashe was crestfallen. He slowly walked to the umpire's chair and, politely, of course, asked if the serve had been out. He was told it was. He never believed a word of it. 'I'll bet all the money I possess that the serve was good,' said Ashe later.

No matter. McEnroe had dodged the bullet. He rallied to take the Masters title, 6–7, 6–3, 7–5. At nineteen, McEnroe now had a calling card that could not be ignored. In seven months as a professional, he had won half a million dollars and rung alarm bells that could be heard throughout the game. 'The Masters calls for a special kind of toughness and McEnroe met the challenge,' said Ashe, 'but we'll figure a way to beat him. If somebody wins too much we all get together in the locker room and work out how to beat him.' McEnroe had no reason to be overly perturbed. Clearly, this combined brains trust hadn't yet found an effective plan to slow down Borg, so it wasn't a threat that would cause McEnroe sleepless nights.

Borg and McEnroe were about to shape and influence the game in their own image. Of course, the Swede remained a model of efficient order with a Viking's rapacious instinct not to be denied in battle; whereas McEnroe now had the confidence to deliver his compelling game with an even more forceful soundtrack from the streets, his tennis mimicking the punk movement. The game was moving to a new dimension and the second instalment of their rivalry took place on an indoor court in Richmond, Virginia. The event was a round in the WCT series, one of eight points-linked tournaments run by Texas oil magnate Lamar Hunt as part of the regular grand prix circuit. Borg met McEnroe in the semis, just a couple of weeks after the New Yorker had captured the Masters.

Borg emerged as the winner, 4–6, 7–6, 6–3. The score line did not begin to reflect the dramatic content of the game.

'That was the first great match we played,' said Borg. 'John had eight match points.' Seven weeks later in New Orleans, in another WCT semifinal, McEnroe came out on the right side of another three-set encounter with Borg: 5–7, 6–1, 7–6. 'I had five match points in that one!' exclaimed Borg. Those raw statistics – Borg saving eight match points and McEnroe saving five – told us that this rivalry had the potential to meet, then surpass, all expectations. McEnroe had shown not only the boldness to take his game to Borg, but he had also demonstrated a resilience that, over time, would build and corrode the Swede's thinking. Borg may have quelled the fiery challenge of Connors, but McEnroe presented him with problems on a new scale.

One week after their meeting in New Orleans, Borg and McEnroe crossed the Atlantic as the WCT erected its big tent in Rotterdam. Johan Kriek, Peter Fleming, Raul Ramirez, Vijay Amritraj, Vitas Gerulaitis and Wojtek Fibak completed the field. One by one they collected their pay cheques as they left the building. Once again, Borg would play McEnroe in the final – and for them it was relatively plain fare, with Borg winning in straight sets, 6–4, 6–2. These WCT tournaments led to the $200,000 singles play-offs in Dallas, the headquarters for Hunt's empire. It was the final occasion the series would be concluded at the Moody Coliseum. Borg was No. 1 seed, ahead of McEnroe, Gerulaitis, Connors, Gene Mayer, Geoff Masters, John Alexander and Brian Gottfried. At twenty-eight, Masters was the oldest competitor.

Almost instantly, Connors managed to get under McEnroe's skin. He was scheduled to play the opening match against Mayer, but successfully applied for a postponement because of an infected callus on the little finger of his left hand. Under the revised programme, McEnroe had to begin proceedings against Alexander. The fact that it took him ten minutes to win the first game did not improve his already fragile mood. When, a couple of games later, McEnroe questioned a line call, the crowd jumped all over him. Their hostility increased as a series of calls bothered McEnroe – who had some justification in voicing his displeasure – but he was never one to let a rowdy crowd throw him off stride. Alexander won a mere six games over three sets. Afterwards, the Australian offered a glowing testimony to the torture that he had endured in the Coliseum: 'I've played against Laver, Borg and Connors and this guy is the equal of them all.'

Borg trounced Masters, while Connors and Gerulaitis also advanced to the semifinals. McEnroe against Connors was the soap opera they most wanted to promote in Dallas and the two charismatic Americans had to play one another in the semifinals. Their antagonism was now undeniable. Connors was the man under greater pressure. As a proven champion, his reputation was on the line. While McEnroe respected Borg and treated the court as though he was in church when he played the Swede, he found no need for such a restrained show of manners against Connors. To Connors, meeting McEnroe on a tennis court was like looking in a mirror. 'We both think we should be perfect all the time and we play like that,' he admitted.

His thoughts that follow were delivered when we met at the French Open in the late 1980s. On this night of reflection, Connors revelled in the intensity of his rivalries with McEnroe and Borg. In the course of this interview, telling and all-embracing, he talked of his marriage and children, saying, 'I was only angry on the court. I only came across like that when I was playing tennis. I was just an animal, but I never carried any of my tennis off the court. The press gave me my image because they were not used to seeing my style or the attitude I brought to the game. I was a brat, a punk. I rode that to the hilt, but then I knew that I had to one day get off the horse and head in another direction.'

In the early 1980s, when Connors's career flared magnificently again and he won Wimbledon for a second time and the US Open twice more, he won the hearts and minds of a new generation of fans. He became the game's older statesman, a husband and a father who showed himself to be extremely humorous, having erased almost all trace of past vulgarities. He never lost his zest for battle, but now he used a rapier not a broadsword. Connors aged with something close to graciousness and there was no one more popular on tennis courts in the heartland of America than him. Into his forties, Connors could still fill a stadium on a Monday evening. I was courtside on a coal-black night in Georgia when he was the victim of a distinctly dubious line call. 'Get mad, Jimmy,' yelled a woman's voice. He stalked the baseline, but there was no belligerence in his step. 'Not any more, lady,' he said, and laughter echoed around the packed stands. He was forty-one years old, still playing the regular tour.

Later, he said, 'A tennis court is our office. Why should anyone think that everything is hunky dory? I know I took things too far many times. We walk a thin line, but what we did was show people we were alive, that craziness and real feelings existed in the game. We weren't robots. Ask me if McEnroe went out of bounds a few times? Sure, he did. Nastase? Sure. Gerulaitis? Sure. But they all gave the game more than just the tennis itself. They drew people in because of what they might do, not because of what they were guaranteed to do. The line was crossed. Did I like that? Damn right I did. I took full responsibility for the good and the bad. Those first five or six years I had a ball. I played the kind of tennis I wanted and the people were there. Whether they wanted to see me win or lose didn't matter. We took the game from the country club and gave it to the blue-collar man.

'Mac and me went through some brutal years. Game versus game; attitude versus attitude; upbringing versus upbringing; some might suggest, punk versus punk. But like all tennis players, we were going into reverse as we spat insults. We got through it all, but it will always be an up and down relationship because of the intensity in everything we do.' Connors was in no danger of starting an argument. The truth of what he said is on film and in print. On that night in Dallas in 1979, Connors had to take most punishment as the winners flowed from McEnroe's half of the court. The match ended when Connors made no attempt to return a service he thought was out, but which was called in. McEnroe had made the final, 6–1, 6–4, 6–4; his first proper win over Connors. For Connors, this was a result that could not be sweetened by a public autopsy, so he skipped the media conference and left town without a word.

McEnroe and Borg had centre stage once more in the final. After three sets and eight games, McEnroe had won a mere three points more than the Swede, but Borg had a weariness about him, having won seventeen straight matches before he arrived in Dallas. McEnroe's service became too hot for Borg and the American completed a superb week by defeating his rival, 7–5, 4–6, 6–2, 7–6, to claim a cheque for £50,000. Borg had no complaints: 'If

you play John you have to be at the top of your game to beat him.'
Borg wasn't talking just for himself. He was talking for everyone
on the tour.

10

HOME FROM HOME AT THE CUMBERLAND CLUB

Just three weeks later, Borg returned to familiar ground in Paris. At the French Open, no one could trouble him for a sustained period if his game was in working order. He had put in the hours to assure that it was. Lennart Bergelin remembered what Italian Corrado Barrazzutti said before he met Borg in the 1978 semifinal of the French Open. 'Barrazzutti said he thought the only way to have a chance was to kill him,' said Bergelin, gently laughing at the stranglehold his man had over his rivals on the clay courts at Roland Garros. Barrazzutti proved to be the prophet of his own doom. He took one game from Borg.

In Paris in the spring of 1979, Czech Tomas Smid at least forced Borg to play four sets in the first round. Smid, tall and languid, hit a heavy ball and was a skilful doubles player, partnering former Wimbledon champion Jan Kodes, before profitably joining forces with Pavel Slozil. McEnroe, along with Roscoe Tanner, John Alexander, Martina Navratilova, Tracy Austin and Evonne Cawley, chose to miss the championships for other assignations, yet the competition in the men's singles was still strong, with Jimmy Connors, Vitas Gerulaitis, Guillermo Vilas, Jose-Luis Clerc, Harold Solomon, Eddie Dibbs and Jose Higueras all in Paris.

Indeed, Borg dropped a second set in the second round when Tom Gullikson caused him an anxious moment or two, but from that moment forward Borg journeyed untroubled to the final. In the semis, his close friend, Vitas Gerulaitis, won a miserly three games from him. Gerulaitis may have been embarrassed with his own tennis, but the truth was Borg played exceptionally well. Connors's hopes of making the French Open final for the first time were dashed by Victor Pecci, an unseeded, six foot, four inch Paraguayan with a hefty first serve.

Pecci must have cursed when he drew his curtains on the morning of the final to find a springtime shower had dampened Paris. Court Central would be sure to play especially slow and the sullen atmosphere would make the balls heavier. In other words, the conditions would suit Borg perfectly. Pecci saw the first two sets vanish and he was trailing, 2–4, in the third when he was finally given an unexpected respite from the storm raging round him. The match was halted for several minutes while a stretcher was summoned for a spectator who had fainted. Borg's momentum was interrupted enough to permit Pecci a glimpse of daylight. Rex Bellamy, the tennis correspondent for *The Times* and a wonderful wordsmith, reported: 'Pecci lashed out with desperate splendour. Borg began to miss – and the authority drained out of him like sand from an egg-timer.' Pecci won the third set, in a tie-break, and as the rain fell he matched Borg game for game in the fourth, but at 4–4, 40–30, Pecci double-faulted. 'He lost six of the next seven points,' wrote Bellamy, 'and, suddenly, there were no more points to play.' Borg had triumphed, 6–3, 6–1, 6–7, 6–4.

Henri Cochet, one of Les Trois Mousquetaires, had been thirty when he won the French Championship for a fourth time in 1932. Borg had just turned twenty-three. As a crumb of consolation for Pecci, Borg described this as his most difficult final at Roland Garros. The next day Borg flew to London with Bergelin and Mariana and checked into the Holiday Inn at Swiss Cottage. As usual, a court at the Cumberland Lawn Tennis Club was booked for him. Bergelin liked the comfort of remaining true to a proven formula. 'We kept Bjorn's tournament commitments down before Paris and he never played a tournament before Wimbledon,' said Bergelin. 'He just practised. That meant he was in good health and feeling good mentally.'

McEnroe took a contrary view. He found the matches to fine-tune his game at the inaugural Stella Artois Championships, staged on the grass courts at Queen's Club, two weeks before Wimbledon. McEnroe was to be the first king of Queen's. If the Stella Artois was good for McEnroe, then McEnroe was definitely good for the Stella Artois. Sir Frank Lowe, president of the tournament committee, said, 'In 1978, after two inauspicious years of sponsorship by Rawlings Tonic Water, I persuaded Whitbread to let me have one more go and to install Stella Artois as the sponsor. So Clive Bernstein, tournament director, Ian Wight, event director, and myself were under no illusions that it was now or never. The god of tennis came to our aid. The weather was better, the entry quite good, the spectator count was up and BBC television covered the last two days. But the biggest change of all was the emergence of a curly haired American in a headband, which, probably even he might admit, should have occasionally been placed over his mouth – John McEnroe. It's almost impossible to emphasise his importance to the Stella Artois.'

While Borg practised in the privacy of the Cumberland Club, McEnroe played his way into the final at Queen's. His opponent: Victor Pecci. The twenty-three-year-old Paraguayan had shaken the clay dust from his shoes and turned his power to good advantage on a surface much more readily suited to his game. He won the first set of the final in a tie-break, but then McEnroe overwhelmed him. The New Yorker permitted Pecci just two more games in the match and then received the quite magnificent trophy on the Centre Court in front of the elegant and very British clubhouse. McEnroe had claimed his first grass court championship in London – and affirmed his position as the man most likely to end Borg's streak in London SW19. 'Setting aside all other aspects of his game, McEnroe had the fastest hands at the net I've ever seen,' said Lowe. McEnroe would appear in the first four finals, winning three in succession. He won the tournament a total of four times as the Stella Artois grew in stature in the tennis calendar. Over time, it became a rich form guide ahead of Wimbledon: men like McEnroe, Connors, Boris Becker, Pete Sampras and Lleyton Hewitt all pulled off the Stella Artois-Wimbledon double at least once.

The Centre Court at Queen's Club, rightly, won a reputation for being hard and true. While the sponsors' brew – and other products from the grape – have sometimes caused players to throw disdainful looks into the stands, there has always been an intimate atmosphere at the tournament. At Queen's you feel up close and personal to the stars of the day. Richard Evans, a veteran of the tennis trenches, having written and broadcast on the game for publications and radio stations across the world for over four decades, tells a story from Queen's that encapsulates the essential McEnroe in just such surroundings.

Evans, who is the author of an authorised biography on McEnroe, said, 'Call it a sixth sense; a vision; an ability to play chess at breakneck speed. Of all our champions I think McEnroe possessed this to an extraordinary degree. And not just because of one funny incident that I will never forget which proved his literal powers of lateral vision. John was serving one day from that baseline, which is directly parallel to the clubhouse doorway which leads up to the locker rooms. The place was full and I had just edged my way through it to stand with a tightly packed cluster of other spectators at the top of the steps. They were five deep in front of me and then all the rows of seats leading down to the court's edge were full, too. Within fifteen seconds of emerging from the clubhouse I sneezed, just as McEnroe threw the ball up to serve.

'He let the ball drop and called out, "Oh thanks, Richard!" How did he know? How could he possibly have picked me out of that mass of faces? Certainly not because he recognised my sneeze! But it was indicative of why McEnroe was so susceptible to on-court blow-ups. He was aware of absolutely everything. Drop a pencil up there in the fifteenth row and he would hear it. Pull a handkerchief from your pocket and it would catch his eye. But his awareness was all part of the mental make-up that made him so different. His vision, in every sense, was exceptional.'

As McEnroe was making headlines at the first Stella Artois championships, Borg was content to stay largely out of sight to the north of the city. His days were regimented and set in stone. 'It was a little like being in the army,' laughed Mariana. 'Bjorn practised for two and a half hours in the morning; and then two and a half to three hours in the afternoon,' she said. 'For Bjorn it was never a question of who was in front of him on the other side of the net. For him, it was the ball.' Club members watched Borg practise without troubling him. In truth, there was not a huge number of people playing at the club during week days.

Chris Bradnam, tennis professional at the Cumberland since 1994, and nowadays gaining stature as a tennis broadcaster as well, said, 'On rainy days at the club, when we sit around having a cup of tea, I hear older members telling stories of how they fancied their chances against Borg! He was that bad when he first arrived from Paris. He was awful, they said. He shanked the ball everywhere, but they also say you could see him improve by the hour.'

In the clubhouse, there are just a couple of small photographs of Borg hanging alongside the portraits of winners of the spring tournament that used to be part of the fabric of the British tennis summer. One is signed: 'To the Cumberland Club, best wishes Bjorn Borg 1977'. Bradnam is in one of the adjacent photos, pictured with Andrew Jarrett after they had become doubles champions in the British Home Stores Tournament that was staged at the Cumberland. 'I had to move seventy-eight other pictures to be hanging next to Bjorn!' said Bradnam, chuckling. 'It's set in cement now.'

The club professional before Bradnam was the late Bill Blake, who, they say, spent fifty years teaching tennis and squash at the Cumberland. The club night he ran on Wednesday evenings was immovable. Legend has it that one night Blake read out the pairings: 'Susan and John will play Eleanor . . . and Bjorn.' Bradnam has no doubt it could have happened. 'Bill ran club night with an iron fist and it was a very important night, and still is an important night, when new members and old get to know one another,' said Bradnam. 'Bill's club night was known around the world of tennis. I have no doubt Bill would have told Bjorn who he was playing with, but Bjorn wouldn't have minded. He didn't just play and leave. He was aware of putting something back.' Mariana added, 'Some days we would shower, then have lunch at the club. Other days we might return to the hotel, but when the afternoon practice ended at 5, we always stayed for Cheddar cheese, biscuits and tea like the English tradition.'

Sometimes, Mariana might persuade Borg to break the monotony of being holed up in their hotel room by going to the cinema. 'But when you went out everyone recognised Bjorn,' she admitted. 'There were always people outside the hotel. It was crazy. He could not get anywhere without being noticed. Bjorn is not like Jimmy or John, who were happy with their fame. Bjorn was irritated. He wanted his private life private. He couldn't understand why people wouldn't leave him alone.'

The less Borg said, the more fascinated people became in him. Call it the Garbo factor. His manager, Peter Worth, recalled: 'Bjorn lived to a very set pattern of events. Starting at the Monte Carlo Open in the spring, he would play four or five clay court events. It was almost a foregone conclusion that he would win. The only person who could possibly beat him was Guillermo Vilas and they had these turgid matches against one another. The French Open was never the problem. The problem was how was he going to win Wimbledon?'

Answer: go to the Cumberland Club and work hour on hour, day on day for two weeks. 'He worked particularly hard for those two weeks,' said Worth. 'Gerulaitis worked a lot with him, but this was a two-way street and not Borg calling in a favour from a friend. Vitas needed to practise as well.' In public, at least, Borg never showed any signs of apprehension or nerves as he went through his routine to make the subtle changes to his game to be able to compete at the highest level on grass. 'With Borg you rarely got any indication of apprehension – or excitement,' insisted Worth. 'I never saw anything other than a fairly bland, dull, polite, nice, friendly man. I can think of many other top sportsmen who get moody. Bjorn didn't. I think one of his strengths was that he lived like that Kipling quotation – he treated triumph and disaster the same way.

'After the first year he won Wimbledon, some things were put in place to shield him. It was no worse from year to year, really. He was pestered, but it was no worse in year five than it was in year two. He couldn't play on an outside court, because no one wanted to take the risk of getting him out and back through the crowd in safety. But no one pestered him in an aggressive manner. No one abused him. At the hotel at Swiss Cottage maybe thirty fans would be hanging around to see him. There was some screaming, that sense of Beatlemania. It was lovely, actually.'

Colin Hess, the committee member from the Cumberland Club who first arranged for Borg to use the courts, felt that Borg appreciated the privacy he was afforded to practise. 'He liked the seclusion the club provided,' said Hess. 'He also liked the way the members behaved very well. The club was founded in 1877 – one of the oldest in England – and Bjorn could drive in near the little cottage that was lived in by the groundsman, Pepe. It's all incredible to recall, really, when you see the way the game has developed, but this is where he would beef up his serve and "flatten" his groundstrokes, so he could play without topspin when he needed. And, if I dare say it, he would learn to volley. He would volley quite a lot at the Cumberland. Borg usually played on what we called our No. 1 court, but if there was a problem with that, he couldn't care less and would play on another court. It sounds smug for me to say so, but they were reckoned to be very good grass courts.'

By the summer of 1979, McEnroe had already been introduced to the social circle of Borg and Gerulaitis, after playing with them in an exhibition in Milan earlier in the year. McEnroe wrote in his book: 'I marked the occasion by indulging in something I'd never tried before (never mind what) – and the next thing I knew, Vitas and Bjorn were carrying me back into the hotel. I felt sick, but wonderful: I had passed the initiation. I was part of the gang. Broadway Vitas and Bjorn! To me, they were like the elder statesmen – it was so exciting to be running with the best tennis players in the world. I prided myself – I still pride myself – on being an energetic, even hyperactive, person, but I didn't have the energy these guys had. I'd eventually say, "I've got to get my sleep."'

McEnroe was No. 2 seed at Wimbledon and therefore seeded to meet Borg in the final. The American was certainly not lacking in confidence after winning the tournament at Queen's Club; what he was short of was decorum. He threw rackets around and yelled at linesmen during a succession of tantrums. As a consequence, he found himself attracting unfavourable headlines in the British tabloid press. One name in particular stuck: Superbrat.

He was playing under huge levels of personal expectation. Having been to the semifinals at Wimbledon on his first visit, as a qualifier, McEnroe knew he had the talent to succeed on the manicured lawns at the All England Club. Talent alone was not sufficient to get the job done, however. After beating American Terry Moor, he dropped a set in the second round against Britain's Buster Mottram, a guy he had wiped out six months earlier in the Davis Cup Final.

Borg, meantime, was his usual vulnerable self. If the good members of the Cumberland Club deluded themselves that they might have the tools to overwhelm the Swede on his arrival in London, seasoned professionals quite clearly did. The three-times champion dropped a set in his first round match with Tom Gorman from the United States, but he was to face a bigger trial in the second round against Vijay Amritraj.

Amritraj came from a Madras tennis-playing dynasty; his brothers Anand and Ashok also played the game to a high standard. Vijay, suave and debonair, had a role in the James Bond film *Octopussy* a few years later. At this Wimbledon, you might say he had been granted a licence to thrill! Borg was cast as the champion backed into a tight corner. Amritraj led two sets to one. Mark Edmondson and Victor Amaya must surely have empathised with the tall Indian, yet Amritraj's ultimate fate was the same as had befallen them at Wimbledon on other days: Borg ushered him out the door in five sets. John Lloyd offered a theory: 'If it had not been Borg staring down the court at them, Edmondson, Amaya and Amritraj would have all won matches from the position they put themselves in, but Borg had this presence on the court. He could make rivals choke in sight of victory.'

In the third round, McEnroe beat Tom Gullikson in straight sets, while Borg removed Hank Pfister without drama. Tim Gullikson was given an opportunity to avenge family honour when he clinched a fourth round appointment with McEnroe. Gullikson duly knocked out McEnroe in straight sets, leaving McEnroe's hopes of meeting Borg on a grass court to be shelved for another year. He had angrily roared around court, but had been toothless when it most mattered. No one was more disappointed than the young man himself. Much, much later, McEnroe tried to make sense of his temper-tantrums: 'I don't know where my rage came from. I grew up with my brothers in a loud Irish-American household and, having lived in New York all my life, I was shocked to discover that other people weren't more like me. If you took a plane and landed at Kennedy Airport, by the time you got to your house you were lucky if ten people hadn't called you an asshole.'

With McEnroe out, fifth seeded Roscoe Tanner forced his way into the final from the bottom half of the draw, behind the fastest service in the game. Borg overcame Brian Teacher, Tom Okker and Connors with surprising ease to claim his now habitual place on the Centre Court for the men's singles final. Hess recalled Borg's routine visit to the Cumberland Club on the morning of the final: 'He would come up around 11a.m. and go on court for forty-five minutes, often with Bergelin. It was a hit and kind of relaxation exercise. The place was packed with juniors and when Bjorn came off court he would sign autographs. Then he would shower and we would feed him. Usually he had a steak and salad. We would wish him luck and he would get in the car – just like someone commuting to the office – and go off to try to win Wimbledon.'

On the morning of Borg's final with Tanner, his mind was troubled by an ongoing row he was involved in with Mariana. 'Bjorn was very stubborn,' she said. 'To live with him was nice, pleasant, but sometimes it was like this.' She banged her fist against the breakfast table for emphasis at Place des Moulins as she sipped coffee during our rendezvous. 'If Bjorn said black was white he wouldn't change.' Mariana had to climb down. 'We were fighting on the drive to Wimbledon for Bjorn's final against Tanner. Finally, I gave up and said to him, "C'mon, it's my fault." Of course, it wasn't, but even when you have right on your side you have to be psychological. It was important that he should not have any problems before his final.'

For the second time in four years, Borg was taken the distance in the Wimbledon final. Indeed, Tanner led by two sets to one. Had we heard this story before? Had we seen others press Borg to the point of extinction, only for the champion to rebound with a vengeance? Tanner was to be cast in a similar plot. He was to understand just what made Borg great, seeing his advantage wiped out as the Swede dug deep into his resources to level at two sets all.

'When we started the fifth set it was the first time I felt nervous playing the Wimbledon final,' said Borg. 'My arm was shaking.' In the stand, Fred Perry was a fascinated spectator. The legendary figure of British tennis had been the last man to win Wimbledon three times in a row and it was appropriate he should be present to witness Borg's attempt to win a fourth successive championship. 'Looking at Fred made me a little nervous,' admitted the Swede.

But Borg's strength of mind would prove critical, again. His last crisis passed when he saved two break points as he served at 4–3 in the final set. Even so, serving for the championship, at 5–4, Borg still managed to give his mother, Margaretha, palpitations as she watched in the player's guest seats on Centre Court. The problem was, Borg had established a pattern with his parents.

After his first championship, they came to London every other year. 'She always eats candy for luck when I play,' said Borg after Tanner's fire had been finally extinguished. 'She spat it out on the floor when I was 40–0 triple match point. Then I lost three straight points. She was so nervous she looked for the candy on the floor, found it and popped it back in her mouth. I won the next two points and the match.' After two hours and forty-nine minutes he had retained the championship, 6–7, 6–1, 3–6, 6–3, 6–4. It represented his twenty-eighth consecutive win at the All England Club. 'Right after the match Fred Perry came up to me and said, "Well done," and he seemed very happy,' said Borg. 'I appreciated that very much.'

Borg later described his emotional response to his march on tennis history in one of his more candid interviews. 'I can't yet believe I have won Wimbledon for the fourth time,' he said. 'It hasn't sunk in yet. There will be a big celebration eventually, probably for the next three or four days. Today I feel much older than I am. I was unbelievably nervous at the end and almost couldn't hold my racket when he came back in the last game from 0–40 to deuce. If he had won that game I could never have won the match.

'I thought I would certainly lose the match when he was ahead two sets to one. I never felt in the fight because the points were over so quickly. He'd ace me or miss! I didn't control anything. Nothing was happening. Nothing worked. But as soon as it was two sets all, I thought I had a good chance of winning, especially when I broke in the first game of the fifth set. He had a lot of chances to break back and I remember hoping each time that he would miss. I just didn't want the ball to come back. When I won for the first time in 1976 I never imagined I could do it four times running. This is the biggest thrill of my life.'

On their way back to the Holiday Inn, Borg dutifully returned to the Cumberland Club with Mariana and Bergelin. 'He'd always look in and say thank you,' said Hess. 'As he left that night, he said as usual, "See you next year."' After having dinner, Borg and Mariana maintained another tradition and went to two of the most fashionable clubs in town. 'We always went to Annabel's and Tramp,' said Mariana. 'One year Petula Clark was with us, one year it was Peter Sellers. Sorry, but I cannot remember which year was which. Anyway, we had fun as always, with lots of champagne and dancing. It was 5a.m. or 6a.m. when we made it home to the hotel. The first thing I did when I woke the next morning – with a hangover of course – was go out and buy all the papers.'

Photographs and stories of Borg, now bearded after he maintained his superstition of not shaving during Wimbledon, dominated the sports pages. 'I didn't mind his beard, because I knew he was clean after taking two or three showers a day,' laughed Mariana. She revealed a secret, too. She was Borg's hairdresser. 'I always cut his hair,' she explained. Worth even made capital from Borg's superstition of growing a beard during the championships. 'I did a deal with Wilkinson Sword for him to shave with their razor after he won Wimbledon – quite a good PR coup really!' he said.

While Borg annexed the headlines with yet another remarkable triumph, McEnroe did not leave Wimbledon empty-handed. With Peter Fleming, he took the doubles championship after defeating Brian Gottfried and Raul Ramirez. McEnroe's name was on the honours board.

11

JUNIOR AND ME

In August 1979, the Canadian Open was played for the first time on Deco Turf II, rather than clay, to establish the tournament as the warm-up event for the US Open. Similar hard courts had been laid already at USTA's new national complex at Flushing Meadow, the site beneath the flight path of LaGuardia Airport that had become the home of the US Open the previous summer. The Canadian tournament organisers were rewarded with the sponsors' dream final in Toronto: Borg versus McEnroe. The final had to be rescheduled for Monday 20 August after rain had disrupted the event, but, nevertheless, all 7,200 seats were sold. McEnroe, from south of the Canadian border, held a 3–2 lead after five matches against Borg, the man from Mars, at least according to Ilie Nastase. Even though they had yet to meet in a Grand Slam championship, there was an increasing sense of anticipation when Borg walked out on court to meet McEnroe. As men, they were patently different. As tennis players, they adopted strategies that were in total contrast. Could the strong, silent Swede outplay McEnroe? Or would the brash New Yorker with his aggressive game cause Borg's defences to crumble and collapse? The questions ran deep.

For once, though, the match-up proved anti-climactic. Borg raced to 4–0 in the opening set and, truly, never looked back. Clearly, the Swede wanted his confidence to be at a peak when he made the short flight from Toronto to New York for the US Open, where the previous year he had finished as runner-up to Connors for a second time. He had caught McEnroe on a day when he was not at his best. Borg kept his service returns arrowed towards McEnroe's shoelaces and directed his two-fisted back-hand and topspin forehand to all corners of the court.

When the Swede was ahead by a set and 5–3, a fan yelled from the stands: 'Finish him off, Borg.' Minutes later victory belonged to Borg, 6–3, 6–3, and his mini-series with McEnroe was tied at three matches all. Afterwards, the two men had a different take on what had happened. 'I thought it was my best match against John so far,' said Borg. McEnroe disagreed. 'Bjorn has played better than that in matches I've won against him,' he suggested. 'Either I missed the easy volley or he put away the next shot. It was not a whole lot of fun playing today.' Borg's value to the tournament was evident by the fact he was paid an estimated $100,000 for endorsements and commercials. His winners' pay cheque paled in comparison: $28,000.

The two men headed for New York where Borg was top seed and McEnroe No. 3, behind Connors. The draw placed the two Americans on a collision course for the semifinals, but McEnroe had an earlier battle to withstand – against Nastase. At thirty-three, Nasty no longer had the speed or dexterity that had made him an irresistible force in the game. However, the man had not lost his instinct to work a crowd – and the crowd that night in the Louis Armstrong Stadium for the second round match between McEnroe and Nastase had plenty of time to slake their thirst before the two men came out to play at 9.

'The 10,000 capacity crowd was in an excitable mood, ready for a show,' recalled Nasty in his autobiography, *Mr Nastase*. 'The press had built the game up as if it was a boxing match. Well, that's almost what they got. Strangely, because McEnroe was a local boy, the crowd was behind me rather than him. In any case, the local bad kid versus the original bad boy of tennis made for a great event as far as they were concerned.' McEnroe and Nastase were in harmony over the choice of umpire. In their minds, Frank Hammond, overweight and balding, had a deep understanding of the game. To them, he was a player's man. He talked to people rather than lectured them. For the first two sets – McEnroe won the first, Nastase the second – the tennis was the story.

But then the script dramatically changed. Bedlam broke out. Anarchy followed. Some loud hecklers distracted Nastase. Being Nasty, he shouted back. Then he felt aggrieved by some line calls and complained to Hammond, but without success. So, a break up, Nastase stalled McEnroe as he attempted to serve. Hammond correctly awarded a penalty point against the Romanian – and fans screamed their disapproval. McEnroe went on to win the third set and he led 3–1 in the fourth when Nastase stalled again. By his own admission, Nasty was close to being out of control. Hammond acted as the rules demanded and hit Nastase with a penalty game. McEnroe was now ahead, 4–1.

Beer cans and paper cups rained on the court. 'The crowd went totally nuts,' recalled Nastase. 'John also got involved and we both went crazy. It was total chaos. For seventeen minutes, while cans, cups, garbage and even bottles were being thrown on to the court, and the police arrived in case there was a riot, I argued, John argued, the crowd screamed at Frank and Frank lost control completely.'

Hammond ordered Nastase to play. 'Too noisy,' said Nastase. Hammond then defaulted Nastase, but this controversial end to the match wasn't the end at all. With the crowd even more angry, sensing they had been short-changed, US Open referee Mike Blanchard came on court to talk with the players. McEnroe agreed to play on. Hammond tried to resume the match, but the crowd's chanting grew louder and louder. Finally, tournament director Bill Talbert took an extraordinary decision. He removed Hammond from the chair to replace him with Blanchard. Hammond left the stadium under a hail of rubbish and abuse. As the clock edged towards 1a.m. Nastase followed him out of the tournament, beaten in four chaotic sets of tennis. After Nastase had showered, he approached McEnroe in the locker room. To McEnroe's astonishment, the Romanian invited him to dinner with his wife, Dominique, and coach, Roy Emerson. 'Sure,' said McEnroe.

In the other side of the draw, Borg made quiet progress, troubling no one and being untroubled himself on the court until he met Tanner in the quarterfinals. The match was scheduled to be played under floodlights. Borg never approved of the day and night aspect of the US Open. Swedish journalist Bjorn Hellberg watched his despairing challenge go unrewarded year after year in New York. 'I always felt Borg had the same amount of good luck at Wimbledon as he lacked at the US Open,' he suggested. 'He had most things go his way at Wimbledon, like not having to play outside a show court after he was champion, and everything conspired against him in New York. Certainly, he didn't like to play under lights.'

Tanner put out Borg's lights in four sets to avenge his defeat in the Wimbledon final. 'The Swede saluted an opponent who had been superior on the occasion – he always does,' said Bud Collins, journalist and broadcaster from Boston, Mass. 'Yet privately he was bitter, and with some justification, about the erratic scheduling. The critics could accept the US Tennis Association's need for added gate receipts to help pay off the huge debt incurred in the construction of the National Centre, but why was there no consistency and little fairness in the scheduling? Why no formula for night play to distribute matches evenly? Why did Borg, for instance, play his quarter at night and Connors play his in sunlight – and that against Pat Dupre, who was given less than twenty-four hours' rest after a tough five-set victory over Harold Solomon? Why, with more time [twenty-three sessions as opposed to fourteen in France and Wimbledon's twelve] and more courts than other major events, was the Open's scheduling so jammed and chaotic?' Why, indeed?

Tanner's tournament was ended by Gerulaitis, who, stoically, came from two sets down to reach the final in his home town. After the pandemonium of his second round match with Nastase, McEnroe's passage was simplified: in the fourth round he had a walkover against Tom Gorman and in the quarters Eddie Dibbs retired injured after a mere three games. With Connors awaiting him in the semifinals, McEnroe respected there was still the potential to fail, but McEnroe no longer feared Connors, as he had that first time they played in the semis at Wimbledon two years earlier, and he trusted his game to acquire the upperhand. McEnroe won in straight sets. It was the first time in six years that Connors would not be appearing in the final.

Instead, the US Open would be disputed by two players who had grown up in the neighbourhood and set out from the same tennis club, Port Washington. Miraculous, McEnroe called it. In essence, the final proved to be one-sided, as McEnroe eclipsed Gerulaitis, 7–5, 6–3, 6–3. At twenty, he was the youngest champion since Pancho Gonzalez won in 1948. McEnroe had earned the right to be talked about now in the same breath as

Borg and Connors. With Fleming, he also won the doubles at the expense of Bob Lutz and Stan Smith. No American had captured the singles and doubles championships at the US Open since Vic Seixas in 1954. John Patrick McEnroe's time had come. Of nineteen grand prix tournaments he played in 1979, he won nine of them.

In doubles, he was almost invincible. The partnership of McEnroe and Fleming gave a new meaning to the term 'team tennis'. Before the 1979 Masters they had won a staggering fourteen titles together in the year. McEnroe picked up a further couple of doubles championships, too: one with Gottfried the other with Gene Mayer. McEnroe said, 'Peter was the best partner I ever had.' Fleming's view was this: 'I was all or nothing. John's major strength was he never missed the ball.'

But the depth of their friendship was beginning to be undermined as the year ended. 'We'd been winning a lot, but, yeah, our friendship came under strain,' explained Fleming. The dynamics of their relationship had been disturbed – at least in the eyes of McEnroe – when Fleming started to court an English girl called Jenny Hudson. They met at Wimbledon that summer and soon became inseparable. Fleming no longer looked to hang out with McEnroe as an automatic option on the road. To McEnroe, this was a conundrum. He was losing contact with the friend he leaned on most – and he was growing jealous.

Their friendship was being challenged on the court, too. Two weeks after McEnroe had won the US Open, Fleming beat him in straight sets to win the Jack Kramer Open in Los Angeles. McEnroe, of course, lost his cool. At one point, he threw his racket with real anger. Not long afterwards, Fleming served for the match against him in the final of the Transamerica Open in San Francisco, but McEnroe survived and proceeded to win the match in three sets. The next flashpoint occurred in Hawaii – without the two of them actually playing. McEnroe had lost in the semifinals to Bill Scanlon, a man he disliked, and he could not bring himself to watch Scanlon play the final against Fleming. Scanlon won, yet years later McEnroe confessed that he was relieved Fleming had been beaten. His friend's love for the daughter of Leeds city councillor David Hudson, later lord mayor of Leeds, was eating at him. It was a condition worsened by the realisation that his own relationship with Stacy Margolin, a player on the women's tour, was in difficulties.

Just how much strain McEnroe was feeling came to the surface when he next played Fleming, in Jamaica. McEnroe felt he had received a bad call on a first serve. He rowed with the umpire, then, finally, asked Fleming to adjudicate in his favour. Fleming claimed he had not seen if the ball was in or out. McEnroe grew more irate and found himself docked a point for a time delay. Even angrier, he demanded if Fleming would accept the point. According to McEnroe, Fleming replied: 'Just because we're friends, don't think I am the Salvation Army.' Fleming won the match – and, he recalled, $70,000 in prize money – but McEnroe lost much more than a game of tennis.

For a time, Fleming's own competitive form in singles, and his happiness with Jenny off the court, made McEnroe look at his friend in a different light. 'He was too happy,' wrote McEnroe. 'He was with Jenny and it was getting on my nerves that he seemed so happy and that I was kind of out in the cold. To be blunt, I guess I was jealous. Doubly jealous: that he had somebody and that she had him.' To McEnroe, the demons could come in all shapes and sizes and not merely manifest themselves through the perceived injustice of a wrong line call.

Twenty-five years later, Fleming sat in the LTA's indoor head-quarters at Queen's Club, kicked off his tennis shoes and reflected hard on the impact of that episode under the Jamaican sun. 'I don't think we ever quite recovered from that,' he admitted. 'It was a little thin crevice in our relationship that slowly got bigger and bigger. It bit deeper than just saying, "Play the calls." He thought I should have given him the call, because we were such good friends. I took it that he was accusing me of cheating. I said to him, "Do you think I would cheat you? I can't accept that."

'So we sort of had a stalemate. Normally, whenever we had arguments, we'd sit down, talk it over and shake. We never quite did that. And that was too bad. It would have been nice if our friendship could have stayed as wonderful as it was, say, in 1978, but I probably wouldn't have met Jenny if that had been the case, so I am pretty much a believer that these things happen for a reason. As for John? Look at his book. He definitely sees things from a different perspective from time to time.'

Today, Fleming lives in London with Jenny, his wife of twenty-two years, and their three children, Joe, twenty, Alex, seventeen, and thirteen-year-old Holly. He is a coach and a broadcaster, who retired from the pro tour with three singles titles and sixty doubles titles. 'I'm still good friends with John and we have dinner once or twice a year,' he said. 'But it's not the same, not the same where you'd do anything for the other guy. We lost a bit of that.' This admission cut deep and he looked genuinely sombre.

During that hugely successful year of 1979, McEnroe won back-to-back titles in Stockholm and London in November. Neither was achieved without controversy. Gene Mayer, who that summer had won the French Open doubles championship with his older brother, Sandy, recalled what happened when he played McEnroe in the final of the Swedish Open: 'John broke his racket on a changeover and was penalised a point. He held serve from 0–15, a reflection of the things he could do because of his will. You were never going to play as well after those things he did. There were unreasonable breaches of the time clock.'

Mayer, from New York, who broke into the world's top five with his double-handed forehand, had this take on McEnroe: 'I saw him when he was very young. He was not an extraordinarily good junior, it was in his late teen years when he started to play well. He was known as a hot head, but I was drawn to him by his tennis. John is probably the most gifted guy with a racket in his hands since Nastase. Then he also had extraordinary concentration and mental ability. Most guys with that talent throw it away. I first played John at Queen's Club in London. You saw the magic of his serve, the pinpoint accuracy and the action he got on the ball. My best shot was my return – and you had to stand in close because once he got set at the net it was awesome. He wasn't terribly difficult to hold serve against, but he was very difficult to break. We had some epic matches, a couple of five-setters at night at the US Open. I lost. He was really an artist and such a complicated personality, but it was clear when he came along that he wanted it badly. He had the variety of game and shots for two players.

'He also had this great self-belief. When the other guy hit the ball it was out. When he hit it was good. He believed this so strongly that he would just lose it. He lost all sight of reality and reason. At different times, he would apologise and say, "I can't believe I did that." Against McEnroe or Connors, when things were going badly there could be five to ten minutes between points. They controlled the clock. Yet after seven minutes of going ballistic, John could come back on the court and play well.

'Were people frightened of McEnroe? Absolutely. Not only were they frightened at damaging the box office, but they were frightened of the embarrassment of dealing with what was going on. Whether it was the umpire, linesmen or the supervisor, everyone was cringing. McEnroe basically conducted the whole thing – and no one wanted to take a stand. Jimmy was able to do the same. In team sports, like basketball, baseball or soccer, officials are pretty quick to eject a player from the game. Guys are dispensable. On a tennis court, they are not. Officials in tennis wondered: "What do I do here? How do I handle it?" The reality was this is what you lived with. You almost had to psyche yourself up to deal with that on top of having to deal with the way John played. It made it even harder. A number of times when he was right, I stepped in on his side to get the dispute over quickly rather than let it drag out. Everyone got so defensive, because he came on like such a lion. He just made everyone uncomfortable.

'But John is likeable and he is very opinionated. We played some doubles and got along. John's a bright guy. To this day, on the senior tour, the same episodes occur. It wasn't the pressure of the time, it's just John. On the senior tour everyone is friends and we seem to have been around for one hundred years. Even if you didn't get along great back in the days we were young, you do now, but when John's in the room there's a tension and an electricity that doesn't exist even with a guy like Connors. John is intense; he's intense about everything. Again, that's part of his genius. He's not afraid to say what he feels in commentary. He's brutally honest. People appreciate his honesty, his belief. That makes a lot of other things disappear from the memory.'

After defeating Mayer in Stockholm, McEnroe flew to London for the Benson & Hedges tournament at Wembley. His victory gave him his second important title in London within five months. Only Wimbledon eluded him in the capital now. The tournament referee at Wembley was Colin Hess, the man who had opened the doors of the Cumberland Club to Borg. Hess had occasion –

and this will come as no surprise – to intervene once or twice when McEnroe was in action: 'On one Friday evening, McEnroe was playing Fibak on live television. McEnroe was toying with him as usual. He did a little drop shot, drew Fibak in, then hit a perfect lob which landed on the baseline. Fibak had a penchant for playing shots over his shoulder, but as he ran back, a voice shouted, "Out." Thinking the ball was fault, Fibak casually returned the ball, but it wasn't the baseline judge who made the call. McEnroe volleyed into the open court. Fibak, who could be difficult, claimed a let.

'Luckily, I happened to be watching. McEnroe went bananas, of course. He demanded to know how many more times he had to win the point. Fibak's argument was that he had only hit the shot over his shoulder for fun. McEnroe said to the umpire, "Get the referee." By this point I was at the umpire's chair. McEnroe asked me, "What are you going to do?" I said that my own views on the matter had best be kept to myself, but I am over-ruling the umpire on the situation. Please play a let. It's a judgement call, however much you may dislike what happened.

'McEnroe said, "Are you serious?" Then, he added, "You don't know the rules." At which point I said that I'd like to see him after the match. John had a doubles match to follow, so it was around 12.30a.m. when I went down to see him in the locker room. I had a rule book with me. I said to John, "I may have my own views on what happened out there, but you told me I didn't know the bloody rules. Come on fella, I don't really like being shouted at on live television and being told I don't know the rules. There's the rule book, will you please show me where this rule is?" I reckon I do know the rules. He looked at me, mumbled and said, "Sorry." I told him that the last thing I wanted was an apology. John shrugged his shoulders and we have been friends ever since.'

McEnroe and Connors had one of their more infamous show-downs at the B&H tournament. They came close to barging one another at the net post on a changeover. They definitely traded insults, if not actual blows. 'McEnroe lost the match from two sets up and it was the only time he lost in the tournament in the doubles with Fleming,' said Hess. 'I saw John afterwards to say goodbye. John said, "Great week, see you next year." I said, "One of us is stark raving mad. Is it you or me? I enjoyed the tournament very much until you played Connors this afternoon, when I hated every minute." McEnroe responded, "All my fault. I was tired. I played too much. I'll see you next year." Then he gave me a big hug. We always had that kind of relationship. John turned into a tremendous commentator, didn't he? It helps he played the game at the highest level, but he's also got a great sense of humour. Mr and Mrs Average watching tennis at home think he's wonderful – and he is.'

12

CRISIS, WHAT CRISIS?

At the beginning of 1980, grand prix chief supervisor, Dick Roberson, declared the intention that the game was going to be policed in a more stringent vein. Roberson explained, 'This past year we have gone to basketball and hockey to study what other "ego" athletes get away with. We have bought seats in the front row and we have talked to officials. We are going to study the information and relate it to tennis. Personally, I feel that we are looking at it more closely and trying to be harder than officials in other sports.'

In fact, the year began with a feast of tennis-related headlines, without a controversy in sight. The Masters at Madison Square Garden in New York was a jamboree of excitement and brilliant tennis. Jimmy Connors was back in town as a father, oozing charm and ambition in equal measure. Bjorn Borg had his wedding to Mariana Simionescu planned for straight after Wimbledon, but no one suspected for a second that he would be distracted from the business at hand. John McEnroe may have had his critics in New York, but the Garden's historic links with the old prize ring made this a place he relished working at.

From the start, the week was to belong to Borg. He won the round robin in the red group by defeating Tanner, Connors and Jose Higueras. In the blue group, there was an unexpected disappointment for McEnroe to endure. Against the odds, he lost to Gerulaitis when Broadway Vitas captured the final two sets of their match in consecutive tie-breaks. Gerulaitis reinforced the seriousness of his challenge when he accounted for Connors in the semifinals. It was only his second triumph in eighteen meetings.

In the other half, New Yorkers received the match they yearned for: Borg versus McEnroe. It transpired to be a minor classic; an appetising hors d'oeuvre before the summer banquet that was to be presented on the Centre Court at Wimbledon. Borg's stately manner was surprisingly popular in a city where the simple courtesies of life can be discarded the moment two people are looking for a cab on Broadway in the rain. In that sense, McEnroe represented the stereotypical New Yorker, yet he had the capacity to curb his natural instinct to conduct a postmortem into the first dubious line call he encountered if the man on the other side of the net had long hair and a Swedish accent. McEnroe's respect for Borg never waned. This meant that the code of conduct – old or new – would be redundant for this much-anticipated semifinal at the Garden.

Borg and McEnroe fought one another to a near standstill. Veteran tennis broadcaster and journalist, John Barrett, wrote from his courtside vantage point: 'So fast were the exchanges, so quick the thought, so brave the recoveries that the 15,437 spectators erupted time and again to acknowledge the daring deeds witnessed. Borg's dipping topspin drives rewrote the laws of gravity. McEnroe's wristy control of the racket face was a miracle of timing.'

McEnroe won the first set, 7–5, in the tie-break, after an hour of absorbing tennis. The second set fell to Borg, 6–3, when McEnroe lost his service in the eighth game. With a degree of inevitability, the deciding set went the distance. The Masters would be decided by a tie-break. McEnroe began it with an ace. It was a rousing, but final, statement of threat from the American, for three errors from McEnroe and four superlative passing shots from Borg meant that the Swede had finally won a tournament in New York City, 6–7,6–3, 7–6, after two hours and forty-one minutes. Rex Bellamy commented in *The Times*: 'In the last crisis, McEnroe looked young and vulnerable and Borg's tennis told him, bluntly, that for the time being there was no room at the top.'

After the Masters, there was routine business to attend to on the tour. Connors beat McEnroe in the final in Philadelphia in February; McEnroe defeated Connors in the final of the US National Indoor Championships in the birthplace of the Blues, Memphis, Tennessee. By the end of March, McEnroe was on the other side of the Atlantic Ocean winning in Milan. In the same week, Borg took the title on offer in Nice.

In late April the action moved to Las Vegas, where battalions of slot machines greet you the moment you leave baggage claim at McCarran International airport. Grab a cab and fifteen minutes later you check your bags – and say goodnight to reality – with the desk clerk at the hotel. Windows at the casino hotels do not open, a feature designed to keep the suicide rate down among punters on a losing streak. Young women wearing high heels and short skirts serve drinks courtesy of the house at the roulette wheel and blackjack and craps tables. Clocks are banned on the casino floors. Neon lights turn night into day. The coffee shops in the casinos never close, with menus promising eggs, cooked any-which-way, burgers and sandwiches with french fries. Casinos muscle one another for the high rollers; free flights into town and complimentary penthouse suites are the norm for those with the highest lines of credit. In the lounge rooms, the biggest cabaret acts are shuttled in and out of town and, as the new decade got underway, Frank Sinatra, Dean Martin, Sammy Davis Junior, Diana Ross, Tom Jones or Bill Cosby could be on stage. Bus tours stop outside the home of Liberace, a confirmed bachelor and an institution in Las Vegas, as much for his diamond and sequin stage wardrobe as his talent as a pianist. Love it or loathe it, Las Vegas knows how to keep the customer satisfied.

Tennis? It was just another arm of the entertainment industry. The desert climate in spring could be relied on. With the name of renowned comedian Alan King, the patronage of Caesar's Palace, one of the most opulent casino hotels on the Strip, and a total prize fund of $300,000, there was never going to be a shortage of stars. The Alan King Classic brought Borg, McEnroe, Gerulaitis and Lendl winging into the city that, according to legend, blossomed in the Nevada Desert through the imagination of the Mob. Dirty dollars may have come into Vegas, but they all left pressed and laundered.

For the guys on the tour, it was a great week to play some tennis and melt into the surreal landscape. Borg found it to be a good preparation for the summer's labours ahead. Not so McEnroe. Harold Solomon obliterated him in the quarterfinals, 6–4, 6–1; it was one of the worst beatings McEnroe took all year.

Solomon made it through to the final to meet Borg, but having won none and lost thirteen against the four times Wimbledon champion, he must have suspected that the odds of breaking the house at Caesar's favoured him better than leaving town as the winner of the tournament. He was not alone in fearing the result was a foregone conclusion. Bookmakers in Las Vegas had installed Borg as unbackable favourite. As American writer, Damon Runyon, had succinctly observed in the first half of the twentieth century, 'The race is not always to the swift, nor the battle to the strong, but that's the way to bet.' And as things turned out, the bookies were correct once again. Borg lost just four games in two sets of tennis with Solomon, then made his way past the slots at McCarran International to return to a world not governed by the turn of a card, the spin of the wheel or the roll of the dice.

In Europe, the tour swung through Hamburg, Florence, Rome and Munich, with the clay court season headed towards its traditional climax at the French Open. Bergelin ensured Borg arrived in Paris rested and prepared as ever. His game would click. That was a given. What had his manager, Peter Worth, said? 'The French was never the problem.' Only for those drawn against him.

McEnroe was No. 2 seed, but never the second favourite in the minds of the cognoscenti – not in Paris. His patience was always suspect; his temperament under the sternest of examinations. He won his first two matches against Patrice Dominguez and Per Hjertquist without the loss of a set, but then his fortune dried up. McEnroe was drawn into a marathon third round match against Australian, Paul McNamee. The duel lasted four hours and eighteen minutes. All four sets they played went to a tie-break; the bad news for McEnroe was that he lost three of them. Now he would have longer than he would have liked to get himself in tune for the grass court season in London. His Swedish rival would not have that luxury, but that was never an issue. Not with the Ice Borg.

Connors, meanwhile, engineered one of the greatest comebacks in the history of the championships. In the second round, Connors faced the guillotine against Frenchman Jean-Francois Caujolle when he served with the score 3–6, 2–6, 2–5, 30–40.

Caujolle had beaten him at the recent Monte Carlo Open, so he was not intimidated by Connors's reputation. Or so it seemed. On that match point, Caujolle narrowly missed with a backhand passing shot. For the Frenchman, that one glimpse of victory was all he was allowed. To the wild delight of the crowd, Connors only lost another two games. Connors was a bad man to arouse on a tennis court . . . and he journeyed without mishap or adventure into the semifinals. Somewhat unexpectedly, and for the second time that year, he was to lose a terrific scuffle with Gerulaitis. Connors led two sets to one, but lost momentum, and Gerulaitis showed his own instinct for battle and secured a famous victory. Connors never made it to the final at Roland Garros.

And Gerulaitis never managed to get the better of his friend, Bjorn Borg. The Swede won his fifth French Open – the fiftieth anniversary edition – without dropping a set in seven matches. Only one man had beaten Borg in his seven visits to the French Open: Italian Adriano Panatta, in 1973 and 1976. In his latest hour of triumph, Borg thumped Gerulaitis, 6–4, 6–1, 6–2. It was the American's fourteenth consecutive loss to Borg and by the time the Swede left the game that record had gone up to fifteen. Some friendships, it seems, can endure the most dreadful professional hardship. Besides, Gerulaitis understood a man's self-esteem was not badly tarnished when he left a tennis court in second place to Borg.

John McEnroe and the rest of the tennis world returned to Britain, which was now in the thirteenth month of Margaret Thatcher's premiership. Even before coming to power she was called the Iron Lady in Soviet propaganda. The nickname fitted her like a Chanel suit. Thatcher had become Britain's first woman prime minister after the House of Commons passed a motion of no confidence in Labour PM James Callaghan. Trade unions had rejected Callaghan's policy of continued pay restraint and a succession of strikes created what became known as the Winter of Discontent. When he returned from an economic summit in Guadeloupe in early 1979, Callaghan was asked, 'How do you respond to the mounting chaos that greets your return, Prime Minister? He responded, 'I promise if you look at it from the outside, I don't think other people in the world would share the view that there is mounting chaos.' The *Sun* newspaper turned his answer into a mocking headline: 'Crisis? What crisis?' Callaghan was in political free fall. Routed in the House, Callaghan was subsequently routed at the ballot box.

Margaret Hilda Thatcher formed a government on 4 May 1979. She had a mandate to reverse Britain's economic decline and to reduce the extent of the state. Thatcher began by increasing interest rates to drive down inflation. This hit businesses, especially in the manufacturing sector, and unemployment rose sharply. By the summer of 1980, a recession was not that far around the corner. So, too, was a war with Argentina over the sovereignty of the Falkland Islands. In May 1980, inflation had risen to almost thirty per cent, while the unemployment figures were heading towards a summer high of two million. An attractive, three-bedroom mews town house in London, close to the Old Brompton Road, was being marketed for £50,000; a Victorian cottage at Kingston-on-Thames could be bought for £34,000; a new Rolls Royce Silver Cloud cost £45,000; a Mercedes 450 SEL had a list price of £20,500; while it was possible to obtain a Vauxhall Royale for £9,700. Petrol was £1.25p a gallon at the turn of the year. Secretarial positions were advertised at £5,000 to £6,000.

Early indications of union unrest had occurred at the outset of the year. Water workers in the General and Municipal Workers Union talked of national strikes unless the National Water Council improved a thirteen per cent pay offer. The Iron and Steel Trades Confederation and National Union of Blastfurnacemen were embroiled in hard negotiations with the British Steel Corporation (BSC), which had announced the axing of over 11,000 jobs. Miners in South Wales were angered by BSC plans to decrease local production at plants like Port Talbot.

In the music world, the anarchic change that swept across the late 1970s was still riding high in the UK. Trail-blazing punk bands like The Sex Pistols may have had their day, but their influence lived on through New Wave bands such as the Clash, the Damned and the Undertones, while Joy Division were just about to have their one and only hit single with *Love Will Tear Us Apart*, re-released after lead-singer Ian Curtis hanged himself in April. However, the punk revolution was not to last very much longer and it was perhaps fitting that the film, *The Empire Strikes Back*, was breaking box office records across the United States.

The Cold War was glowing red hot, with Soviet troops in bitter combat in Afghanistan, following their invasion. As a show of its displeasure, the United States decided to curtail the sale of grain to the Soviet Union and declared its intention to send military aid to neighbouring Pakistan. The knife-edge diplomacy encompassed sport, too. President Jimmy Carter ordered US athletes to boycott the Olympic Games in Moscow that summer. Thatcher told the Commons that she was in favour of moving the games from Moscow. For Britain's athletes, in general, the political crisis enveloping the Super Powers, the USA and the Soviet Union was a threat to all they had worked for over the past four years. For Steve Ovett and Sebastian Coe, in particular, it was devastating, as they ruled middle-distance running. Ovett versus Coe on the track, with their duel timed to reach a climax at the games, was a rivalry as rich in potential as that of Borg and McEnroe at Wimbledon that same summer.

Ovett, from Brighton, had an unpretentious attitude to life – apart from when he walked on the track. Often he waved to the crowd in the final metres before taking the tape. Coe, born in London, brought up in Sheffield and educated at Loughborough, was an aristocrat of the track and later a real life peer of the realm. They chased the same rainbow: Olympic gold. In forty-one days in the summer of 1979, Coe had sensationally broken three world records: 800m (1minute 42.33 seconds), mile (3.49) and 1500m (3.32.03). He was the first man in fifty years to achieve world records at 800m and 1500m. Ovett, incredibly, would later lower Coe's world records for the mile and 1500m. These were giants of athletics, yet ostensibly they were very different to one another. They were also portrayed as the most bitter of rivals. The truth was less colourful. Ovett and Coe hardly spoke to one another as they hardly knew one another. Like Connors and McEnroe, they could never have a friendship when they were racing for the same records and prizes, but their rivalry was defined by the beauty of their running, by their devilment and commitment, and by an unwillingness to concede a yard.

Ovett or Coe? Who is your favourite? It was a debate to be heard amongst sports fans in the same way as you took your pick between Borg and McEnroe. At that time, Jonathan Edwards was at school in Devon and still twenty years away from winning his own gold medal in the triple jump at the Millennium Olympic Games in Sydney, but he identified his favourites. 'I always warmed to John McEnroe,' he said. 'Being a McEnroe man was like choosing between Steve Ovett and Sebastian Coe and coming down in favour of Ovett. Both McEnroe and Ovett were unconventional and anti-establishment.'

Edwards's selections may be considered unconventional for a man of deep religious conviction, who's never been known to curse or even cast a stern look at officialdom, but while he has the utmost respect for Borg and Coe, a man he knows well, Edwards fell under the spell of the more Bohemian Ovett and McEnroe. 'What I love in watching athletes is pure talent,' said Edwards. 'Sport is more art than science and McEnroe was the ultimate artist. I know some people may be surprised at my choice, but I never saw McEnroe as a role model. When he had those tantrums, I felt sorry for him, but they were a child's tantrums. He wasn't getting his own way and he had to deal with what he saw as stupidity, so he was stamping his feet. He got infuriated with the umpires; and it must be horrible to feel you've been dealt a cruel blow when every point matters. I wouldn't encourage my children to behave in the way that McEnroe did, because it was out of perspective. That was never my way as a sportsman. Even so, what McEnroe did was to express something that was an innate part of him, of the talent he had, and he did it with passion. I love the aesthetics of sport and for me John McEnroe painted a most beautiful picture when he played.'

While Carter insisted on a US boycott of the Moscow Games, Thatcher's government supported the ban, but allowed athletes to decided for themselves whether or not they should go to the Olympics. Ovett and Coe, for the record, both won gold medals in Moscow; Ovett taking the 800m, supposedly Coe's stronger event, and Coe winning the 1500m. They were races that still make the hairs on the back of your neck stand upright when you see them.

Borg had to delay his journey to London that summer, because after he won the French Open he flew home to represent Sweden in the Davis Cup against Germany. Borg defeated Klaus Eberhard, 6–2, 5–7, 6–0, 6–0, and never played for his country again. 'Borg started and finished in the Davis Cup in Bastad,' said Bjorn

Hellberg. 'In all, he won thirty-seven matches and lost just three singles in Davis Cup.' His differences with the Swedish Federation just ran too deep, it seems. With the tie behind him, Borg belatedly headed to the Holiday Inn to start his Wimbledon preparations as usual at the Cumberland Club.

McEnroe was already in action defending his Stella Artois title at Queen's Club. Ian Wight, events director for the Stella Artois tournament, admitted that overtures were made to entice Borg to play in the tournament. 'But it was very much a lost cause,' he confessed. 'The reality was that Borg had a winning formula and didn't want to change it. It was easy to be sympathetic to that, but we did ask him to play.'

After a quarter of a century, the event is established as part of the British summer calendar, but, with neat self-deprecation, Wight said: 'We were all very new at the business when we began. I knew three-fifths of nothing about tennis; Clive Bernstein [tournament director] knew three-fifths of nothing about putting on an event. How we got a banner to stand upright was a minor miracle.' Nowadays, the banner flies high over Queen's Club with the Stella Artois recognised as the second most important grass-court tennis tournament in the world. Wight realised that the tournament had become part of the fabric of a London summer when Jak, the *Evening Standard*'s late, celebrated cartoonist, featured McEnroe. Wight said, 'There was a Colonel Blimp character in the umpire's chair – and let's face it, that's what many of them were like in those days – and he was saying, "I know which racket he sponsors, I know which shoes and clothes he sponsors, but which charm school is he representing?" I knew then that we'd made it.'

McEnroe successfully defended his Stella Artois crown, beating Kim Warwick, 6–3, 6–1, in the final, but there was no denying that his brilliance came with some excess baggage. There lurked a beast within his beautiful game. McEnroe won £8,000. Over the same weekend, Jack Nicklaus, forty, won the US Open at Baltusrol, New Jersey. It was Nicklaus's eighteenth major championship; an example of longevity without parallel in modern sport.

Before Wimbledon began, McEnroe sounded in a conciliatory mood. 'It's going to be different this year,' he pledged. 'No arguments with umpires or linesmen, nor with spectators. I'm tired of all the tantrum headlines.' He also considered it wearisome to be constantly portrayed as the bad guy, as he told the *Daily Mail*: 'People don't understand. Is it so terrible to question a call? When I do it, it's because I believe I am right. I tell you, I think the public wants a villain, needs one, and I have been given the role. I don't like it. Who would? Borg is the epitome of the tennis player, but if everybody were like him the game wouldn't be so exciting. You'd have a bunch of robots with everybody afraid to say something. I'll probably miss all this in ten years' time, when nobody knows who I am, or cares, but that's down the road.'

McEnroe, still only twenty-one years old, had an old head on young shoulders. Was it a virtue or a curse? Of course, Borg never involved himself in such forums. At this stage in his life, he had a fairly uncomplicated existence. His only controversial moments occurred in the Swedish media and, rarely, if at all, travelled beyond the country's borders. Bergelin was a faithful foil, creating a barrier between Borg and those without real business with him. His manager, Peter Worth, with support from the IMG heavy cavalry in Cleveland, Ohio, kept his commercial value at a premium. And Mariana continued to place her boyfriend's welfare first, as their wedding plans took shape.

Worth and his secretary Daphne were instrumental in the fine detail for Borg's fairytale wedding to Mariana, booked to take place after Wimbledon at the president's country retreat outside Bucharest. Today, celebrities have the option of selling exclusive access to their wedding photographs to publications like *Hello!* and *OK*. In 1980, Worth sold the picture rights to Sigma, an international agency with a global marketplace. 'I secured a $100,000 deal for the photos,' he recalled. That was an indication of the size of Borg's celebrity status. 'Without an exclusive arrangement there would have been a mass of photographers around,' added Worth. After the wedding, parties were scheduled for Monaco, then in Marbella at the invitation of famous socialite of the time Regine, who owned prestigious clubs in places such as Paris and Monte Carlo. Borg moved in these circles reserved for the rich and famous, even if in these times he exercised great discretion and never partied when there was serious work to be done.

Wimbledon represented the most serious work of all, yet not even Borg's position as four times champion could shield him from the stringent rules of the All England Club. Seventy-two hours before he was due to open the 1980 championships, Borg was ordered off court at Wimbledon! My late friend and colleague, John Parsons, who died in Miami in the early days of 2004, reported the story on the front page of the *Daily Mail*. Parsons dedicated a great part of his working life to reporting tennis from around the world, spent almost a quarter of a century as lawn tennis correspondent of the *Daily Telegraph* and was on assignment until his death.

He reported, 'Borg got his marching orders from an official at the All England Club as he practised with American Vitas Gerulaitis and Colin Dowdeswell of Zimbabwe. The trio were told to leave the court because they had over-run the time allowed. The three were allowed one and a half hours – half-an-hour each – but officials said they had been playing one and three quarter hours. Borg, who is chasing his fifth successive crown, kept his cool. But Fred Stolle, coach to Gerulaitis, was fuming after the incident. He said: "They've made this ridiculous rule, whereby each competitor is allowed only half an hour's total practice on the Wimbledon courts. It's stupid to expect players like Borg and Gerulaitis to come into an event like Wimbledon with only half an hour on these particular courts."'

Gerulaitis was indignant, explaining: 'I said to the guy who told us to get off, "Aren't you embarrassed to tell Bjorn Borg to get off a court at Wimbledon?" I wouldn't have the guts to do something like this. After all, Borg has helped build half the new stands here.' Typically, Bergelin was more taciturn. 'At least we had one and a half hours' practice, so it wasn't too bad,' he suggested. 'And you have to abide by the rules.'

"I know about the racquet, the balls, the shirt, but whose charm school is he advertising?"

13

MIND OF A CHAMPION

Could anyone beat Bjorn Borg at Wimbledon? The question had a resonance like no other in sport. The bookmakers passed their judgement, installing Borg as 8–11 favourite. After all, he had not lost a match at the All England Club since Arthur Ashe, the eventual champion, had beaten him in the quarterfinals five years earlier. Borg occupied an extraordinary position within the game. Everyone knew all about him, yet everyone knew so little.

American Brian Gottfried typifies those who spent their professional lives entwined with Borg. Gottfried talks of Borg as a man of mystery. 'I don't think Bjorn said ten words to me in ten years on tour,' said Gottfried. 'He really kept to himself. What I found out later was how little we knew about him. For instance, he probably played for two or three years with pimpled tennis shoes – the first grass court shoes that were made – before any of the rest of us knew there was such a thing. I would assume he was pretty smart, but he just never said anything. Nobody played like him either. He really changed the game. On grass, he played a sliced backhand and his volley was a lot more effective than on a hard court.

'Of course, the guys talked about him. You don't win Wimbledon four times and guys don't talk about you. You know, what? We couldn't help but think he couldn't go on winning. He wasn't a natural grass courter. At the time, there were a lot of guys who were more comfortable on the grass. It seemed like he always had a match each year that he was almost out of: Edmondson, Amaya, Gerulaitis, Amritraj all had him in deep trouble.' Yet each year Borg extricated himself from the hole that he had fallen into. This was why he was the most feared – and mysterious – man to set foot on the grass at Wimbledon.

Rain. It's a four-letter word meaning misery when used in association with Wimbledon. So, when rain fell on that opening day of Monday 23 June 1980, the championships stuttered rather than burst into life. As tradition demanded, Borg raised the curtain on Centre Court. His opponent was Ismael El Shafei, one of just three men to have beaten him at Wimbledon. Admittedly, El Shafei had capitalised when Borg had precious little grass court experience and had just spent the previous two weeks of the summer of 1974 winning his first French Open championship. El Shafei, now thirty-two, a father of two and no longer a regular on the tour, had emerged from the ordeal of the qualifying tournament at Roehampton to take his place in the first round. He felt short-changed when he was told the news that his reward was a re-match with Borg. 'Frankly, I am disappointed,' he said. 'I had hoped for a better break. I can only go out and do my best and remember our match in 1974.'

On that day, Borg had astounded the crowd on No. 1 Court by seeming to be uninterested in the result as he lost in three one-sided sets. 'If it wasn't a surrender, it was the nearest thing I've seen to it,' reported Laurie Pignon. There was zero chance of the Swede adopting the same mind set again. His draw had never been easier, but the fine details still had to be addressed, something Bergelin and Borg never overlooked. On arrival in England, Bergelin had all Borg's rackets re-strung to an even greater tension. 'It's because we've found the balls they'll be using at Wimbledon this year appear to be a bit lighter than last time,' explained Bergelin. 'We came with the rackets strung at seventy pound tension, but we've had them re-done at around seventy-six pound.'

But no player or coach can totally legislate for rain and Borg's meticulous planning had been thrown out of synch. In the soggy countdown to the championships, Bergelin, usually the most taci-turn of men, moaned, 'Your English rain is ruining our prepara-tion.' Borg's nerves were not soothed by having to open his defence against El Shafei, whose left-handed, heavy serving style of tennis was the brand of game with the potential to disturb him most.

The championships began nine minutes late and play was

restricted to the two show courts. Just twenty-one minutes later the skies opened again and the covers were pulled back across the courts by ground staff drilled to operate with military precision. No one knew it then, but a pattern was emerging. Rain was to plague these championships. Borg is a man of infinite patience. On the court, especially a clay court, he offers the impression of a man willing to stay until nightfall if that's what it takes to get the job done. Similarly, he has the patience to ride out the delays that showers induce.

After he had taken the first set from El Shafei, the match was interrupted for over two and a half hours. On his return to the court, his racket disintegrated as the strings exploded after one of his topspin forehands. Borg the Iceman looked at the buckled frame and smiled. It was a small moment of light relief for El Shafei, too. Of course, he had no response to Borg's game. The Swede had tailored his strategy to meet the conditions. Sensibly, he came to the net more than he normally does. Afterwards, he sounded relaxed. 'For me that was a satisfactory start,' he said after a straight-sets win. 'The court was very soft and because of the low bounce it was difficult to make shots from the back. Although it was damp and I have not had as much preparation as I would like, I was never scared on the grass. I don't think there is as much pressure on me as last year. Four Wimbledons in a row was something that no one in modern history has managed. Although I hope to make it five, it is not quite the same thing.'

McEnroe also secured an opening day victory, darting between the heavy showers. For the first time, service line judges had the benefit of the 'magic eye', an electronic device invented by Bill Carlton to try to reduce the element of human error. The eye was placed at the line judge's feet and linked by an earpiece. It worked like this: an electronic beam was relayed across the service line and when the ball was struck up to six inches long, the line judge would hear a beep in the headphones he was wearing. This gave the line judge confirmation of a service fault. Unsurprisingly, the eye experienced teething problems with the players from the start.

Ironically, McEnroe's opponent, Butch Walts, shot an ugly look or two towards the machine, while the No. 2 seed remained nonplussed in the presence of new technology. Walts was so concerned that he sent for referee Fred Hoyles to ask for the device to be disconnected. His request was refused. Walts said, 'It is supposed to be foolproof, but not so far as I am concerned. It may be alright in concept, but it's useless in practice.' But McEnroe, having dispensed with Walts in straight sets, suggested optimistically: 'It's going to take a very bad call before I do anything and I am not going to worry about a few questionable calls here and there. To win Wimbledon you have to be in good shape and I am.' Only twenty-two of the sixty-four scheduled matches were completed on this first day.

With a degree of inevitability, Ilie Nastase could not be kept out of the news. Nastase took public exception to the eye, looking down the socket and bouncing balls on its cover. He accused the machine of being made by the Russians – the ultimate exponents of sinister Big Brother technology as far as those raised behind the Iron Curtain were concerned. He courted further attention when, on the third day of the championships he escorted the reigning Miss UK, Carolyn Seaward, to Wimbledon. When he was asked about his wife, Dominique, he admitted he was no longer living with her. Then he turned to the newsmen and demanded: 'What of it?' Nastase liked the company of beautiful women. He never viewed this as a crime, but at Wimbledon he was naive to suppose that his presence in the company of Miss Seaward would not attract a battalion of photographers or inquisitive reporters. The truth of it was that Nastase really did not care. He was where tennis and show business met. He played hard and lived harder still.

Against this diversion of gossip and mild controversy, the rain still kept on falling. And falling. Matches were constantly delayed and stretched over seemingly endless hours. When Buster Mottram lost, 13–11, in the fifth set against American Nick Saviano, the match clock stopped at four hours and twenty-three minutes, but the contest had been spread over two days. With Mottram's demise, British interest in the men's singles failed to stretch into the third round for the third time in five years. Indeed, Virginia Wade became Britain's only survivor in the singles event when she beat Helena Anliot, Borg's erstwhile girlfriend, to reach the third round.

Roger Taylor had succumbed to Australian Terry Rocavert in a five-set first round marathon. Rocavert supposed his second round

match with McEnroe was such a dubious reward that on the day of
the game he sent his wife to organise their air tickets to leave London
for the next tournament in the United States. His prospects of
causing an upset were not enhanced when a Wimbledon courtesy
car did not arrive at his rented Bayswater flat at the appointed hour.
His day worsened still when the taxi he hired to take him to the All
England Club became hopelessly lost.

Rocavert arrived just fifteen minutes before he had to go on
court, yet, remarkably, McEnroe ran into a greater crisis – his
game didn't show up. Rocavert, twenty-five, ranked number
ninety-eight in the world, led two sets to one when the fourth set
went into a tie-break, with Rocavert having two serves to open
up a 4–1 lead. He lost them both – and never recovered. McEnroe
scraped home in five sets that lasted three and a half hours on
Court No. 3. For the Australian, it was confirmation that, while
he could play a decent game of tennis, he didn't possess the mental
capacity to break through on the tour. He knew then that he
would return to Australia and make a different life for himself and
his family. Rocavert became a club coach. In the Sydney suburbs
where he is an accomplished and respected coach, he is occasionally asked to tell the story of the day McEnroe got away from him.
He does so quietly, without bravado or resentment and without
regret. 'I was not meant to be a champion, John McEnroe was,'
said Rocavert. 'You have to be a certain kind of person to fit into
all this. You are put up on a stand and people look at you, and
that's the kind of thing I have trouble with.'

McEnroe had not been impressed to find himself on Court
No. 3. When he dug a hole on the soft baseline while serving, he
had to change his angle of attack to maintain a foothold. As the
excitement mounted, a crowd estimated to be over one thousand
strong blocked the concourse around the court. Some youngsters
heckled McEnroe's errors. Eventually, the American's patience
snapped and when he smacked a ball into the net in frustration at
missing a volley, umpire George Armstrong gave McEnroe a
warning for unsporting conduct. Twelve months earlier, McEnroe
had been hustled out of the championships on Court No. 2 and he
was fearful that he was blowing another opportunity. 'Court 3
was worse – and I never thought I would say that after last year,'
he said afterwards.

Borg's progress into the third round was without any such drama as the Swede overcame former Israeli army sergeant Shlomo Glickstein in three sets. McEnroe's third round opponent was Tom Okker, whose speed around the court earned him the nickname 'the Flying Dutchman'. Okker had first played at Wimbledon as a junior in 1961. He played at the All England Club for the last time in 2004. In the intervening forty-three years, he missed appearing at Wimbledon just twice. At sixty years old, he received a letter from the club telling him he would no longer be invited to play. 'It's normal. I am playing guys forty-five years old and I am now more like the Dying Dutchman!' he exclaimed with good humour.

Okker, who for the past twenty years has owned an art gallery in Amsterdam, was taking tea with friends in the players' lounge after his last-ever match when he reflected on his collisions with McEnroe and Borg. Twice he met the Swede in big matches at Wimbledon, losing to Borg in the semifinals in 1978 and the quarters a year later. 'Borg was one of the few who could stay back and win points on grass,' said Okker. 'In our day, you almost always had to come to the net to win a point. These days hardly anyone does that any more. Borg was physically much stronger than me. His serve improved over the years and, of course, he was so fast he had plenty of time to do different things with the ball. I think that was his strongest point.'

And McEnroe? 'When we played in 1980, I was on my way down,' explained Okker. The American trounced him, 6–0, 7–6, 6–1. 'He killed me, uh,' says Okker. 'He was very talented and difficult to play against, especially on the grass. The ball stays low and McEnroe could move it around very nicely with his wrist. Actually, it was nice to play against him, because technically he was so good. Sometimes, he could be annoying for his opponents, but I always thought that the umpires should control the match and if he could get away with it, fine. In those days you could get away with a lot. You could get the umpire changed if you wanted.'

Borg's third round encounter with Australian Rod Frawley posed him some awkward questions. 'He was nervous playing me. He knew I was a good grass courter,' said Frawley. He travelled and shared an apartment with New Zealander Chris Lewis (who three years later lost to McEnroe in the Wimbledon final). 'I wasn't very professional compared to Bjorn,' said Frawley, 'but who was? We had no money, no trainers, no backup. We just went out and did it ourselves. Borg was very quiet around the locker room, saying little other than hello and goodbye, but guys like Nastase and Vitas would tell you that without a championship on the line he was a little more relaxed. Borg had an aura, though. He also had people around him. McEnroe didn't – because no one could put up with him. He said himself, "I couldn't have a coach, I'd probably kill him!" I do think Borg and McEnroe shared one thing – a fear of losing.'

Frawley's preparation to play Borg was less than ideal, as the day before he had been on court for what seemed an eternity, against Tony Graham, finally eliminating the American 13–11, in the fifth. Borg took the first set from the Australian, but Frawley took the second in a tie-break after saving a set point. 'I had won a set from Borg at Wimbledon!' exclaimed Frawley. This small triumph had come at a cost, however. He had stirred Borg into retaliatory action. The Swede lost just one game in the third set and recovered from 1–4 in the fourth to knock out Frawley, 6–4, 6–7, 6–1, 7–5. 'I don't think I was professional enough in the third set. I didn't stay with Borg,' reflected Frawley. 'As I say, I don't think he liked to lose. The guy was so quick on the grass and he was having to cover a lot of ground and angles as he stood five metres outside the baseline. I served well and he still covered the angles. He bristled with determination.'

Borg had equalled his idol Rod Laver's record of thirty-one consecutive wins at Wimbledon. 'He had that record on his mind and talked about wanting to break it,' recalled Mariana. He remained on course. He was dealing with the rain and he was dealing with keeping his body together. Remember, here was a man who had already won seven matches back-to-back on the debilitating clay at Roland Garros and then went on to play in the Davis Cup, before heading to Wimbledon.

One man who understood the toll this took on Borg's physique better than most is ATP trainer Bill Norris, still keeping players of the modern generation on the court twenty-five years after he joined the tour. 'Bjorn was a work horse,' he explained. Norris had worked in various professional sports in America: baseball, football and basketball. 'Tennis players are probably some of the best athletes I have worked with,' he said. 'After the French Open, a player gets a lot of soreness. A change of surface requires so much different involvement. The thing with Bjorn was that even when he had an injury that may have been debilitating to another player, he could still play. He had niggling injuries through his career. He trained hard. He would put a strain on his lower abdominal muscles and they are difficult to treat. All you can do is apply ice and some electrical therapy. With Borg we gave him a lot of electrical therapy and medications, but during this two weeks at Wimbledon you really don't get much time to rest. It really was a credit to his perseverance and his fortitude that he came through. He had an inner strength.

'During the early part of 1980 he had a few niggling injuries on and off. He had a blister on his hand once in a while; sometimes he would play with white adhesive tape across his hand to prevent them recurring. He was not fragile. He was a tough guy. I knew that physiologically Borg was one of the finest specimens we had come across. His low resting pulse was perhaps part of his success. He was definitely a pioneer in his training methods.'

Unsurprisingly, perhaps, Norris felt McEnroe and Connors had the same resilience as Borg; that same capacity to run a yard more when it mattered most. 'All three men were intense characters who could find a way to win,' said Norris. 'McEnroe had a lot of strength. He had played a lot of soccer as a kid. I think that helped his hand-eye coordination. He just never developed his training methods until a little later. He had the ability that is indigenous to a lot of athletes – a great talent and the capacity to think things out. He did not need much time to practise and prepare, but John had a few niggling things. He would strain his thigh muscles, but he would play through those things, because, like Borg and Connors, he possessed great perseverance.

'I remember one time helping him when he was playing with Vilas on what was marketed as "Tour over America", an exhibition week when they travelled from city to city. John developed a gastro-intestinal type of bile condition. He had eaten some seafood and it was making him sick. We were in Minneapolis. The stands were packed. So what did he do? He went into the bathroom and just retched everything out of his system and then he went on court. He had lost all his electrolytes, but he knew there was a show to be put on that night. It was a real privilege to serve those fellas, as it is now.'

South African Kevin Curren awaited McEnroe in the fourth round at Wimbledon. Five years down the road, Curren would appear in the historic Wimbledon final that witnessed the coronation of a seventeen-year-old German called Boris Becker. Curren beat McEnroe in the quarterfinals that summer before he succumbed to the power and the will of Becker. In 1980, Curren was good enough to stretch McEnroe over three close sets, but no more. His perspective is fascinating and his experiences against McEnroe give an insight into the emotional kaleidoscope of the life and times of the mercurial American.

'I had come through qualifying in 1980, but I was young and inexperienced when I went to play McEnroe on Court No. 1. It was the first show court I ever played on. I had played McEnroe in college, but only in doubles. I was at Texas, he was at Stanford. He had this presence and he was able not only to control what was happening on the court, but the crowd as well. He used to push the rules to the limit. It was intimidating playing him, although I seem to remember he wasn't too bad in that particular match. It was close, 7–5, 7–6, 7–6, in McEnroe's favour. Even he said afterwards that he had battled with my serve. I think if I'd had more confidence I would have had a better chance.

'But here he was setting himself up for this great rivalry with Borg. McEnroe was probably one of the greatest serve and volley players I have come across. Nevertheless, I had a game that on grass was very effective. He didn't get a lot of chances against me that day. I surprised myself it was that close. On an outside court, I might have had more of an edge, but we were playing with wooden rackets and it was a very different game in those days. You couldn't just blow a rival away with power. A lot more skill was needed – and McEnroe had phenomenal skill.

'Yet I was a great fan of Bjorn, the epitome of an athlete. Borg and McEnroe were a classic match-up. Borg had this baseline game and great physical talent; he was quick, strong and in great condition. Against him was this artist. One man was ice cool, the other ready to go off at anything. I am talking about guys you'd put your life on when the pressure is at its most intense in a game of tennis. These are guys that actually raise their game when the stakes are highest. You can throw Connors and Becker into that same category. Very few guys have that attribute – a game without fear. They believed that to be a champion was their destiny.

'In 1985, I was a different player and a different man. John was different, too. I was ready mentally to play McEnroe. I'd played him the previous year in San Francisco and we were in a tie-break when he went ballistic. The match was stopped for half an hour. He should have been defaulted, but he wasn't. The match was on national television, a semifinal. The umpire gave him a warning and a point penalty and it was my turn to serve. McEnroe wouldn't get up from his chair, so I waited. Then they gave me the game. Now I've got to changeover and he hasn't got up yet. I'd won the first set and I was now a game up in the second. I thought, "Shit, I'm going to finally beat the guy." I thought he had to be rattled. Well, John took that set, 6–2, and I lost the match. With John, he has the ability to have an argument and his blood pressure doesn't rise. You get upset, but it doesn't affect him. He has a way of manipulating a situation, no question.

'So, at Wimbledon in 1985 he could see I had come to play. I was a set up. He wasn't returning my serve and I was all over his. I missed a first serve at 15–30, I think. He started walking about and talking to someone in the crowd. I was waiting to serve. I said to the umpire, "This is an undue break of play." He agreed and the umpire awarded me two serves.

'McEnroe started shouting and screaming. Referee Alan Mills came on to the court. I went and sat down and put a towel over my head. I didn't want to interact with the umpire. I saw what had happened that last time in San Francisco. His issue was with the umpire. Alan confirmed it was two serves. I went out and hit a first serve winner, so it was back to 30–all. Alan walked off and John said something as he left. Alan walked back to the chair and told the umpire to give McEnroe a warning and to invoke the code of conduct if he stepped out of line again. I think John realised he couldn't push it any further. I played really well, but in his book John talked about the fact he had a lot of off-court distractions and that his focus was wrong.'

McEnroe later confided to me that he had left Wimbledon in 1985 a physical wreck, vowing not to return. 'My stomach went haywire and I couldn't move,' he said. 'I understood for the first time how you could become sick from stress. I was mentally gone and I realised that I was no longer capable of handling the pressure. I just didn't want to deal with what went on around me at Wimbledon. I knew it wasn't worth this and I wasn't coming back. To me, the whole event had become a circus.'

McEnroe had been defending champion, a man who had played in five successive finals at Wimbledon. His romance had begun with Oscar-winning actress Tatum O'Neal, but to deflect unwanted publicity they decided she should remain in the United States. 'I'd never been in the *National Enquirer* before we met, never experienced this kind of paparazzi treatment, so I arrived in England alone,' explained McEnroe. 'I told the press, "I haven't brought Tatum. I am here to play tennis."' He took sanctuary in an exclusive hotel in Chelsea where rock stars like David Bowie felt comfortably secure. 'It got to the point where I didn't want to go out. I wasn't grown up enough to realise the reality of the situation. I thought if I didn't have Tatum with me that things would be easier. That was a mistake. It couldn't have been any worse and I was lonely without her.' After he lost to Curren, he was physically ill. 'I was throwing up in the dressing room. It was the pressure, I think. As a young guy of twenty-six this hit me like a ton of bricks and made me aware of the effects of stress. My attitude stank in that quarterfinal.'

If McEnroe's mind was fragile in 1985, in the summer of 1980 there was no shame attached to Curren in defeat. He knew he was playing a man whose game was rising to challenge Borg's supremacy. He played fearless tennis and, when the match was halted in the fading evening light, he was two sets to the good over Curren. The next day dawned miserable yet again and McEnroe said waspishly, 'When we went out on court it was raining pretty hard and I asked myself, "What are we doing going out here?" I suppose they must be getting a little desperate to get matches played and they are having to throw you out whether it's raining or not. All the waiting around can be trying. You just have to try and keep calm through it all. Who knows what's going to happen next? I suppose snow is the next probability.' McEnroe required thirty-five minutes on court to put paid to Curren, a player ranked just inside the world's top 200. Now McEnroe was set to meet his old friend Peter Fleming in the quarterfinals.

'John was great for the game and he still is,' said Curren, who declared himself honoured to be South Africa's Davis Cup captain when he returned to Wimbledon to participate in the over forty-fives event last summer. 'His commentary is very insightful, brilliant to listen to even as a former professional. He is a complex personality, no question, but he has a lovely family and his brother, Patrick, is a great guy. I think John is a little like a chameleon. He changes with circumstances. He can put his arm around you and the next moment tear your throat out, but he was lovely to watch play the game and he brought more fans to the game than just tennis enthusiasts. That's what made him so great – and that's what helped make tennis popular in those years. It was just that he was a guy you didn't want to play against every week, because he could be a pain in the arse!'

When Balazs Taroczy beat Ramesh Krishnan in the third round, he assumed he would be playing his next match on Centre Court, because he had to meet Borg in the last sixteen and Borg was attempting to win a record thirty-second consecutive match at the championships. 'I had never played on Centre, so I was looking forward to that,' said Taroczy, one of Borg's regular sparring partners, of course, but the obstinate weather continued to wreak havoc with the schedule and Taroczy had to settle for playing on Court No. 1. He admitted unashamedly, 'If I am honest I didn't think I had a chance, but at the same time I never felt that Bjorn should be so good on grass. He had a good first serve, but his second was not that special. And, I mean, he had a ridiculous looking volley! I knew the only chance I had was coming to the net on my sliced backhand. That was a good shot of mine and on the grass it was the right tactic, but against him I was a little bit too slow to get into the net. I served, waiting one shot, and then went in with the backhand slice. Really, I never played against him in a way I was thinking of winning. I was almost surprised with every game I won.'

Taroczy watched McEnroe's progress in the draw with increasing respect and his appreciation of the American's brand of tennis grew through the passing years. 'For me, McEnroe is the greatest talent I saw,' said the Hungarian. 'He was also an incredible competitor. He could be an asshole, but he was tough. He made it difficult for everyone: for his opponent, for the umpire and for the referee. The guy wanted to win and he was not afraid to show it. I am sure he was acting, playing at being an asshole some of the time. He knew that intimidation would get him where he wanted.

'He was forgiven, because I think everybody respected him as a player. If you beat someone, then you can tell them you are this or that, but when you lose? When you lose to someone and then want a row, you look ridiculous. Come on, the guy just beat the shit out of you, so what can you say? That was just one part of the man. Technically, he was gifted. He could take the ball so early. If Bjorn would come back today with his game, even though he was a great competitor, I am not so sure he could be so dominant as he was. I am convinced that with his ability McEnroe would be No. 1.'

Taroczy duly entered Wimbledon history as Borg's thirty-second straight victim, when he was beaten, 6–1, 7–5, 6–2. Afterwards the Swede was effervescent – for him. Borg said, 'Rod Laver was the greatest who ever played the game. To beat his overall record means so much to me because he won so many titles. It's important for me to break a record like this, because I'm a player who must have goals. That's why I am always anxious to win major titles and why my main target now is to win the US Open.' That was one ambition which was to elude him.

With no improvement in the weather, some players began to agitate for an extension of the tournament. Leading the protest was defending women's champion, Martina Navratilova, who finished her quarterfinal against Billie Jean King on the second Wednesday of the championships in drizzle and fading light. 'It was raining really hard,' she said. 'Water was splashing in my eyes. We shouldn't have started the match, it was so dangerous.' She campaigned for officers of the ATP and WTA, the players' associations for the men's and women's tours respectively, to have a greater voice in the scheduling. Yet Wimbledon referee Fred Hoyles dismissed suggestions that players were being placed at risk. 'We are careful not to ask players to play when it's not safe,' he said. Even so, the backlog of matches was becoming critical. Connors said, ruefully, 'I'll either be in great shape if I make the final or dead.' As you might expect, Borg was pragmatic. 'I'm not getting married until the 24th [July] so I have plenty of time,' he said.

riana on the town
h Borg

lats Wilander, the first Swede
to pick up the torch from Borg

Vitas Gerulaitis
with Borg, sparring
partners on and
off court

McEnroe sampling
the night life with
Broadway Vitas

Jimmy Connors ended McEnroe's fairytale entrance at Wimbledon in the 77 semis

Three of a kind: Borg, McEnroe and Connors chilling out

Borg reunited with McEnroe at Wimbledon for the Millennium Parade of Champions

Lennart Bergelin and Borg at the Cumberland Club, their London home
from home, with committee member Colin Hess

McEnroe declaring he is the victim of a rough call at Wimbledon

Malcolm Folley

Hulton Deutsch Collection/Corbis

Jimmy Connors offers McEnroe some advice on etiquette on the
Centre Court in a turbulent semifinal in 1980

Peter Fleming at one with the man he calls Junior

McEnroe and Borg march out for their date with destiny at Wimbledon

...rg in his majestic moment of triumph... seconds before the scoreboard has ...gistered the final score

Borg's noble love affair with Wimbledon sealed with a kiss

Fleming had never before reached a quarterfinal in a Grand Slam tournament and admitted to feeling proud. 'I thought it was a big deal for me,' he said. 'As I had a good record against Junior I also thought I had a good chance to reach the semis.' Fleming had one private concern: the legacy of an old foot injury. He had sustained the injury in February and played little tennis for the next few months. Relief came when a doctor showed him how to protect his foot with a pad, but when he arrived in the locker room to prepare for his match with McEnroe, Fleming realised something was wrong. 'I had lost the pad I used on my foot,' he said. 'I was freaking out for fifteen to twenty minutes. Where is my pad? I couldn't find it anywhere. I could make them – it only took ten minutes – but instead of making one at 1.30p.m. – we were going on court at 2p.m. – I looked for the missing one for twenty minutes. Then it was panic stations. I'd just finished putting it on, when I was told, "You're on court."'

McEnroe was in the locker room. He said nothing. Fleming's theory is this: 'It might have been one of the first times he was able to be ruthless against me. Before, he was maybe ambivalent as we were incredibly close. From his perspective, now I was just another guy to play at Wimbledon.' Fleming's self-induced panic over the missing pad meant he walked on court in the wrong frame of mind. 'I wasn't ready to compete,' he explained. 'I dumped my serve in the first game.' However, he doesn't offer this as mitigation for his defeat. 'When Junior served for the first set, I had a point to get back on serve,' said Fleming. 'I didn't break back. Thereafter, he steamrollered me. He wasn't nervous anymore. He got into the flow. He moved up a couple of gears – gears I didn't have. In the second and third sets he played some stunning tennis. He was just better by a long way.' McEnroe had reached his second semifinal at Wimbledon, 6–3, 6–2, 6–2.

To Gene Mayer, a quarterfinal against Borg on the Centre Court at Wimbledon was an opportunity, not a professional death sentence. 'I thought I could beat him,' said Mayer, who remembers the reasons for his optimism with great clarity. 'For someone to beat Borg at the French Open was almost inconceivable,' said Mayer. 'If he had won twelve French Opens that wouldn't have surprised anyone, but I think that even after Bjorn had won four Wimbledons, the idea that he could win a fifth was still a shock.

He was certainly not suited to playing there. To win the title as often as he did was just a super-human effort.

'Compared with most other players, he never impressed you with the quality of his shots. His strength was the number of balls he hit, his consistency, his fight, determination and speed. I had opportunities galore against him that day. I was up a break in all three sets. He just found a way to make the right shot at the right time. He wore you down. In some ways, he let you beat yourself. He would never choke. Bjorn had a mystique. Unlike Connors or McEnroe, who were both outspoken personalities, Borg drew people in by not letting them know very much. He was certainly one of the great gentlemen to play the game.

'Borg moved so well on a tennis court. You couldn't gradually build the point on percentage balls – his passing shots were too good. When you had the ball, you had to try to punish him. I tried to come in more and I did get lots of hittable volleys, but he'd get a running pass or somehow come up with something extraordinary. So, then you'd stay back, even though you knew that's what he wanted. You really had to do the damage with the first volley.'

Or else you went home. Borg journeyed into a semifinal with Brian Gottfried by beating Mayer, 7–5, 6–3, 7–5. Gottfried, unseeded, had not dropped a set. No one was more surprised than the twenty-eight-year-old American, renowned for being one of the nice guys of the game as well as one of the most dedicated. On his wedding day, he practised for four hours before the ceremony and then drove fifty miles each day on his honeymoon to train with his coach, Nick Bollettieri. His wife, Windy, said, 'No matter how he's playing or what's happening, he's always the same placid fella.'

Regrettably for Gottfried, the doubles programme was behind schedule. The night before his semifinal with Borg, Gottfried and his partner, Raul Ramirez, went five sets against the Amritraj brothers, Anand and Vijay, winning 19–17 in the decider. 'When you play Bjorn on any surface you like to be fresh,' he lamented. Borg drew the sting from his opponent's game. He was remorseless and he was never going to buckle mentally. 'Points were pretty short on grass most of the time except against Borg,' said Gottfried. 'You went from playing four or five matches serving and volleying, then all of a sudden you had to make six- or seven-ball rallies. My second serve wasn't big enough, so I was stuck having to stay back if I missed my first. Wimbledon was like final exam week. By the end, you couldn't do anything but lie in bed.

'Although I was an attacking player, I wasn't a natural grass court player. Anyway, we used to say that Borg didn't get any bad bounces on his side of the court! You never ended up on the winning side, that's for sure. With Borg, it was a different game.' Gottfried was level at set-all when Borg accelerated away from him like a Ferrari leaving behind a Ford at a set of traffic lights. Gottfried won a mere two games in the final two sets. 'You have to work so hard against him,' said the American. 'So many balls come back . . . and they take their toll. It's like taking too many body punches.'

Borg would play in his fifth consecutive Wimbledon final. He also had the luxury of finishing work on Thursday, giving him two days to prepare for the final. McEnroe and Connors had to play their semifinal twenty-four hours later due to the backlog of matches – and it was never going to be less than a dog fight. It hardly mattered that a place in the final of the world's most prestigious tournament was at stake. McEnroe and Connors would have brawled over a first round match in Wilmington, North Carolina. No one needed a thermometer to recognise that the temperature on court in this unseasonally cold summer was going to reach boiling point. McEnroe cast himself as the villain. He became incensed when he thought he had aced Connors, only for a linesman to call the serve out. At the change of ends, McEnroe shouted at umpire Pat Smyth, a bespectacled grey-haired man: 'I am not going to play until you get the referee out here. I want the referee right now.' Smyth then made Wimbledon history by making McEnroe the first recipient of an official warning for bad conduct on the Centre Court. The tension never lightened.

Connors did not find it difficult to become infuriated with McEnroe. At one point, he told him, 'I'll let my son play you next time. You are both the same age.' Brett Connors was eleven months old. In the emotional maelstrom, referee Hoyles did appear on court. It was a gesture of appeasement, but Hoyles was never going to douse the players' passion for the fight. Connors had the crowd on his side, but McEnroe had never allowed that to destabilise him. He appeared deaf to the jeering, booing and slow hand-clapping. In his autobiography, McEnroe wrote, 'At that point, my relationship with Connors was the exact opposite of my relationship with Borg – there was little respect for the man or the occasion of playing him. Like two club fighters, we trash-talked each other at the changeovers. Jimmy called me a baby and I told him what he could kiss.' McEnroe won in what he called 'four draining' sets. He had made an appointment to meet Borg in the Wimbledon final.

Twenty-four years later, Connors came back to Wimbledon with a wistful smile and reflected on days of past thunder and lightning, like that bruising semifinal. Connors, who won a record 109 tournaments in one of the most illustrious careers in the history of the sport, placed Borg and McEnroe neck and neck in his assessment. 'If Ilie had been a bit more focused he might have become the greatest of all time,' said Connors. So if not Nastase, who takes the honours? 'One is Pancho Gonzales, because of his size and the way he moved. The second is a tie between Borg and McEnroe. To have a rivalry with one player is something special, but to have two at the same time is something incredible. We brought the best out of each other. They helped me push myself to the limit and I would hope they would say the same thing about me.' In the same spirit of entente cordiale, McEnroe admitted, 'Our rivalry brought the best out of us on court, but we just didn't see eye to eye off the court. But we're older now and I have the utmost respect for Jimmy.'

Back in the summer of 1980, McEnroe's day had not ended with his turbulent triumph over Connors. He had a doubles semifinal to play with Fleming against Australians Peter McNamara and Paul McNamee. 'It was weird. Basically, I put in a really poor effort,' recalled Fleming. 'I barely tried and John was asking, "C'mon, what's going on here?" The truth was I felt guilt by association for John having to play doubles. I'm sure it was this Jenny thing, but I didn't want to be the reason he lost the final the next day through being tired. My mind was like, if we go five sets this is going to be too much for me to handle. I don't want to take anything away from the other guys – they came out and played really well – but I was concerned for Mac more than he was. I don't ever remember him trying less than one hundred per cent, but we went down in three straight. It was quick, very quick. My mind wasn't on the court.'

To illustrate how even the hardiest of champions are affected under this intense scrutiny of their mind and talent, John Lloyd described the stark disappointment experienced by his wife, Chris Evert, after her defeat in the women's final against Evonne Cawley, earlier that same day. Lloyd's own ranking had gone south on the men's tour as he travelled as coach with his wife of the time. 'Chris experienced total elation when she beat Martina Navratilova in the semis – she'd lost to her some ridiculous amount of times in a row and no one thought she had a shot,' said Lloyd. 'We didn't get back to our house at Kingston-on-Thames until gone 9p.m. and she had to play the Wimbledon final the next day. The phones were ringing from Florida as friends called her. Normally, you'd get twenty-four hours to savour a semifinal win, but I tried to tell Chris she didn't have that luxury. She went, yeah, yeah, but carried on anyway.

'Next morning she was flat. She didn't have that look in her eyes. No disrespect to Evonne, but Chris should never have lost that final. Talk about experiencing the opposite reaction and feelings inside twenty-four hours. There was a match that she should never have won, then a match she should never have lost. Chris took her losses badly. She cried and took it out on those closest to her, basically, for a couple of days. As her coach, I told her she had the US Open to look forward to playing. I took three years off my career as her coach – three good years – but I got a great feeling working with her. She won Grand Slams and I thought it was me that had won. You are a team and this is the reward for the hours put in.

'I was aware that Borg and McEnroe had come together for this great final, but I was wrapped up in Chris's Wimbledon. I remember getting on the plane home to Florida, thinking that if I had just lost a final like that I'd be having a couple of weeks on the beach, but Chris said that when we land, I want to go straight to the courts and play. She said, "I never want to lose to her again." That was the mind of a champion.' That was precisely the way Borg thought, the way Connors thought and now it was the way McEnroe was beginning to think.

14

'I CAN'T STAND LOSING . . .'

On Saturday 5 July 1980 Peter Harrfey awoke in his house at Eastbourne, on the south coast of England, and wondered how his back would feel. He had spent the previous day propped up on cushions in his lounge, after receiving treatment on a trapped nerve in his back. This was not the most ideal of preparations for the biggest appointment of his life. Harrfey had been told on Wednesday that he had been selected to umpire the Wimbledon final. He was fifty-five years old and a health service dental board administrator. He took leave to umpire and this would be the fourth time he had been invited to control a Wimbledon final. The previous summer he had umpired the women's final when Martina Navratilova defeated Chris Evert, but, with no disrespect intended, Harrfey was looking at the men's final as the jewel in his officiating career.

He did not umpire for the money involved; no one did. In common with his colleagues, he received £35 per day expenses and one second class return rail fare from his home. He normally stayed in lodgings close to the courts throughout the Championships, but, when his back began to play up after he had been told he would be in the chair for the final, he had chosen to return home for treatment from a local physiotherapist. 'On Friday morning, the pain was such that I thought I'd have to miss the final,' admitted Harrfey. After another visit to his physiotherapist, he went home and made himself as comfortable as possible between a bedding of cushions. He turned on the television. McEnroe was playing at full volume against Connors, who was not exactly acting the part of a shrinking violet. Harrfey's heart went out to umpire Pat Smyth.

He said, 'I was horrified. McEnroe was in high dudgeon and I was aching for poor Pat, an old friend who has since died.' Another thought hit Harrfey as he watched his television: 'By god, if this happens again tomorrow when there are about forty million people around the world tuned in to the final, I shall just want the court to open up and the chair to slide straight down the hole.' But the next morning, with his back no longer causing him discomfort, Harrfey moved his Hillman Super Minx out of his drive with a sense of anticipation. Two hours later, he pulled into No. 1 car park beside the All England Club. It was close to 11a.m. Harrfey had little appetite, butterflies taking most of the available room in his stomach.

At this time in North London, Borg was getting ready to go to the Cumberland Club for a light workout before the final. Mariana packed his kit with ritual precision. She had five plastic bags each containing the same items. 'Everything had to be in the same order – wristbands, headband, socks, shorts, shirt and shoes,' she explained. 'He had to have a change of clothes after practice, then a change if it was raining. I decided he should take five changes. It was better that way.' Mariana confirmed there was an air of tension. 'We didn't speak too much.'

After hitting for around forty-five minutes at the Cumberland, Borg patiently signed autographs for all the junior club members who were around. He showered and was looked after as usual by club steward, Tom Nutley. He had steak and vegetables for lunch. Bergelin said, 'Tommy was a little fellow, a very nice guy who always came with us to Wimbledon. Bjorn was a little nervous. That is normal. He was quiet and concentrated. With Mariana, he mostly talked in Swedish. She had learned the language very quickly.' Inside the car on the way from the club, there was silence. 'It was like a funeral. Even Lennart wasn't talking,' reported Mariana, 'and he talks all the time! I felt like my stomach was upside down. Every match I am tense, but when he gets to the final it is really a terrible feeling.' The journey took approximately an hour. Once at Wimbledon, Mariana gave Borg a kiss and said goodbye in Swedish. Borg headed for the locker room with Bergelin. 'I went to have a cup of tea and some strawberries,' said Mariana.

Peter Fleming was staying with his girlfriend, Jenny Hudson, in a rented flat near the Gloucester Hotel, in South Kensington, where a vast majority of players stayed during the championships. He was excited for his friend John. 'Here was this guy I'd first met as a twelve-year-old in Port Washington, going to play the Wimbledon final.' Fleming may have been beaten by McEnroe in the quarterfinals, but his friendship was not affected by his own disappointment. He knew McEnroe was playing tennis on a level he could only fantasise about. Fleming drove in good spirit to the All England Club to warm up his doubles partner for the greatest match of his life.

McEnroe and Fleming had often travelled in the same car to the club during the tournament and Fleming remembered hearing one hit record being continually played on the radio, to the increasing irritation of McEnroe. 'This song by the Police, *I can't Stand Losing You*, was on the radio constantly during that fortnight,' said Fleming. He broke into a slow, deep refrain: 'I can't . . . I can't . . . I can't stand losing . . .' sang Fleming, 'and the DJ would come on and say, "Sounds like a song for Superbrat." That angered John. He was just everywhere that summer; in this country he was as recognisable as anyone alive. It was a big deal walking down the street with John in those two weeks and he hated that name more than anything. He was like, "Superbrat? What is this?" He really struggled to see anyone else's perspective on him. He could just see the world with the benefit of his twenty-one years from Douglaston, New York. Now he has a better perspective on where other people might have been coming from, but then he looked pretty straight ahead.'

Once at Wimbledon, Fleming joined McEnroe on an outside court to assist McEnroe in loosening up. 'I thought John's chances were really good,' he said. 'No, I never mentioned tactics with him. I wasn't in his league in that game. He had his coach, Tony Palafox, that he trusted and had a great relationship with. Who the hell am I? Tony rarely came with John anywhere – he was happy to be out of the limelight – but Junior knew he could talk with him whenever he felt a need.' When McEnroe felt sufficiently prepared, Fleming wished him good luck and went back to central London. He preferred to watch the final on television in his rented flat with Jenny and his parents, who were in town from the United States.

Chris Gorringe was administrating at his first championships, having taken over as secretary of the All England Club from Major David Mills in the autumn of 1979. His mind was consumed with the timetable, which had to run with military-like precision and culminate in the presentation ceremony on Centre Court. Gorringe's planning was complicated by the fact that, due to poor weather, the mixed doubles final had to be accommodated before Borg walked out with McEnroe to try to win his fifth consecutive championship.

Over the coming years, Gorringe would get to know McEnroe, father and son. 'I came to know Mr McEnroe Senior early on,' he said. 'One was in dialogue with him much more than one was with John Junior. Let's face it, in my opinion, some of McEnroe's behaviour was totally unacceptable, but if you look back, one of the positive things that can be said is that McEnroe played a big hand in improving the quality of officials at all tournaments around the world. I think the officiating is incredibly higher than it was in the late 1970s and early 1980s and, to a large part, that was due to McEnroe.'

Gorringe is a man with a low profile, but as chief executive he has played a significant role in the modernisation of Wimbledon, to the point where he can retire in the summer of 2005 knowing that it is a model facility for players and spectators in the twenty-first century. He may not be readily identifiable, but those who have been to Wimbledon will recognise Gorringe's voice. During rain delays, it is Gorringe who takes to the public address system to declare earnestly, 'Ladies and Gentlemen, if I may have your attention, the latest news from the London Weather Centre is not very encouraging...'

His office, within the Centre Court complex, characterises the man: unfussy, but pristine and orderly in its organisation. On one wall is a photograph he values with great affection. Borg is on his knees on the Centre Court, his hands clasped in prayer and his racket still air borne. He had just thrashed Connors to win his third championship, in 1978. 'This picture epitomises Borg for me,' said Gorringe. 'Borg was a phenomenon. He transcended the sporting acumen he undoubtedly had to become a sort of pop idol. Why? He didn't court it; his manager and agents didn't court it. He wasn't out on the town as he had a steady girlfriend. He took his privacy seriously. Yet there he was at the centre of Borgmania, something we'd never experienced before. Within the All England Club, Borg was held in high esteem, on and off the court. With Borg, you wouldn't know by looking at his face whether he was winning or losing. It must be frustrating for his opponent to play a fantastic shot to put him on the ropes and then the guy just doesn't flinch or do anything. Borg never showed off, did he? He never acknowledged the applause. He was totally focused.'

As Tracy Austin and John Austin edged closer to winning the mixed doubles title at the expense of Diane Fromholz and Mark Edmondson, Peter Morgan, director general of the Litesome Sportswear Business, made his way to the men's locker room, to escort Borg and McEnroe to the innermost sanctum of Wimbledon: the waiting room. In a line, the three men walked up the seven steps towards the Centre Court, with Borg leading McEnroe past the shining championship cup they were about to play for. They passed through the glass-panelled mahogany doors, above which are inscribed Kipling's lines: 'If you can meet with triumph and disaster and treat those two impostors just the same . . .' Before them were the doors leading on to the Centre Court, but Morgan led them instead through another door on their left. Borg and McEnroe were now in the waiting room.

It is perhaps fifteen feet by eight feet, sparingly furnished with two cushioned chairs and a green-covered couch that also serves as a store for blankets for the royal box. On a glass-topped table was a bowl of flowers, a telephone and, strangest of all, an ashtray. The walls were decorated with a mirror and four framed photos of Mo Connolly, Christine Truman, Fred Perry and the Queen with Virginia Wade after her triumph in the Silver Jubilee year of 1977. For Borg, the room was as familiar as his apartment in Monte Carlo. In the previous summer, on his fourth visit to the waiting room, Borg had tried to ease the tension by discussing the merits of Roscoe Tanner's season with the American. For McEnroe, the suspense had to be killing. As he sat and waited he was counting dead time. He had dreamed of this moment and now he just wanted to play tennis.

McEnroe was probably never more relieved in his life to see Fred Hoyles. The presence of the referee meant Borg and

McEnroe would shortly be invited to walk out of the waiting room and turn left through the green double doors leading into the back of the Centre Court. On Hoyles's signal, the waiting game was declared over and McEnroe went out through the doors first, with Borg half a pace behind.

15

HOW TO WIN FRIENDS AND INFLUENCE PEOPLE – McENROE STYLE

As John McEnroe came into view, some spectators in the 15,000 crowd began booing and jeering. No one had been subjected to such treatment in the history of Wimbledon, but McEnroe's behaviour had clearly offended the sensibilities of more than a few. However, it was also clear from the cheers that greeted his introduction that the American had a large body of support within the capacity crowd. One banner proclaimed: McEnroe for president. My own vantage point was in neutral territory, on a stone step in the over-subscribed press box.

At his rented flat in South Kensington, Peter Fleming watched with fascination. 'This is a match in time,' he thought. 'It was post-Sex Pistols, right? In the standing area on the court there were mostly kids and there were a lot of punk haircuts. Junior was their man. He was anti-establishment. Margaret Thatcher had just come to power and she was tearing hearts out. Bjorn was Mr Nice Guy. He was by no means the establishment, but he was middle England's hero. Everyone loved him. He had this aura – and what's not to love about him? Seemingly, Junior was the opposite – what's not to hate! But there he was and he had his own fans. It was an incredibly tense environment. If you are into the idea of group energy you had 15,000 on the Centre Court who were soon riveted. Not just riveted, they were involved: emotionally, mentally, even physically. Shouting. It was like a football match.'

Untold millions were tuning into the match around the world.

On Robben Island, off Cape Town, Nelson Mandela, the most celebrated prisoner in the world, settled down to listen to the final on his radio. In Fort Worth, Texas, Patrick McEnroe sat in front of a television to watch *Breakfast at Wimbledon*. He explained, 'I was playing in the Boys National Hardcourt 14 & Under Championships and I was staying in one of those cheap American roadside motels with the little swimming pool outside the door.' He was travelling with a friend, who had his coach with him. 'I was jumping up and down on my little bed,' said Patrick. 'I'd watched Borg for so many years – so had John – but I can't say it was a shock that my brother was in the final. He'd made it to the semis as a qualifier and we had always known grass was a great surface for John. We had come to expect it in some way, which is weird. Only when I got older and realised how hard the game was did I think, "Jeez, you know that was pretty damn amazing that every year John was in the semis or the final of the US Open and Wimbledon."' His father, John McEnroe Senior, sat in the back row of the competitors' box on Centre Court, half hidden under his trademark white, floppy sun hat.

In front of McEnroe, Bergelin and Mariana sat poker faced as usual. Both suspected that the afternoon stretching before them would be an ordeal. 'I remembered John coming to Wimbledon as a little boy [1977],' said Mariana. 'He was funny with that hair and headband, but he played good tennis. He had a good touch and it was a game made for Wimbledon. I never thought he was bad. Everyone cannot be like Bjorn, a model of self-control. This was the way John was made and he had to take it out on the court, but for me John was never a bad boy, never.'

Bergelin knew that McEnroe would be tactically astute, a man capable of making adaptations if required. It was Borg's eighth meeting with the American. 'At the beginning, I remember McEnroe served and all the time ran to the net,' said Bergelin. 'And Bjorn passed him. But later on, McEnroe learned to play even from the baseline. He could hold the ball in play. From then, he started to be more difficult for Bjorn.'

In the commentary box, John Barrett suggested, 'It's Scandinavian sang-froid taking on New World brashness.' The ninety-fourth men's Wimbledon final promised to be special, but no one could have predicted just how memorable an occasion it would be. No one could dared to have forecast that we were about to witness the most dramatic subplot in Wimbledon history; a match within a match.

McEnroe kept his shock of hair out of his eyes with the aid of a bright red headband; an accessory that Borg himself had popularised. He was oblivious to the jeering that greeted him. At twenty-one, he was absorbed only by the challenge of dealing with Borg's game. He sensed his hour was at hand. He knew, just knew, that his tennis stacked up impressively against the Swede on grass. He came to the Centre Court, the court of King Bjorn, without fear. As for Borg, the occasion was now second nature. He was at home, among friends. His left hand was protected by a ribbon of white tape wrapped round his knuckles and across his palm as a precaution. His right thumb was also taped. Borg's beard made him look more like a Viking than ever. His shirt had a faint pinstripe.

Umpire Peter Harrfey allowed the players a few, final moments to complete their knock-up. On his table on his perch above the Centre Court, were four lights linked to the magic eye, two for each side of the court. One light indicated that a service was in, the other told him it was out. He had in front of him a standard score sheet and two pencils. 'I knew I had to concentrate on every single shot. There was no question of allowing your mind to stray,' he said. 'Such was my concentration with what I had to do beforehand – make sure the net was the right height, supervise the coin toss and mark up the score sheet for the change of balls – that once we got started I didn't have any tension. It was a job I had been doing for twenty years. It was not unfamiliar.' Harrfey and his team of line judges all wore jackets and ties.

As he waited to receive, Borg shifted his weight from foot to foot. McEnroe's insides may have been churning, but he offered us a portrait of a man calmly in control of his destiny. At 2.19p.m. – a late start due to the mixed doubles final turning into a three-set marathon, won by the Austins – McEnroe tossed the ball into the air to begin a Wimbledon final that will never be forgotten.

His unique service clicked from the start. He rocked forward and bent low, with his arms locked in an embrace on either side of his racket handle. As he uncoiled, he tossed the ball into the air. His racket head materialised in a blur. His motion carried him speedily into the court behind the ball. He lost two points in the opening game, but his ability to win his first service game was a soothing tonic.

In sharp contrast, Borg served from an upright position, standing tall like a guardsman. At 30–30 on Borg's opening service game, McEnroe gave himself a chance to break with a backhand passing shot. He cashed in with a forehand lob that Borg turned and chased, but found too difficult to hit back into court. McEnroe's start was flawless. When McEnroe held his next service game to love, with Borg standing two yards behind the baseline to receive, the American had raced into a 3–0 lead.

At the changeover, if Borg was ruffled he didn't show it. He sat on his chair and banged one racket against another, taken from the dozen in his bag, listening for the note each one made with the ear of a man tuning a piano. His face was expressionless. Borg came back to the court to win his first game of the final. He opted to follow his first serve to the net to be in position to volley. Borg is never at his most comfortable at the net, but he realised he could not let McEnroe have possession of the forecourt at all times.

In the next game, Borg missed a chance to earn a break point on McEnroe's serve when he missed a backhand pass, with the American looking vulnerably placed at the net. On the next point, McEnroe showed sound judgement to allow a backhand from Borg to drift past him into the tramlines. The American was ahead, 4–1. His belief that his game, constructed around his serve and volley, could unhinge Borg was looking more than the bluff or bravado of youthful exuberance. It was a boast beginning to resonate with authenticity, sounding like an echo of Muhammad Ali's insistence that he would tame Sonny Liston. Borg was a more subtle exponent of his art than Liston, a bear of a man with the heart of an assassin, but he was still taking an undue amount of punishment from McEnroe in these opening exchanges.

Those who came to the Centre Court to support McEnroe were being rewarded. His tennis was brisk and purposeful and he was not giving the umpire reason to do anything other than call the score. In the next game, Borg was coerced into surrendering his serve for a second time. McEnroe's now-electrifying tennis was winning friends around the Centre Court, even gaining grudging admiration from those who had booed him on sight. He owned the first set, 6–1, when he placed a delicate backhand shot across the court from his position at the net. To applause, McEnroe walked with quiet dignity to his chair. Borg had won a mere seven points from McEnroe's first four service games. After twenty-seven minutes, there was a lop-sided balance to this final that no one would have forecast.

In her seat, Mariana took a discreet draw on a cigarette. 'John was all over Bjorn,' she said. 'In the first set Bjorn wanted to check out strategy, work out how to play. He knew it was going to be a difficult match. John has a game built on improvisation. You don't know where the ball is going. It's there . . . there . . . and suddenly over there. Then there is his unbelievable touch. He can change the game. He can do things you don't expect. Bjorn was losing, because he didn't find a way – yet. But what we were watching didn't mean anything to get afraid over. He just had to get into the match.' As ever, Bergelin watched behind a face devoid of emotion. 'Bjorn had respect for John. He knew to beat McEnroe was not going to be easy,' he said. 'He just had to be ready to take his chance when it came along.'

On court, Borg was not given to panic. After all, he had been here before. Connors had captured the first set from him in the 1977 final, while only the previous summer Tanner had also gone ahead by a set. Borg had known he would need to be patient and watchful against McEnroe. Connors and Tanner had their own strengths, created their own puzzle for Borg to solve, but McEnroe was an enigma on a tennis court, as in life. He was wholly unpredictable, a player like no other Borg had encountered. Borg had to sustain his concentration; and no one knew how to do that better than the Swede. An example of Borg's unblinking approach soon presented itself. Serving the second point of the first game of the second set, Borg's racket flew from his hand, bounced and landed at a right angle outside the court. The Swede walked over, bent down, picked up his racket and returned to the service line. He offered neither a smile nor a grimace. It was as though this was something that happened to him on a regular basis. Was his palm sweating through nerves? Borg would not have countenanced the question. All that mattered to him was his next serve.

But Borg lost that point as well when he over-struck a backhand drive. The scoreboard now showed him at 1–6, 0–30. McEnroe had Borg in peril and knew it. Instinctively, he went to strike another body blow, but his backhand was hit too carelessly and an opportunity was missed. Borg rattled off the next three points to critically hold his service. 'C'mon McEnroe,' shouted a lone voice. 'C'mon Borg,' yelled a chorus in response. Outside the press seats, there was no room for neutrality.

In South Kensington, Fleming understood the magnitude of the moments he had just witnessed. '6–1, 2–0, would have been a pretty decisive lead,' he said. 'That night we had a party – it would have been a celebration party, but it was a commiseration party – and we started talking about the match. I said to John, "My God, early in the second set it was right there, that was a chance to bury him." We knew what each other were thinking a lot of the time. We had a real good empathy and understanding. John said to me that before he went to hit that backhand, he thought to himself, "It's too soon, I'm not ready to be No. 1 in the world." That's what flashed through his mind almost when the ball was on his racket and he missed it. John had to bury, bury, bury, bury him. Dead.'

Even though he had been reprieved at the start of the set, Borg struggled to read or return McEnroe's service. The American engineered a break point for a 3–2 lead in the second set. Yet again McEnroe's talent betrayed him. He netted a backhand return to take the score to deuce. The American looked at the heavens and sighed aloud, 'Uhhhhh.' Let off the hook, Borg held his service to go ahead, 3–2.

At his chair, McEnroe fidgeted with his shoes during the changeover. In the BBC commentary booth, Barrett was saying, 'We really do have a classic confrontation here. The best server in the world against the best returner in the world; the best volleyer against the man with the best passing shots; and the most volatile player in the world against the calmest. The dilemma for Borg is that he dare not stay at the back of the court against a man serving and volleying and playing his approaches as well as McEnroe is today. He's having to come in and we have seen quite clearly how unhappy he is in that forecourt position, even though he has been practising it for most of Wimbledon.'

At 4–4 in the set, McEnroe had lost a mere five points on his serve. He had good reason to suspect he held his fate in his own hands. 'At 6–1, 4–4, I was killing Bjorn,' McEnroe told me years later. 'I thought I was going to win in straight sets.' In that ninth game, he had three break points on Borg's serve, but the Swede never batted an eyelid. He saved the third of those points with a nerveless serve wide to McEnroe's forehand. The American couldn't handle the power or the angle and netted his return. McEnroe also netted the next point and lost the game with a forehand struck into the tramlines. Borg headed to his chair to a resounding ovation. McEnroe sat parallel to the court. He took off his right shoe and peered inside before replacing it. He towelled down, then re-tied his left shoelace. He rarely sat still. Not far away, Borg stared across the court, dabbed some sweat with a towel and moved back into the arena. Crisis, what crisis?

The next two games went with serve and then McEnroe suddenly felt the full force of Borg's competitive nature. At 5–6, 15–0, McEnroe lost three points in succession, the last a stunning backhand return from Borg hit over the high part of the net off an outswinging trademark serve. McEnroe saved the first set point with a serve into Borg's body that forced an error from the Swede. McEnroe missed his next first serve and the noise level rose several decibels higher. Borg swayed as he waited for McEnroe's second serve, the set at his mercy. Borg returned on his backhand side and McEnroe came forward to volley . . . but his touch was imperfect and his backhand volley hit the net.

Borg's supporters screamed ecstatically. Against the bedlam, umpire Harrfey struggled to announce the score. 'Game . . .' And Harrfey's voice vanished. Eventually, he made himself heard and called the score at one set apiece. In reality, it was a superfluous action. There was not one person in the Centre Court who needed to be told the score.

The momentum had moved dramatically in Borg's favour. He jumped out to a 3–0 lead in the third set and that meant McEnroe had lost five games in succession. Was the intense, energy-draining semifinal with Connors and the disappointing doubles match beginning to catch up with him? His mind was being stretched as well as his body. After he had held serve to trail, 2–4, McEnroe was clearly unhappy when Harrfey declared, 'New balls.' McEnroe asked the umpire, 'How come it's new balls now?' Harrfey told him that the old balls had been in play for the requisite number of games, nine. It was the closest McEnroe had come to creating a scene – and frankly didn't register at all on his personal Richter scale. Borg's service came under threat, new balls or not. The game lasted nine minutes and McEnroe had five break points before the Swede held his advantage. In the competitors' box, Mariana stubbed out another cigarette and chewed on her fingers.

After McEnroe won his own service to love, Borg accepted the opportunity to serve out the third set. Just three minutes shy of two hours tennis, Borg had gone ahead, 1–6, 7–5, 6–3. Fleming began to sense McEnroe's hopes were fading as he watched in his rented flat. 'In my opinion, as I was watching it, the big chance for John had gone in that second set,' said Fleming. 'Once Bjorn got into the match, he was a different guy. He was a great champion. His serve was a bomb.' Regardless of the score, McEnroe had already achieved a momentous triumph: he had won over the crowd. His earlier misdemeanours had been forgiven. Superbrat had an alter ego and that man played tennis of the highest calibre and with an unqualified dignity. At the start of the fourth set, McEnroe was drowned in cheers.

By this point, there was little to choose between them. At 1–1, McEnroe did go down 0–30 on his serve, but he had the arsenal to keep Borg at bay. At times, the American felt a need to stretch his thigh muscles. His hard work the previous day had to be taking a toll. Also, to combat Borg's topspin ground strokes McEnroe was covering the court at speed, to try to take the ball as early as possible. The set progressed on serve to 4–4.

And then McEnroe succumbed to an onslaught from Borg. At break point down, McEnroe served wide to Borg's backhand with his left-handed away-swinger. Borg was in position fast. His two-handed return dipped towards McEnroe's ankles and the New Yorker could only push the ball along the ground. Borg's supporters jumped to their feet, yelling and screaming. Bergelin watched through unblinking eyes. At 5–4, Borg was serving for the match. He arrived at 40–15 with a fabulous forehand hit down the line from his own baseline. Championship point one, Borg.

*

In the chair, Peter Harrfey looked at the clock. 'We'd had two and a half hours' play,' he said. 'Well, that's been quite good entertainment, I thought. We've got away with it. No fracas. Everyone's had a good afternoon. That will do, thank you.' Borg's first serve flew into the corner of the service box where the service line meets the side line. The ball skidded away. Girls screamed. It was a case of premature celebration. A fault was called. Borg turned unemotionally and set himself upright to serve again. Had he looked into the competitors' box, he would have seen Mariana had her eyes shut. He was on the threshold of immortality, but some moments in time are wreathed with too much tension to be able to bear witness to them. Behind a backhand approach, Borg worked his way to the net on his second serve. McEnroe remained in the back court, but he was far from finished. He squeezed a bold backhand pass between Borg and the sideline to keep himself in the final. Championship point two, Borg.

With great perception, McEnroe ended a pulsating rally by driving a forehand volley down the court to level the game at deuce. Borg conceded the next point with a forehand hit from the baseline that never cleared the net. The Swede's next first serve was good, but McEnroe had anticipated the play and moved into position to strike an unanswerable backhand return cross-court. As the ball landed for a winner, McEnroe yelled, 'C'mon!' His voice was barely audible above the din that erupted. The score-board ticked over to 5–5. McEnroe walked along the baseline with his hands on his hips. Mariana's hands were clasped over her mouth. It was 4.55p.m.

McEnroe, being driven by an invisible force, served out his next game to love to go ahead, 6–5. From being two championship points down, he had won eight points in a row. At the changeover, Borg took a drink and towelled his racket handle and his hands. His face was a blank page. Whatever thoughts raged in his mind, he was not going to show them to the outside world. Now Mariana was not the only person on the Centre Court unable to look. A scan of the crowd showed people hiding their faces or snuggling into the shoulders of their friends or loved ones. Borg seemed to have the coolest head on the premises. At 40–0, McEnroe chased a Borg volley to his right, falling over as he managed to get the ball back over the net. He was still on the ground when Borg tapped the ball into the empty court. Six games all, tie-break. McEnroe was down, but he wasn't out.

16

THE TIE-BREAK

Mariana braced herself for the tie-break, her face still and without a trace of emotion. Borg could look across the court at any time and he could take strength from her apparent calmness. She was a pillar for her man, but where was she to take her strength from, she worried. Behind her fixed stare, she was an emotional wreck. 'I was completely numb,' she said. 'It was like I was up in the sky looking down. I tell you it was terrible.' All around Mariana, people were screaming. First for Borg, then for McEnroe, and then a respectful silence descended over the court just as the protocol of the game demands. McEnroe had the balls in his possession; the tie-break was ready to commence. The most riveting twenty-two minutes of Wimbledon history was about to unfold before our eyes. They are twenty-two minutes of tennis that deserve to be told point by point.

What was at stake can be compressed into simple arithmetic. McEnroe had to win the tie-break to prevent Borg from becoming Wimbledon champion for a fifth summer in succession. His pulse racing, but his head clear, McEnroe tossed the ball into the air. The serve was a fault, but his second landed safe and the American drew first blood with an athletic overhead smash, hit as he reversed into the court. It was a statement of his intent, a reflection of his belief and an indication of his athleticism. Borg was far from home and dry: 1–0, McEnroe.

As ever, it was totally impossible to guess Borg's state of mind by looking into his eyes. Under interrogation, here was a man who was never going to tell you more than his name, rank and number. His first service of the tie-break was returned into the net: 1–1.

McEnroe netted a backhand on the next point and gripped his own throat, a pro's signal that he has 'choked' and conceded an opportunity. With people all around the court yelling themselves hoarse, umpire Harffey called for the crowd to be quiet: Borg, 2–1.

'It was a stupid comment,' admitted Harrfey. 'I was usually quick off the mark with the score, but in that tie-break it was impossible, really. I gave up. It was almost like being in a football stadium. It was unique in my experience.' McEnroe was untroubled by the increasing noise. He made his first serve and won the fourth point with a forehand drop volley: 2–2.

Borg couldn't deal with McEnroe's serve down the middle: McEnroe, 3–2.

After Borg made his first serve, the Swede responded to McEnroe's return with a stop volley of his own. McEnroe ran down the ball, but his cross-court backhand went wide. As the players changed ends, McEnroe walked down the tramlines as he liked to do. He then slapped his thigh in frustration: 3–3.

McEnroe hit a backhand return wide off a good serve from Borg, which was so close to the line that it threw up chalk dust: Borg, 4–3

Borg was taken out of court by McEnroe's fine serve and the Swede struck his return long: 4–4.

McEnroe's first serve was called a let. He took a deep breath and took aim again. From the back of the court, Borg's backhand was too heavy for McEnroe's forehand volley. Borg had struck a decisive blow, winning a point on the American's service: Borg, 5–4.

In Las Vegas, a young boy was watching intently as this emotional inferno raged across the Centre Court. 'I enjoyed watching Bjorn play. He was the person I looked up to most in tennis as I grew up,' said Andre Agassi, destined to win Wimbledon himself one day. 'I used to watch him play, then in the commercial break go out on the court and work on my topspin. I was rooting for Bjorn. That's just the way it was.' And now Borg had two serves for the title to follow. Typically, McEnroe reacted boldly. His backhand return was a punishing shot and when Borg played a half volley, McEnroe raced the ball down to whip a winning backhand cross-court. Borg had just lost his advantage: 5–5.

On the next point, Borg's second serve 'kicked' into the grass. He pounced on McEnroe's return to overpower the American with his backhand approach: Borg, 6–5.

Championship point three, Borg. Up in the stand Bergelin was motionless, but he was talking to himself. 'Please let it be now,' he was thinking. 'It was not so good for the heart, for sure.' Bergelin's plea went unanswered, even though McEnroe failed with his first serve. People edged forwards in their seats or leaned closer to the court in the standing area. The buzz you could hear were voices muttering excitedly all over the old arena. Borg met McEnroe's second serve to the advantage court on his forehand and the Swede went cross-court. At full stretch, McEnroe brilliantly pushed a forehand volley away for a winner to stay in the match. He came to a halt only inches in front of the net, his arms outstretched to ensure he didn't come into contact with it. McEnroe's anticipation had been exceptional. His girlfriend, Stacy Margolin, flashed a winning smile from her seat behind Mariana and Bergelin: 6–6.

On McEnroe's next serve, Borg made a backhand return and then, when the ball came back to him, the Swede drove a phenomenal backhand that flew passed the American. 'Aaaargh,' screeched McEnroe: Borg, 7–6.

Championship point four, Borg. Tall and emotionless, Borg stepped forward to serve for the Wimbledon title. McEnroe met the ball with his backhand. Borg had come forward behind his serve to play a volley. Still in the back court, McEnroe played another backhand designed to test the Swede's volleying prowes – and this time Borg's volley never made it over the net. McEnroe stood with his hands on his hips as his now considerable army of supporters roared their approval: 7–7.

Borg's first serve prompted a forehand return from McEnroe. At the net, Borg crunched a forehand volley that McEnroe, instinctively and defensively, lobbed back at the Swede. Going backwards, Borg rose off one leg and smashed the ball back down the centre of the court. McEnroe played a backhand down the centre. Borg played his own backhand response to McEnroe's forehand . . . and the crowd yelled louder. McEnroe was ready to deliver a forehand cross-court. Borg had the shot covered, but, unwisely, as he struck his backhand he moved towards the net. He was bluffing on an approach play that was no better than average. McEnroe administered instant justice. His backhand cross-court pass left Borg defenceless. McEnroe bent over and threw a left jab into the air. The crowd rose in admiration: McEnroe, 8–7.

Set point one, McEnroe. The American could take the final into a fifth set and then all possibilities were open to him once more, yet he was startled by the ferocity of Borg's forehand return off his first serve. McEnroe hurled himself at the ball – and even threw his racket – but to no avail. He climbed to his feet, at that moment looking an older man. He shook his head in wonderment, wiped his mouth and dusted his shirt: 8–8.

Bjorn Hellberg was broadcasting on the Centre Court. 'On the radio, I described myself as feeling sick, you were so nervous,' he said. 'It was an electrifying atmosphere. People were white-faced with excitement. This was not any match. This was the final of Wimbledon between two great rivals.' With a classic serve and volley, McEnroe recovered from his obvious and deep disappointment at losing the opportunity to get on level terms. He had nosed once more into a position of superiority: McEnroe, 9–8.

Set point two, McEnroe. Remarkably, Borg opted to apply the same serve and volley strategy. Rushing to the net behind his serve, he hit a backhand volley down the line that was never coming back. He could play McEnroe at his own game: 9–9.

Borg's next serve, hit deep and hard, was knocked out by McEnroe: Borg, 10–9.

Championship point five, Borg. McEnroe waited for the noise to die a little, fidgeted on the baseline and contemplated his next move. In her seat, Mariana took another gulp of air. Borg blew on his fingers; it was a habit of his. Nervelessly, McEnroe placed his first serve as wide as possible. Borg's return never troubled the boundaries of the court: 10–10.

The American could breath again, but it was a luxury not afforded him for long. He hit his first serve into the net. 'Oh god,' he said, loud enough for those closest to hear. His second serve was just in and McEnroe made his first volley, but he missed the second one: Borg, 11–10.

Championship point six, Borg. The Swede's first serve ended in the net. There were audible groans from all sides of the court. After he made his second serve, there were a couple of tentative shots from both men. Then a backhand from McEnroe hit the top of the tape and leapt upwards. The ball fell on Borg's side of the net, dropping like a stone. McEnroe had dodged the bullet once more: 11–11.

McEnroe had but a brief respite. When Borg made a cross-court volley behind his own service, the American's attempted riposte never cleared the net: Borg, 12–11.

Championship point seven, Borg. As Borg waited to receive, he shuffled. McEnroe had to be feeling the heat now. Sure enough, McEnroe missed his first serve. No one around the court dared blink. Was this the moment of history before us? Borg had a clean swing at the American's second serve, but McEnroe's speed allowed him to conjure a marvellous back-hand volley that was uncatchable. Seven times Borg had stood on the threshold of the championship – and seven times McEnroe had turned him back. A day that had begun so darkly for the American was now coloured by a golden rainbow of his own creation: 12–12.

McEnroe won the next point with a forehand volley executed as he fought to retain his footing: McEnroe, 13–12.

Set point three, McEnroe. 'When McEnroe won a point, we didn't move,' said Mariana. 'Lennart was white. We never spoke. We just felt each other with a hand on the knee, but I remember he was white. It was like you had picked him out of the grave.' Borg served. McEnroe returned. Borg's volley clipped the baseline and McEnroe's backhand hit the net. The American, hands on hips, shook his head, but he said nothing: 13–13.

The Swede backed himself into a corner when he netted a volley. The noise inside the court was incredible: McEnroe, 14–13.

Set point four, McEnroe. Going to a tried and trusted formula, McEnroe aimed his serve wide on Borg's backhand side. When the Swede made contact, McEnroe was already approaching the net. He went for a text-book forehand – only he miscalculated by a fraction. The ball landed out. Borg had been defenceless and

McEnroe knew it. The American shut his eyes in disbelief, his anguish evident to all. Above the commotion someone yelled, 'C'mon McEnroe, you can do it': 14–14.

Frank Deford, one of America's finest sportswriters, recorded the mounting tension in his dispatch for *Sports Illustrated*: 'The pressure! They won serving, passing, volleying, off both sides, down the line, cross-court. Neither would yield, neither would even swallow hard. The crowd would cry out and then absolutely hush, the alternating unnatural silences that tennis demands taking much more out of the place than unrestrained yelling ever could have. The tie-breaker was as excruciating a battle as ever was staged in athletics.' Yet more drama overtook the match on the next point. McEnroe's first serve threw up a puff of chalk dust. Borg delivered a backhand return that McEnroe put into the net with a backhand volley. Had there been a shout when the serve landed with its powdery trail? A linesman indicated he had called a 'fault'. Umpire Harrfey, believing the ball had been good, corrected the call. His decision was to instruct the players to play a let. Borg never registered a murmur of complaint. McEnroe took full advantage of the turn of events with a winning stop volley: McEnroe, 15–14.

Set point five, McEnroe. Borg's serve drew an error from McEnroe. Uncertain at first, the two men changed ends again as the rules demanded. Alternately, the crowd called out the names of each of them as though a choir in rehearsal: 15–15.

Peter Fleming felt as though he had been transported from his flat to the court, so engrossed had he become in the moment: 'It was such an incredibly intense environment that I felt I was there. The entertainment value was incredible. Forget tennis. This will be remembered as one of the iconic events in all of sport.' In front of us, McEnroe was growing in stature with every point; Borg was simply reinforcing his reputation as the champion of the age. This was sport at its compelling best. Borg served into the deuce court and McEnroe returned the ball at the Swede's feet. Instinctively, Borg lowered himself adroitly to place a backhand volley cross-court. McEnroe responded with lightning pace. He sprinted to his left and, still running, he controlled a forehand that arrowed down the line to reclaim the lead once more. McEnroe's momentum almost carried him into the crowd. For a moment he stood there at the side of the court with his fists clenched above his head. 'Please!' he said: McEnroe, 16–15.

Set point six, McEnroe. 'I could feel the excitement coming off those people in waves – to the extent that I actually had to make an effort not to get too excited myself,' said McEnroe. 'The further we got into that tie-breaker, though, the less I could hold it in. I did feel it was becoming something that was really special. I just had this magical feeling you don't feel that often.' With the set at his mercy yet again, McEnroe sprayed a backhand volley way out of court. His eyes burned with rage: 16–16.

Borg remained unmoved, outwardly at least, but he was still vulnerable and negligently he put a return off McEnroe's second serve out of court: McEnroe, 17–16.

Set point seven, McEnroe. Borg opted to serve down the middle. McEnroe's backhand return looked innocuous. Borg had time and he had court position to make a forehand volley. He would have played thousands, no, tens of thousands of volleys just like this on the courts at the Cumberland Club. He was trained to play them in his sleep, but at that moment, with 15,000 people on Centre Court holding their breath and the world watching through the lens of a camera, Borg lost his fabled control. His volley fell lamely into the basement of the net. In the competitors' box, John McEnroe Senior jumped to his feet and Stacy released a coy smile. McEnroe walked towards his chair to a standing ovation. He had captured the most momentous tie-break ever played, 18–16. McEnroe could still become Wimbledon champion.

Patrick McEnroe was watching as an excited boy in his motel room in Fort Worth, Texas, but it was his assessment of his brother at Wimbledon twenty-four years later that cast some insight into the mind of John McEnroe. 'John made us proud, sure he did,' said Patrick. 'He also made us upset. I think the most thing I felt for him was disappointment that he wasn't happy, with his trials and tribulations, if you will. He was a little restless, but, you know, in a way that has really been a part of who he is. That's what drives him to this day. John is constantly full of energy, in some ways conflict is good for him. Not everyone is like that. When you understand he is wired like that

you understand him a lot better and you see all of his good sides, his loyalty and his greatness as a dad. You understand that a lot more.'

17

THE FINAL CURTAIN

At the moment he surrendered the tie-break, Borg dropped the second ball he was holding and trudged to his chair. He walked so heavily he could have been wearing diving boots. He was lost in his own bleak world and deaf to the cacophony on the Centre Court. Dan Maskell, the doyen of the BBC commentary team, watched on his monitor as the director summoned a close-up of the Swede. 'What must Borg be thinking?' asked Maskell. And that was the point. No one ever knew. But years later Borg admitted, 'I think I never felt so bad in my life. That was the worst moment I had since I was born. Losing seven match points . . . playing my fifth Wimbledon final . . . against John McEnroe . . . so I think I am going to lose this match. I mean I had no chance.'

Unsurprisingly, McEnroe felt like a million dollars. He had sensed from his earliest days as a professional that he possessed a game that would cut through the defences of most men at Wimbledon. His serve had sting and he had the capacity to disguise it as well as any man playing. His serve out wide to a right-handed player in the advantage court hurt a man so hard he bled inside. His volley was simply the best in the game and his speed around the court was comparable to that of Borg. And then there was McEnroe's competitive nature. He hated losing. Hated it.

Having saved seven championship points against the great man, the man he had grown up idolising for his tennis and for being, in McEnroe's words, a matinee idol, he returned to the court with a sense of destiny. 'I thought there's no way I can lose now,' said

McEnroe. 'Borg's won Wimbledon four straight times. He's just lost an 18–16 tie-breaker. I thought the guy's got to let down. I was hoping he was going to fold.' McEnroe had forgotten his own fatigue. On the other side of the net, it was Borg who suddenly felt leaden and mentally drained. He left his chair to serve the first game of the fifth set, but, unusually for him, his mind had lost focus. 'I was still thinking about the fourth set,' he said.

Borg made a lamentable start. McEnroe's cross-court backhand, struck while off balance, proved too good for Borg's volley: 0–15. Then McEnroe drove a backhand volley on the move for a winner: 0–30. McEnroe was confidence personified. Mariana's discomfort in her seat was becoming worse. 'You just wait and you watch,' she said. 'It is like something happened to you in life that you don't want to do, but you are obliged to be there.'

But Borg is not a man to wallow in his own stupor for long. Like the champion he is, he found a higher gear from nowhere. McEnroe lost the next four points, three of them to winners from Borg. The game belonged to the Swede. Bergelin looked on with a mixture of disbelief and awe. 'For me, it was the most fantastic thing that Bjorn could come back after the fourth set. He showed the fighter he is – and after all those match balls, too! He never gave up. He thinks over what is going on. He thinks only of the next ball. Finally, he find himself. On his double-handed backhand, he could wait them all out. Wait with the stroke. The other players never know if it is straight down the line or cross-court or if he lobs. The other one never knows. Bjorn could mask it so well.'

McEnroe was not to know, but that first game of the decisive set was to be the last window of opportunity he would get on Borg's serve. The drama, though, continued unabated. In the second game, McEnroe was now the man under siege. After two glorious winners from Borg, the American served a double fault. McEnroe shook his head at such carelessness. He now faced three break points. He saved the first with an ace that swung past Borg's backhand; Borg conceded the next point by hitting a backhand return wide; and then McEnroe fired another ace that was swinging even more wickedly than his first one. Borg, however, was unimpressed. He stood with his hands on his hips, staring hard at the line. Clearly, he thought the serve was out. He contemplated speaking to the umpire, but in the end kept his counsel. 'Deuce,' said Peter Harrfey. McEnroe proceeded to serve another double to give Borg a fourth chance to break his service. The American missed his first serve, then his second was called a let. The strain was etched on his face, yet he showed great agility to level the score with a backhand volley and then won the next point with soft hands allowing him to beat Borg with a drop volley. When the Swede struck McEnroe's next service wide, the American was on terms at one game all.

That tortuous tie-break would have broken most men, but Borg had a mind of iron. He won his next three service games without losing a point. McEnroe only dropped one point in his next two, but his next crisis was around the corner. At 3–4, his serve came under the most exacting scrutiny. As always, McEnroe bounced the ball on his racket as he evaluated his options. Each serve was sent down with a strategic plan behind it. On the first point, he was in place to make a forehand volley, but he fluffed it. Borg squeezed the noose tighter with a backhand passing shot from the baseline that McEnroe could only nudge sideways. The American's despair deepened when he totally mishit a backhand volley yards out. McEnroe cupped his hands and berated himself. 'Oh, no!' It was 0–40. Had McEnroe cracked?

Borg had seen McEnroe's work as an escapologist too many times in one afternoon to make any such assumption. His respect for McEnroe's tennis had been healthy before this final started. Now he understood that the size of the American's heart matched his own. After missing his first serve at 0–40, McEnroe went daringly deep with his second and Borg, perhaps caught out, slotted his return into the net. The American won the next two points on his volley and an ace gave him advantage point. Borg brought the score back to deuce with a topspin forehand return smuggled down the line, but two more volleys from McEnroe's racket won him the game. At 4–4, the championship was still wide open.

In Sweden, however, the belief in Borg remained unequivocal, according to Mats Wilander. 'No way he was going to lose,' he said. 'It was never going to end. We were not going to see him beaten, ever.' Wilander is not a blind patriot. He has lived for much of the past twenty years in the United States – inasmuch as tennis players live anywhere for any length of time – and as much as he admires the tennis McEnroe produced he presents Borg as the all-time greatest. He explained, 'I think there's no question Borg is in a higher league. I'd put him ahead of them all, the No. 1 of all time. I never saw Rod Laver play – and he did win the Grand Slam twice – but Borg never went to the Australian Open. He would have picked up at least three or four titles in Australia. Then, he'd have fifteen Grand Slam titles instead of eleven. You could put Pete Sampras [fourteen Grand Slam championships] to bed. Sampras never won on clay. Borg never won the US Open, but he got to the final four times. In my eyes, I put him higher than Sampras for sure.

'McEnroe is a way, way better player than Borg. McEnroe was the complete player, whereas Bjorn was very limited, I think, but for me Borg is the best because of his domination. No one dominated the sport like him – that's the way I see it. He hardly lost, he really didn't, and when he lost there was a reason and it was legitimate. McEnroe was to have that fantastic year in 1984, but he did not dominate over the time Bjorn did. Bjorn was generous towards me, he telexed to congratulate me in the days before faxes existed! He makes me feel I achieved more than he did. He had eleven Slams, I won seven . . . but he thinks that's not far behind. There's a mile between us, yet he tells me I was unbelievable. No, that was him.'

Borg repaid the faith placed in him in Sweden, and across vast swathes of the rest of the world, by holding his serve comfortably to go ahead, 5–4. McEnroe had to serve to stay in the championship. He did just that without a hint of nerves: 5–5. Borg held again to love, when McEnroe cried after one backhand return, 'Go in!' He was whistling in the wind: Borg, 6–5.

McEnroe was looking down the barrel again. When the American netted a backhand volley under pressure from a huge backhand return down the line, the scoreboard on the Centre Court flicked to 30–30. Someone shouted, 'C'mon on my son.' McEnroe's next service crashed into the net. 'Oh yeah,' he said. Borg could see the door to the trophy opening, yet on McEnroe's second serve the Swede hit a wild, looping forehand. McEnroe watched it in the air, saw it pass him and land where he had hoped . . . in the tramlines. The American won the game with an incredible backhand volley placed in the furthest corner of the court from Borg. With his speed, Borg reached the ball, but had no chance to play it back into court.

Borg swiftly had the lead again at 7–6, having won his fifth love game of the set. After losing those two points in the first game of this set, he conceded just one more to McEnroe. 'I just didn't have enough gas left in the tank,' explained McEnroe. 'I was barely hanging on.' What about the expectation that Borg would fold? 'I was sadly disappointed,' said McEnroe. 'He was able to master a game plan and stick to it – and to do something I doubt anyone will ever do again. It showed the type of champion Bjorn was. That he was able to come back on what was my best surface. It says a lot about Bjorn.'

It said much about McEnroe, too. Deford wrote tellingly in *Sports Illustrated*, 'All those championship points were not merely lost by Borg. They were won, too, every one of them, by as gallant a loser – and sportsman, too, this particular day – as ever came to Wimbledon. McEnroe swaggered on to the court to boos and slumped off it to cheers, and with that metamorphosis he can never be the same.' For Borg, this final had truly become a trial of his inner-strength. McEnroe had cut to the core of the man. 'I kept telling myself not to get tight or nervous,' said Borg. 'Like Connors, McEnroe never gives up until the final point. It was exhausting, not physically, but mentally.'

Mariana was maintaining her poker face, but internally she was ready to explode. As Borg's hour of triumph approached, she thought of the hours of remorseless sacrifice they had both made on his behalf. 'I know the suffering and I know the work we put in together as a team with Lennart. Of course, Bjorn was the one, but three of us were one. I was so proud of him, really proud because I knew what it meant. I knew that he was breaking the record and I knew that he would stay in the history, and for him that was very important.' Bergelin, with so many memories of so many fabulous times with Borg, was in no doubt of the significance of what he was seeing. 'It was the most dramatic match ever, that fighting from end to end,' he said. 'It takes time for your heart to return to the normal rate. It is difficult to talk. I just swallowed hard.'

The stories behind the story were apparently endless. Patrick McEnroe understood that his brother had met a hostile crowd at the start of the afternoon, but long before the end had won them over with his tennis and his on-court dignity. 'I'll never forget the ovation John received,' he said. 'That was really an emotional time and all the crap he had been through with the press and the fans came full circle where everyone was on his side. He behaved so well and played one of the greatest matches ever seen.'

Peter Fleming had seen his friend climb almost to the summit, then lose his footing. 'In this fifth set, the momentum had changed in John's direction after he took the tie-break, but it quickly snapped back. John was physically tired, but then he had played seven sets the day before, four of them in an emotional match with Connors. That was two alter egos colliding. Junior wanted young people to give him respect, but he gave very little respect to anybody else other than Borg. With Junior, it was just a case of "Hey, you're the next guy to beat. I am the new gunslinger. You are the next guy who is going to get shot." I don't feel comfortable taking anything away from Bjorn in this final, but I think John might have been physically and mentally fried in the fifth.'

In the chair, Peter Harrfey was gasping for a drink. 'I was dying for a cup of tea,' he said, the epitome of an Englishman. 'It was a pleasure to be there, though. I mean, I had the best seat in the house. It was an outstanding event, an outstanding day in your life. It was. It is.' Nowadays umpires are given a commemorative medal, but all Harrfey received was a handshake on court from the Duchess of Kent. Afterwards, he even had to queue in the buttery to get that cup of tea he craved, but Harrfey did persuade Borg and McEnroe to sign the scorecard. 'Only recently I gave it away to a young girl, a tennis fanatic. No one had looked at it for donkeys' years.'

Chris Gorringe, the club secretary, was almost as nervous as the two men battling for the championship. In his first year of office, he was responsible for the post-match protocol. 'I watched as much of the match as I could on the monitor in my office or in the players' waiting room behind the Centre Court,' he explained. 'Being my first year, I was nervous for other reasons. I had to concern myself with the presentation ceremony.'

Peter Worth never sat in the competitors' box. In his role as agent, it was just not done; he was outside the immediate entourage. Besides, for much of the championships he usually had corporate business to attend to, but he was on court for the final. 'Remember the Jimmy Connors-Ken Rosewall final [1974]? We all wanted Rosewall to win, but Connors just blew him away. We were close to having a similar story with McEnroe and Borg. McEnroe had put himself way out in front – the difference was Borg just hung on. I thought it was over, before the tie-break. Funnily enough, the tie-break was the turning point of the match. It's easy in hindsight to say that. The fact that Mac won the tie-break, I thought he was just going to take over. The greatness of Borg was that he was never going to allow that to happen. Don't underestimate his serve. I think you'll find it's a lot harder than anyone who never played against him realised. I think McEnroe tightened. You could never say Borg's volleying was good, it was adequate. He didn't have the hands of Laver or McEnroe at the net. McEnroe became a tad tentative and took a little pace off the ball and allowed that extra split second for Borg to get his racket in place. From a commercial point of view, we weren't nervous.

'The secret of this story is McEnroe's respect for Borg. If you look back over the history of Grand Slam tennis, you appreciate it is where every great player has to make a mark. You play the best of five sets and have to play seven matches over two weeks. There are huge crowds and huge press and television intrusion. It's the ultimate challenge in tennis and McEnroe took on a bigger challenge as he played doubles as well. Very few people understand the pressure, both physical and mental, that a player endures. McEnroe, being very clever, very bright, knew after his first Wimbledon what it would take to win Wimbledon. And he had seen Borg win back-to-back French and Wimbledon titles. Borg was a god in his world. That's where the respect comes from.'

As the final reached its climax, Worth had no suspicion that we were witness to the closure of an era. Borg had won four titles at Wimbledon and now he stood on the threshold of a fifth – so what? Borg was only twenty-four years old. 'This was not the end,' said Worth. 'This was the continuation. It was not extra special.' But that is precisely what it was, as history now tells us. For McEnroe, the task of having to serve yet again to remain in the championship was to be a bridge too far. 'It seems like I lost that match twenty times more than I lost any other,' said McEnroe, in a *Sunday Telegraph* column before Wimbledon 2004. 'You'd think after all these years I'd be sick and tired of the mention of it, but I'm not. When you have a rivalry as good as ours it's an honour to know it's still remembered – even the defeats. In fact, it helps ease the pain of losing.' The pain on this unforgettable day in the history of tennis arrived as the clock on Centre Court registered 6.11p.m. Teenage girls were screaming out Borg's name. McEnroe had to serve at 15–40.

Championship point eight, Borg. McEnroe served to Borg's backhand. McEnroe volleyed the ball back down the centre of the court. On the baseline, Borg picked his spot with the deliberation of a sniper. His backhand pass ripped beyond McEnroe to land in history. The scoreboard was swift to offer the final statistics, but not the story: Borg had won, 1–6, 7–5, 6–3, 6–7 (18–16), 8–6, in three hours fifty-three minutes. And down there on the Centre Court, Borg had turned towards his own baseline and fallen to his knees as Mariana and Bergelin leapt to their feet in celebration, in relief. Borg's eyes were shut tight and he yelled hard, but we never knew what he said because the noise on Centre Court would have drowned the engines of a jumbo. At that moment, Borg was the king. He had won the greatest final of all time, in the most revered theatre, in a grand manner, but the final twist to this story was that the man who lost was also a winner. John Patrick McEnroe had laid claim to the crown and Bjorn Borg would never deny him in a major championship again.

WIMBLEDON 1980:

Round One	Round Two	Round Three	Round Fo

Borg defeats
El Shafei
6–3; 6–4; 6–4

Borg defeats
Glickstein
6–3; 6–1; 7–5

Borg defeats
Frawley
6–4; 6–7; 6–1; 7–5

Borg defea
Taroczy
6–1; 7–5; 6

McEnroe
Curren
7–5; 7–6; ?

McEnroe defeats
Okker
6–0; 7–6; 6–1

McEnroe defeats
Rocavert
4–6; 7–5; 6–7; 7–6; 6–3

McEnroe defeats
Walts
6–3; 6–3; 6–0

ROUTE TO THE FINAL

Quarterfinal	Semifinal	Final

Borg defeats
G. Mayer
7–5; 6–3; 7–5

Borg defeats
Gottfried
6–2; 4–6; 6–2; 6–0

Borg defeats
McEnroe
1–6; 7–5; 6–3;
6–7 (18–16); 8–6

McEnroe defeats
Connors
6–3; 3–6; 6–3; 6–4

McEnroe defeats
Fleming
6–3; 6–2; 6–3

BORG VERSUS McENROE – MATCH RECORD

1978: Stockholm, hard, semifinal McEnroe 6–3, 6–4

1979: Richmond, VA, WCT, carpet, semifinal Borg 4–6, 7–6, 6–3

1979: New Orleans, carpet, semifinal McEnroe 5–7, 6–1, 7–6

1979: Rotterdam, carpet, final Borg 6–4, 6–2

1979: Dallas, carpet, final McEnroe 7–5, 4–6, 6–2, 7–6

1979: Montreal/Toronto, hard, final Borg 6–3, 6–3

1979: Masters, New York, carpet, semifinal Borg 6–7, 6–3, 7–6

1980: Wimbledon, grass, final Borg 1–6, 7–5, 6–3, 6–7, 8–6

1980: US Open, hard, final McEnroe 7–6, 6–1, 6–7, 5–7, 6–4

1980: Stockholm, carpet, final Borg 6–3, 6–4

1980: (Jan 1981) Masters, New York, carpet, final Borg 6–4, 6–7, 7–6

1981: Milan, carpet, final McEnroe 7–6, 6–4

1981: Wimbledon, grass, final McEnroe 4–6, 7–6, 7–6, 6–4

1981: US Open, hard, final McEnroe 4–6, 6–2, 6–4, 6–3.

INDEX